# BEYOND HAPPY

ALSO BY MARK FABIAN

*A Theory of Subjective Wellbeing*

Mark Fabian

# BEYOND HAPPY

## How to Rethink Happiness and Find Fulfilment

First published in the UK in 2025 by Bedford Square Publishers Ltd,
London, UK

bedfordsquarepublishers.co.uk
@bedfordsquarepublishers
info@bedfordsquarepublishers.co.uk

© Mark Fabian, 2025

The right of Mark Fabian to be identified as the author of this work has been asserted in accordance with the Copyright, Designs and Patents Act 1988. All rights reserved. No part of this book may be reproduced, stored in or introduced into a retrieval system, or transmitted, in any form or by any means (electronic, mechanical, photocopying, recording or otherwise) without the written permission of the publishers.

Any person who does any unauthorised act in relation to this publication may be liable to criminal prosecution and civil claims for damages.

A CIP catalogue record for this book is available from the British Library.

The manufacturer's authorised representative in the EU for product safety is Easy Access System Europe, Mustamäe tee 50, 10621 Tallinn, Estonia
gpsr.requests@easproject.com

ISBN
978-1-83501-049-5 (Hardback)
978-1-83501-050-1 (Trade Paperback)
978-1-83501-051-8 (eBook)

2 4 6 8 10 9 7 5 3 1

Printed in Great Britain by CPI Group (UK) Ltd, Croydon, CR0 4YY

To Maddy, who healed me.

It was Maddy who observed that 'wellbeing is about wholeness, not happiness, and wholeness is so much more demanding than happiness'.

# Contents

Introduction ... ix

**Part I: A Pleasant Life**

1. Disposition ... 3
2. Character ... 27
3. Emotion ... 53

**Part II: A Fulfilling Life**

4. Self-Actualisation ... 87
5. The Inner Empire ... 113
6. Better Together ... 143

**Part III: A Valuable Life**

7. Nihilism ... 179
8. The Free Spirit ... 211
9. Metamodernity ... 251

Conclusion ... 299

Endnotes ... 303
Bibliography ... 313
Acknowledgements ... 327

# Introduction

> Salvation is for the feeble, that's what I think. I don't want salvation. I want life, all of life, the miserable as well as the superb.
>
> Tom Robbins, *Jitterbug Perfume*

The popularity of self-help books speaks to a common malaise in our society. Many people feel that their lives could be better — more pleasant, fulfilling or valuable, or have more meaning or purpose. Or perhaps life isn't making sense to them, and that's a bother. Everything seems a bit chaotic or stressful or mundane. Even more broadly, they might feel like society has lost its common purpose and isn't providing a clear path towards well-being for everybody. What should they do with their lives? And why?

I had similar thoughts in my adolescence, which triggered a depressive episode that lasted several years. This was out of character for me, as until then I had generally been happy-go-lucky and upbeat. My depression wasn't chemical in origin; it was philosophical. As I became more politically minded, I began to see the world as run not by enlightened heroes, but by venal and corrupt individuals only kept in check by fragile institutions. This coincided with some painful first forays into love, making me question my self-worth. There soon followed the looming requirement that I graduate from high school and enter the 'real world', meaning that I had to figure out what I was going to do with my life, which also meant answering some rather fundamental questions. I wanted to do something good. I wanted to be good. But what even is 'good'?

Different people and cultures have been fumbling with the answer to that question for millennia, but the search has become increasingly pronounced in the West since the decline of religion from the late nineteenth century. Our culture used to tell us what to do. Religion especially, with its clear rules about right and wrong and its ritualistic practices, ordered our lives. But our contemporary culture is committed to the idea of finding your own path, following your heart and doing what you think is right. This may be wonderfully liberating, but it's also difficult and puzzling, because then the answers to all life's big questions are up to you. As the character Dmitri pondered in Fyodor Dostoevsky's 1879 novel *The Brothers Karamazov*: 'but what will become of men then? Without God and immortal life, all things are permitted – and they can do what they like?'

Down the rabbit hole I went, and my search for answers led me to enrol in a philosophy degree. As a student, I read voraciously – although usually not my course's set texts. Instead, I plundered the collection of great literature sold on the cheap by a second-hand bookseller who came to campus once a week. My reading ranged from the ancient Roman Stoic philosopher Marcus Aurelius to the twentieth-century psychoanalyst and Holocaust survivor Viktor Frankl, and across to thinkers in the liberal tradition like Adam Smith, with a smattering of the Chinese Zhuangzi, the Buddha and other writings that introduced me to different cultural perspectives. They were college years well spent, I'd say, despite my dumpster fire of an academic record.

Yet the more I researched, the more frustrated I became with the often very long and arcane books I was reading. They rarely seemed to provide more than one piece of life's giant jigsaw puzzle. Putting it all together, I realised, was going to be an arduous task. There was plenty to read about what not to do (Shakespeare was particularly good about that), but stories that I could relate to, of slowly putting a life together one piece at a time, were scarce.

During my exploratory period, the scientific study of wellbeing was still in its infancy, and much of the research that I came across was too limited to be of practical use. Science tends to restrict itself to narrow questions that can be answered with precision. For example, rather than asking, 'How can you live well in old age?', science will instead ask something like, 'How do different perceptions of aging in midlife predict stress levels in retirement?' Over a long period, this can achieve remarkable things. But I didn't have time to wait, and what was available was rather meagre. In particular, most of the studies were about happiness, not wellbeing. This was because, as I discovered later, the pioneering American psychologist Ed Diener worried (correctly) that his colleagues wouldn't take him seriously if he said he studied 'happiness'. Instead, he chose the more technical sounding term 'subjective wellbeing', and most of the research into wellbeing that followed built on Diener's narrow definition.[1]

There are, however, crucial distinctions between happiness and wellbeing. Happiness is about our mood and emotional state. We smile when we are happy; it's hard not to smile when we're happy. Wellbeing is broader. It is about whether your life is going well. It includes happiness, certainly, and the broader notion of 'hedonic satisfaction', which is considering your life to be pleasant. But wellbeing also includes the very broad notion of 'existential satisfaction' – how fulfilling your life is, and how valuable, which includes deeper concepts like purpose and righteousness. People who have an abundance of wellbeing don't necessarily smile all the time, nor are they always in a good mood. You don't always smile while you're pursuing your hobby, but that hobby is a critical part of your wellbeing. I'm an avid rock climber, and find rock climbing integral to my wellbeing, but when I'm climbing I don't stop and think 'I'm so happy', because I'd fall.

In fact, happiness and wellbeing are often in conflict. If you pursue happiness exclusively, you will neglect your wellbeing because you will flee from the pain that is involved in self-renovation. Setbacks and slogs are an unavoidable part of achieving worthwhile things, and the personal sacrifices that are required to make the world a better place. For this reason, few expressions irritate me more than 'I just want to be happy', despite this sentiment being written into the culture of many countries at an institutional level (such as the 'unalienable Rights' in the US Declaration of Independence to 'Life, Liberty and the pursuit of Happiness').

Ultimately, the pursuit of happiness often ends in boredom. The things that make for a full life, like being involved in a community, seeing the world, family life, intimate relationships, career success and memorable experiences in general, typically involve a mix of emotions. If you seek only the pleasant ones, you'll end up with tranquillity, not happiness. Maybe that's genuinely what you want. No judgement. But I want a bit more. I want all of life. And, given that you're reading this book, I suspect you do too.

The result of my seeking has been an academic career studying wellbeing and, in turn, a book published by Oxford University Press, called *A Theory of Subjective Wellbeing*. (If you want to cross-reference anything I say here, I recommend you look there. It's a very long and thorough book – the reference list alone is more than 15,000 words). Having searched in vain for a single, consistent theory of wellbeing, that book was my attempt to produce the theory myself. It was the result of fifteen years of research that I started late in high school, and that I continue in my present-day academic work.

I'm proud of *A Theory of Subjective Wellbeing*, but it's a very academic book. It is written for a scholarly audience that is fastidiously careful about what can be claimed on the basis of our current scientific evidence. The book dwells on complexities of measurement, tricky problems in the philosophy of science

# INTRODUCTION

and pedantic issues in ethical philosophy that aren't of much interest to most people. It doesn't say as much as I'd like about how wellbeing works, or how to get more of it, or people's 'lived experience' of their own wellbeing, because these are 'applied' questions that many academics and philosophers think should only come after the academic work is done.

So I wrote this book too – a popular version of my theory of wellbeing. In fact, this is the book I've always wanted to write: a sort of one-stop shop for readers interested in their wellbeing, but who don't have the time or inclination to wade through hundreds of pages by the Danish philosopher Søren Kierkegaard, or spend four years studying remedial mathematics just to understand the statistical evidence for why earning more money doesn't necessarily make you happier. This book's purpose is to capture in a single volume the most important insights from over two millennia of scholarly and philosophical work on wellbeing, and explain how you can achieve it.

Be warned though, wellbeing is tough, complicated and time-consuming. There is no silver bullet or mental trick to attain it. Instead, there are dozens of practices that are required to achieve the good life. Wellbeing is something you must practise to get better at, and like most skills it takes a long time and many failures to master. Most self-help books strike me as broadly deceptive about this fact. Single, simple ideas that can be effectively summarised in a page are given entire volumes and marketed as 'the science of happiness' or some such nonsense. Inspirational anecdotes, often the length of chapters, are used in place of analysis. A recent trend is to transform a slice of ancient wisdom through the profuse use of the word 'f*ck', and then market this as an original insight.

Few of these books present an account of what kind of organism the human is, and therefore what sort of things we need to be well. They don't touch on how people interact with society and politics to produce individual and collective wellbeing. And they don't fit the huge range of insights we have on wellbeing from multiple disciplines into a consistent theory supported by the facts.

This book is (hopefully) different. I will cover a lot of ground, because wellbeing is a vast topic combining multiple subjects. A central finding of my research is that philosophers, psychologists, economists, anthropologists, sociologists and theologians all have valuable insights to contribute to wellbeing, and that the subject can only be understood by looking across the many rich traditions that have studied it. I will also be honest about the many challenges involved in achieving wellbeing. For example, one of the first steps is to bring all the things you dislike about yourself into loving self-awareness, and then either make peace with them or resolve to change them. Persevering through this personal renovation can be miserable, but ultimately it will pay off through personal growth, self-esteem and serenity.

I have divided the book into three parts that correspond to what I call the three dimensions of wellbeing: a pleasant life, a fulfilling life and a valuable life. Although these parts speak to different types of human experience, you will only gain a complete understanding of wellbeing by reading them all. You might even discover a whole aspect of your life that you've never even considered.

Part I, 'A Pleasant Life', is for those people that might be broadly satisfied with their lives but want to be a bit happier. It covers methods of mood management that have been developed by psychologists like Sonya Lyubomirsky and Robert Emmons over the past four decades or so, who focus on hedonic psychology, which is concerned with our feelings and how we experience them. Many of the techniques that come from this area of psychological science reflect ancient wisdom, so Part I will explore this too, notably ideas from stoicism and Buddhism (especially mindfulness).

The ancients, though, were concerned with much more than mood, and we can glean other insights from them. These include techniques for how to cultivate virtues of character, like integrity and self-compassion, and build a constructive attitude or disposition towards life through traits such as curiosity. Using these techniques will make you more pleasant to be around; it is easier to enjoy the company of someone who is reliable, transparent, open and able to engage in self-criticism, than it is to befriend someone who merely wants something from you, assumes the world is against them and carries around a notebook full of grudges. These techniques will also help you to ride the unavoidable randomness of life. For example, if you're a curious person, then you will see new information, people, places and events not as threats to your carefully constructed worldview, but as sources of new ideas and stimuli. This disposition will keep you open to personal growth throughout life, and the wellbeing that results.

The shortcoming of the mood management techniques in Part I is that they assume you don't have deeper underlying issues in your psyche that continuously generate bad moods. If you don't have any such issues and just want to be a bit happier most of the time, these techniques will take you from a neutral state to feeling really quite good, and help you to sustain your pleasant mental states for longer. But if, for example, you're feeling lost or restless, or you are haunted by feelings of emptiness, then mood management will only treat your symptoms. To get at the cause of your unease, you will need something deeper.

Part II, 'A Fulfilling Life', will bridge this gap. For most people, the roadblock to wellbeing is that they haven't discovered or aren't pursuing values that 'fit' them. The word 'values' might sound a bit vague or lofty, but once we think about it in terms of our behaviours, the connection with wellbeing becomes clearer.

Imagine you have no interest in football, but you spend a lot of time researching it because your work colleagues are really invested in their fantasy football league and you want to fit in. Your behaviour is out of line with your values, and the emotional consequence is that you're bored. The solution is to bring your values and behaviours into harmony. But what are your values?

Maybe you don't know yet. Our culture gives people a lot of freedom to hold and express whatever values they want, but it doesn't give them many skills or tools to identify which values are most appropriate for them.

The ambition of Part II is to encourage you to discover or create your values, so that you can refine your lifestyle to align with them. It will help guide you towards identifying the things that you want to do for their own sake, and that can lead you on your journey towards wellbeing. This will require a substantial turn inwards, as you become more aware of yourself: the good, the bad and the ugly. Perhaps you have a real talent and love for gardening. This is the sort of information around which you can build a fulfilling life. But knowledge of your weaknesses, vices and quirks can be just as useful. If you know that you have a short attention span, for example, and flit about from activity to activity, you should avoid occupations that require a high degree of focus on urgent tasks, like corporate law.

Only once we understand ourselves can we authentically turn outwards and find our people. To assist with this process, Part II will conclude with an exploration of aspects of wellbeing that depend on our relationships with others, such as belonging, friendship, camaraderie, love and community. The overarching theme of Part II is what psychologists call self-actualisation: the process by which we come to define and know ourselves, integrate our emotions, motivations and thoughts, secure purpose, and enmesh ourselves in nourishing communities of people who we love and who love us back.

Part III, 'A Valuable Life', is about overcoming nihilism, both individually and as a society. Most people experience their life as meaningful and regard their day-to-day actions as valuable. This is usually because they have been socialised into a system of meaning and value that enchants their world. Their life may be full of rituals that mark matters of importance – even simple things like family dinner, watching a game at the weekend or regular attendance at a religious service. Their community might show them respect and appreciation for various occupations or behaviours they perform, like being a doctor or volunteering at the school fête. And their culture celebrates particular achievements in life, such as graduating, getting married, having children or buying their first house. In all these subtle ways we are encouraged towards particular values, and as long as we are successful in pursuing those values, we never question their worth – we simply get on with it, progressing from goal to goal.

In contrast, nihilism is the sense that life lacks inherent value and meaning, and that one can't justify one set of values over another. Nihilists perceive the world as fundamentally incoherent in some way, without purpose, unserious and insignificant. They find it difficult to direct their lives and settle on a desired identity to pursue. They can't answer the existential questions: Who am I? What is right? What should I do?

Nihilism emerges when the systems of meaning and value that people use to organise their lives have their integrity undermined. It has been spreading in Western society for centuries as feudalism, religion, nationalism, materialism and traditional family values have each in turn lost their grip on our culture. The prevalence of nihilism in society today is evident in the popularity of media that celebrate nihilistic themes, such as the animated television series *Rick and Morty* (Morty's line, 'Nobody exists on purpose, nobody belongs anywhere, everybody's gonna die. Come watch TV', is a favourite of the show's fans), the 'Nihilist Memes' page on Facebook which has almost two million followers, and the nihilism subreddit with over 100,000 subscribers. If you think these social media platforms are a bit passé, TikToks marked with nihilistic hashtags boast over fifty million views at the time of writing. Nihilism has a role to play in our mental illness epidemic, the wildfire popularity of prophetic public intellectuals like Jordan Peterson (whose most popular book is subtitled *An Antidote to Chaos*) and the increasingly religious fervour of our political partisanship.

A classic, cheerful nihilism meme

How do we fill this cultural vacuum? The answer I will present towards the book's conclusion is found in what the Dutch cultural theorists Timotheus Vermeulen and Robin van den Akker have called the 'metamodern' cultural mode, which is emerging in the wake of 'postmodernism'.[2] Metamodernism is characterised by acknowledging that there is no meaning or value written into the firmament, and yet people nonetheless want to feel meaning and connection by practising their values socially, especially by being invested in enriching social projects like a sports team, a creative community or a national spirit. In metamodernism, individuals re-enchant the world by affirming their notion of what is good and building communities around it. Unlike in traditional societies where people are socialised into value systems and their compliance with those systems is policed, metamodernism is characterised by self-expression and voluntary association, allowing us to affirm our values in a wholehearted and sincere way.

The 'XKCD Meetup' is a good example. XKCD is a nerdy webcomic drawn with stick figures. In one episode, 'Dream Girl', a character dreams that he meets a girl in a dying world, and just before reality is torn apart she whispers a stream of numbers in his ear. It turns out they are the coordinates of a place, date and time. He goes to the site at the appointed hour and... nothing happens. In the final panel, he muses, 'it turns out wanting something doesn't make it real'. This is all very nihilistic. But in real life, thousands of XKCD fans, unbidden and unorganised, descended on those coordinates (Cambridge Park in Boston) from across the globe in a spontaneous celebration of their love for the webcomic. They dressed up, re-enacted their favourite scenes and held a wonderful party. To top off the event, Randall Munroe, XKCD's author, redrew the final panel of the comic but left thirty-five feet of whiteboard for people to fill in what happened when the character in the comic went to the place at the appointed time. To me, this incident beautifully demonstrates the power of metamodernism to imbue life and communities with a palpable sense of meaning and value.

Such movements and cultural expressions aren't as all-encompassing as the world's religions, which claim to explain all of existence. But that's the point. A liberal society that preaches pluralism and tolerance and seems to acknowledge, on some intuitive level, that values are subjective, needs a culture that permits different value systems to compete, collaborate and mix without giving way to conflict. This new landscape empowers people to self-actualise in a way that the stringent cultures and dogmas of old did not, and it also holds nihilism at bay, by empowering people to find communities that will nurture their wellbeing.

But let's not get ahead of ourselves. Nihilism is weighty and complex, and we have Parts One and Two to get through first. Let's learn to walk, and hopefully by the end of this book we'll be soaring.

## *Interlude: This is not a work of popular science*

I mean by intellectual integrity the habit of deciding vexed questions in accordance with the evidence, or of leaving them undecided where the evidence is inconclusive. This virtue, though it is underestimated by almost all adherents

of any system of dogma, is to my mind of the very greatest social importance and far more likely to benefit the world than Christianity or any other system of organized beliefs.
Bertrand Russell, *Why I am Not a Christian*

Before moving on, I want to quickly stress that this book is *not* a work of popular science. It is hopefully a work of wisdom. There are three reasons why I need to underline this. The first is that the science of wellbeing is frankly pretty shoddy. It has made enormous advances, to be sure. The study of mood, in particular, is streets ahead of where it was in the mid-twentieth century. But the aspects of our scientific knowledge in which we can have the most confidence often concern the (in my opinion) relatively less important aspects of wellbeing, notably being 'happy'. Big ticket items, like self-actualisation and conscience, are more poorly understood. I want to talk about those important things, and I will draw on scientific research, but I don't want to pretend that what I'm saying is 'science'. It's my educated intuition.

The second reason is that wellbeing is in many ways more philosophical than scientific. Wellbeing is what is *good* for you; what makes your life go well. It's impossible to define wellbeing, or talk about it honestly, without making value judgements, which, crudely speaking, run counter to the scientific method. But on many occasions in this book, I am going to make very strong value claims. Notably, I'm going to be speaking vehemently about how I think you should live. This isn't the business of scientists. I would be corrupting the institution of science and my own scientific credentials if I implied that what I'm doing here is science communication.

The corruption of science leads me to the third reason. We are living through a scary high tide of populism and anti-elite sentiment. Some of this is driven by the unfortunate tendency of scientists to engage in debates about values without taking off their scientist hats and while misrepresenting their values as facts. In my day job, I work among scientists on wellbeing public policy. I often argue that the scholarship we do is far too technocratic. We spend nearly all our time appealing to politicians and bureaucrats, trying to convince them to change policy so that it aligns with scientific evidence. But what this ultimately amounts to is sneaking a change in *values* into government – we are promoting our view of what makes a life go well. Values in a democracy can only legitimately come from *citizens*. What we need to do much more of is deliberate with *citizens* so that they are wiser about wellbeing. Their values will then drive wellbeing public policy democratically. This book is an attempt on my part to do that. But I need to take off my scientist hat. We can't have a genuine, wholehearted conversation about values if I present myself as a scientist, occupying a position of power over you based on my 'knowledge'. So I come to you simply as another citizen of a (hopefully) liberal-democrat nation, and I make my appeal to you as part of public discourse.

# PART I

## A Pleasant Life

It is impossible to live a pleasant life without living wisely and well and justly. And it is impossible to live wisely and well and justly without living a pleasant life.

Epicurus, *Principal Doctrines*, no. 5

# 1
## Disposition

> The essential thing 'in heaven and in earth' is that there should be long *obedience* in the same direction. There thereby results, and has always resulted in the long run, something which has made life worth living. For instance, virtue, art, music, dancing, reason, spirituality – anything whatever that is transfiguring, refined, foolish, or divine.
> Friedrich Nietzsche, *Beyond Good and Evil*

When I first started drafting this book, Part I was called 'basic skills', and I think that remains an accurate way of describing the content of these sections, except that they're not really skills, more a mindset or an orientation. It's important to understand that wellbeing is a process as much as it is a state of being – you need to *live* in a well way if you ever want to *be* a well way. Another way of making this point that wellbeing is a process is the almost cliché phrase: 'life is a journey'. Well, if it's a journey, then you'd better make sure you get on the right path, or that you've got a compass that works and some way to know which way is north. That's what Part I is about. We begin with disposition – the attitude you should take to life.

You've got to understand the nature of the journey that you're on, especially that *it doesn't end*. Western culture has long held out heaven as the reward for a life of hard work. More recently, materialism brought that heaven ahead to earth in the form of a comfortable retirement. These visions both emphasise working hard to get *somewhere*. The journey of life is presented as a path you walk down before arriving at the end. Buddhism, a much wiser doctrine than materialism, teaches that desires are never ending, and so you don't ever arrive, at least not for long. Some new desire beckons and you start walking a bit further down the road. Better to get off the road entirely, counsels Buddhism. I'm going to suggest something quite different, which is to make the journey as enjoyable as possible and accept that you're going to be on it for a lifetime, heading nowhere that's especially clear. Your guide on this journey is your internal compass, which steers you towards the things that work for you and helps to bring them into harmony. So the first step on the path to wellbeing is to turn inwards.

## 1.1. Happy but dissatisfied

> Human beings will always complain. There is no Garden of Eden, there is no paradise, there is no heaven except for a passing moment or two. Whatever satisfactions are given to human beings, it is inconceivable that they should be perfectly content with these'.
> Abraham Maslow, *The Farther Reaches of Human Nature*

You are wired to be happy but dissatisfied. What this means is that while you will be in an upbeat (not ecstatic) mood most the time, you are also prone to feeling that something is missing, or that there could be more.[1]

The evolutionary roots of this are straightforward. It is not beneficial to be in a good or bad mood for long. The ecstatic tend to be indolent – when you're having a great time you don't want to interrupt it to do the relatively boring labour that is necessary for survival. The depressed tend to be lethargic. They do not engage in that boring labour with sufficient energy.

Mania and anxiety are constructive in the short term as they both incline the individual to activity, but they are exhausting. They are heightened states designed for niche situations, like avoiding a predator or recovering from a social faux pas. A moderate mood is thus optimal from a sustained activity point of view.

But merely sustaining the current level of activity gets you left behind. More ambitious and energetic humans get the power, the resources and the mates. So our positive mood is complemented by a gentle background level of disappointment. A little genetic daemon on our shoulder is always pushing us to get more: be sexier, richer, more adventurous, athletic, glamourous, famous, influential.

We usually have moderate background levels of positive mood, and our mood tends to *return* to this high background level in short order after shocks. Psychologists refer to this as 'homeostatically protected mood'.[2] You don't stay angry for long when you miss the bus. The buoyant mood you have after a comedy show doesn't last through to breakfast the next morning. Mood disorders, notably depression, are characterised by the persistence of extreme emotions (anger management problems, mania, depression, anxiety) and a tendency to fall into them. They are related to a breakdown in the homeostatic protection of our mood, as are periods of sustained stress, like solitary confinement, poverty or oppression.

Our overall satisfaction with life is trickier. We rely on mood for information about how life is going, so if we are mostly in a good mood then we are more likely to think that life is going well (and vice versa). And we tend to think more about all the ways life could be better when we are in a bad mood. But even people whose lives are going well and are characterised by good moods can still be struck by existential disquiet. That's the essence of the mid-life crisis (or the increasingly common quarter-life crisis). Its stereotypical form is for a middle-aged salaried man with kids to leave his wife, buy a sports car and bump uglies with a younger woman. That story has got evolution's fingerprints all over it. His genes, who only care about maximising their odds of replication, are whispering in his ear: 'This is nice, Dave. Good job on procreating, but don't you want something a bit *more* exciting? Like, I don't know, how about a younger, more fertile woman?'

This tendency towards mild dissatisfaction goes well beyond the mid-life crisis. Starting in 2022 and continuing to the present day, I have conducted research where I interview people as they answer life satisfaction questions while thinking out loud.[3] The most common form of this question is: 'Taking all things together, how satisfied are you with your life right now on a scale from 1–10?' One of the most striking findings of this research is that a great many respondents said that they would never give 10/10 and that they could only see themselves being 9/10 for an hour or a couple of days after some particularly exhilarating achievement or experience. This wasn't because their lives were bad. Indeed, they generally said that life was good. It was just that they could always see it getting better and liked the feeling of having projects and making progress. Of course, making that progress didn't result in them giving higher scores. It was rather that being able to make progress rather than being stuck meant they were an 8/10 rather than a 7/10.

These interviews were with residents of the United Kingdom, one of the most developed nations on earth, where the average life satisfaction of the population in 2018 was 7.7/10, according to the annual population survey. So it seems that the average UK resident, and I presume the average resident of most wealthy nations, is broadly satisfied with life but on the lookout for ways to make it better. Some of this might be peculiar to what academics refer to as Western, Educated, Industrialised, Rich, Democratic (WEIRD) psychology.[4] Anthropologists come across people outside of WEIRD cultures with a more steady state or sufficient attitude to life – 'this is enough'.[5] I think that attitude is worth investigating in much more detail, but this book is written for WEIRDos, so I'll take a psychology of happy yearning for granted from here on out.

## 1.2. Learning to love the treadmill

> Was *that* life? Well then, once more, from the beginning!
> Friedrich Nietzsche, *Thus Spoke Zarathustra*

Once you understand the concept of homeostatically protected mood and the impossibility of complete satisfaction, you realise that the common saying, 'I just want to be happy', is a bit silly. You *are* just happy.

Now, of course I am being unfair here. When people say they just want to be happy, they mean wellbeing, not happiness. They are also, I suspect, saying that they would like to simply *be satisfied*. To get off the 'hedonic treadmill', as psychologists call it. This is the 'happy but dissatisfied' psychology that I outlined in the previous section. It gives you a sugar spike of good mood and satisfaction when you achieve a goal, but then quickly makes you curious again for something extra, and a little bit agitated as a result. When people say they just want to be happy, they want out of this agitation. They desire *tranquillity*. This is a major theme of Buddhism, in which a sophisticated and psychologically rich version of tranquillity is the goal of practice, as well as many self-help books. The German spiritual teacher Eckhart Tolle's famous book *The Power of Now*[6] is a riff on this idea. In developed countries, our life is broadly pleasant, so settle into the positive experience that is your day-to-day existence – live in the now. Stop wanting. Just be. As Buddhism counsels: desire is the root of all suffering. A WEIRDer version of this Buddhist argument is available in the popular books of American management academic Arthur Brooks, notably his *From Strength to Strength: Finding Success, Happiness, and Deep Purpose in the Second Half of Life*.[7] He provides 'three ways to want less', one of which is to 'get smaller' – deriving joy and fulfilment from smaller or at least less ambitious things.

I don't want to criticise this attitude of tranquillity because a) I think it has a lot of merit, and b) it genuinely seems to be a critical step in the right direction for a lot of people. However, I'm going to argue in this book for something quite different: *learning to enjoy the treadmill*. That we experience both mild positive mood and mild dissatisfaction with life is a fact of our biology. You can of course practise good psychological and spiritual hygiene to dampen this fact, but you can't get rid of it. So let's embrace it instead. What does that mean, succinctly?:

*It's not about embracing that you'll always need to strive for something new. It's about enjoying the act of running.*

This is not living in the now. It's understanding that 1) your life needs to be dynamic and 2) establishing a dynamic that you find pleasant, brings you fulfilment and is valuable to you. Let's take each of these two points in turn.

Pleasure is first about having your basic material needs met. Poverty makes everything shit. That doesn't mean that you should be materialistic! It just means having the means to do the things you authentically, deeply, want to do. Pleasure is also about your physical and mental health. The latter is often about things in this book, but it is even more often about healing from trauma, unwinding neuroses and unlearning bad patterns of thought. You need a therapist for that, not this book.

More broadly, and where this book starts to come in, pleasure is about mood management. There are ways to nudge that modest background level of positive mood up to a slightly higher level such that you're not so much 'happy' as 'joyful'. Gratitude, for example, and other methods for focusing your attention on the good things in your life, will perk you up. There are also ways to extend your good moods. Savouring, for example, which involves being mindfully present in the experience of positive emotions. And there are ways of being prone to fall into good moods. Developing the skills of 'basking', which is where you delight in the positive experience of others, for example, increases the opportunities in your life to feel good. These techniques can also be practised in reverse to reduce the intensity of your bad moods, shorten their duration and limit their frequency. All this adds up to make life on the treadmill broadly enjoyable.

Even more broadly, pleasure is about what I call 'hedonic satisfaction'. This is mostly a matter of getting rid of bad things, especially things that periodically produce 'shit' for you to deal with. Pay attention to the sources of negativity in your life and deliberately, consciously, work away from them. For example, if the end of your workday is met with relief rather than a sort of happy exhaustion, try to change jobs. If there is a pattern of behaviour with relatives or friends that grinds your gears, confront the other party and respectfully and graciously establish a different pattern.

Hedonic satisfaction is about the baseline of your life being gentle. You don't want the treadmill randomly going up a steep gradient, unexpectedly accelerating or otherwise throwing you off course. You should be able to increase the challenge when you want to in ways that you want to, but otherwise be settled in a steady state of activity that brings you positive experiences. That's a nice treadmill to run on. Importantly, when you deliberately try to take time away from the dynamics of the treadmill, like on weekends, work leave or quiet time in the evenings, your life should be restorative. If there's always new chaos to order, threats to deal with or unexpected obstacles to overcome, then your life will be dissatisfying.

Beyond hedonic satisfaction is what I call 'existential' satisfaction, and this is where fulfilment and value come into play.

Fulfilment, as we'll cover in Part II, is about self-actualisation and meeting your basic psychological needs for autonomy, competence and relatedness. What this amounts to is that you're running on a treadmill that you chose, not one that other people or your culture says you should use. You're getting better at the things you value. And you're spending time with people you respect, care for and appreciate, and investing in those relationships so that they grow and become more rewarding. It is easy to find *motivation* for these things. Life isn't a struggle when you're pursuing your interests and hanging with your buddies. You don't need to draw on your willpower to get through the day in the hope of achieving something down the way. You just live, and life is good.

The last piece of the puzzle is value. The dynamism of life on the treadmill can sometimes feel like so much busywork. What is the point? We are trapped by our biology like a hamster on a wheel, working ourselves to nowhere. This sort of nihilistic realisation can undermine our sense of pleasure and fulfilment and drive us into depression. To ward it off, we need to have a purpose. This might be a goal, like revitalising our local community or getting into shape, but the goal isn't the point – *living* in pursuit of that goal is. Purpose brings us motivation to go about our daily life and wards off the sense that running on a treadmill is a worthless activity. Our purpose should ideally come with feedback – indications that we are making progress. We want to see our community looking after shared spaces or our business opening a new branch, for example. You can't stop jogging through life, but it's lovely to see the scenery get nicer as you go.

In summary, wellbeing is not about getting off the treadmill, it's about making the treadmill a place you want to be. Compare this to the 'American Dream': you want to get to a big house, a successful career, a happy family, a full wardrobe, vacations in Hawaii, a luxury car, etc. Many people live a life that isn't so positive in order to *get to* these things – they work long hours, take few holidays, live a long commute from work, spend endless hours hunting for bargains online. That's an unpleasant treadmill to run on, and all these material achievements are never enough. The treadmill chugs on and eventually you just want to get off. But you can't no matter how comfortable your new sofa is. What we need to do is not change the goal so that it's easier to attain, or make a futile effort to purge the treadmill from our being, but to change our experience of the treadmill.

The clue is in the name: well*being* is not something you achieve, it's a way of life.

## 1.3. If you had all the time and money, what would you spend it on?

The unexamined life is not worth living.

Socrates

The main reason why people get stuck running on an unpleasant treadmill is that they live their lives unconsciously. They devote insufficient thought to what they want to do and why. They just fall into something over time.

Worse, too many people live their lives acquisitively. They simply try to get more stuff. This is ecologically unsustainable, but it's also not good for your wellbeing.

When you put these two modes together – unconscious acquisitiveness – you end up with people thinking first about how to get more and never thinking about what they want to use it for. This gets life and wellbeing backwards.

*You need to think about what you want to do with your life and then how to get the resources you need to live that life.*

This means living consciously and only acquiring as much as you need.

Unfortunately, even a lot of well-intentioned anti-materialist commentary fails to understand this. For example, the Harvard Business School psychologist Ashley Whillans has a fun little book called *Time Smart*.[8] It's full of helpful tips for increasing your 'time affluence' and is well worth a read. But it makes the mistake of suggesting that all people need to do to improve their wellbeing is to prioritise time over money. This is wrong. Time and money are *both* a means of exchange. What matters to your wellbeing is what you exchange time and money for. That will be different for each of us, and if you exchange unconsciously it won't have much of an effect.

You need to understand your authentic values and then figure out how to get the time and money that will allow you to live in accordance with those values.

It's quite likely that you won't even need that many resources. Few expensive things express values. When you buy fashionable clothes unconsciously you express the tastes of others, not yourself. When you indulge in fine dining you are obtaining a fleeting sensory pleasure, not taking steps towards a long-term goal. Some of us authentically value things like haute couture, racing sports cars or interior design, but for most people these expenditures can be dispensed with to free up resources for more authentic pursuits.

It is also possible to find ways to bring your life into alignment with expensive values without needing to make loads of money. For example, when I was completely obsessed with tennis – a very expensive hobby – I started working as a tennis coach. This got me access to free court hire, sponsored merchandise and opportunities to get paid to practise. If you want to sail, work crew. If you like expensive wine, become a sommelier. Beautiful buildings? Enrol in architecture. Avoid doing something you hate for eight or more hours a day just to facilitate the purchase of things you barely have time to enjoy.

Delightfully, your authentic values are usually things you have motivation for and want to get better at. This means you will become skilful at them over time, which allows you to eventually command a high salary anyway.

Knowing what you want to do with your life is an alternate route to what public intellectual Nassim Taleb calls 'f\*\*k you money'.[9] He argues that you should seek financial independence so that when an employer asks you to do something lame, you can simply walk. Among the finance bros who worship Taleb, having lots of money is the key to this freedom. But you can also achieve it by simply not needing much money to live your values. Most hobbies, relationships and personal strivings can be facilitated on modest budgets. This makes it easy to walk away from bad deals.

A corollary bonus from the authentic approach to life, money and time is that it will inoculate you against cynical attempts by employers to sucker you into exploitative arrangements through appeals to your wellbeing. Firms have cottoned on to the fact that people want their work to be meaningful, to have quality relationships and for their lives to be pleasant. They're also aware of emerging evidence that happier workers are more productive.[10] So they're trying to dress up drudge work as full of purpose, presenting the firm as your family and populating the office with ping pong tables. If they genuinely care about your wellbeing this can be great, but too often it's just a way to press more labour out of you on the cheap. If your goals, relationships and leisure are all at the office, why would you ever leave? Knowing your intrinsic motivations allows you to find employers who are your kindred and see through the bullshit of those who aren't.

I'm not saying that work is bad. I 'work' a lot. But it's because I've been able to organise my life so that I can do the things I want to do and just happen to get paid for it. I have a hair-trigger sensitivity for the intrusion of drudgery into my life, because I know exactly what I want from employment and which aspects of my job are the unavoidable costs associated with being able to live the way I want to.

I'm reminded of some wisdom my old friend Dan came up with: a good indicator of a job that's right for you is that you enjoy the lowest level of that job. Many high-school graduates dream of being diplomats, for example, but they don't realise that the first rung of that career ladder is processing paperwork in the foreign ministry. If that paperwork excites you, then maybe you're onto a winner. It's likely that you have some deep fascination with the minutiae of foreign policy.

How can you discover your authentic values and intrinsic motivations? That's the subject of Part II of this book. For now, let's continue elaborating on the attitude we need to live well. *Do the things you value.* If you don't know what your authentic values are, then find out. Find ways to make your day-to-day life contribute directly to those values rather than merely giving you resources to spend in your limited free time.

## 1.4. Do not hack yourself to perfection

> There is nothing noble in being superior to some other man. True nobility is in being superior to your previous self.
> W. L. Sheldon, *What to Believe: An Ethical Creed*

Wellbeing involves self-improvement of a sort, specifically self-actualisation: the discovery and creation of our authentic self. This is a growth process and frequently involves being better than you were yesterday – closer to the perfection of who you are. But a common mistake in wellbeing circles, especially amidst American capitalism, is to conflate self-actualisation and self-*optimisation*. Countless self-help books, podcasts and blogs suggest ways that you can optimise your memory, your posture, your timetable, your diet, your sleep, your sex life, the exact minute of the day in which you consume coffee, and on and on.

This isn't the perfection of who you are, but of your general capabilities. Insofar as those capabilities help you become who you are, this is all good and well. If sleeping better makes you the less irritable person you would ideally like to be, then all power to you. The problem with self-optimisation is twofold. First, it is general rather than tailored to you, so you're ultimately meeting society's idea of what an 'optimal' person is rather than your own. Second, optimisation is almost inevitably tied up in competition: being 'superior' to those around you. These two problems tend to contribute to illbeing.

Society's expectations need to be constantly validated by other people, which leads to anxiety, striving, narcissism, fragile ego, fragile self-esteem and a host of other issues. It makes you pay more attention to what other people think, do and value than to your inner compass. It makes you want to be popular instead of happy.

Competition makes you envious, selfish and easily exploitable by a simple carrot. This is the problem of American capitalism and all cultures of 'high achievement'. You confuse being the best with being well. Then when you lack motivation to do things other people care about and suddenly stop being successful in their eyes, your personality collapses. You chase the praise of authority figures like a lovesick teenager because your whole identity hinges on being good at tasks. So when Goldman Sachs congratulates their new graduate hires by saying 'welcome to the 1%', those kids are ready to work ninety hours a week so that some numbers on a spreadsheet get larger.

I met a lot of students who combined social expectations and competitiveness while I was teaching at the University of Cambridge. There were a lot of genuine stars among them, but the mass of students was different. They were brilliant, sure. They'd always been top of the top. But nobody ever helped them articulate their values, personality or ambitions. So many of them wanted to be famous and spent their days figuring out how to turn their prodigious skill set into something that would 'hit' with the public. They didn't think about how to turn their skills into a life that was authentic to them, and they certainly didn't think about how to use their talents for collective benefit. Chasing popularity in this way makes your happiness contingent on the praise of self-absorbed people, which inevitably leads to your own misery.

I suspect that what bothers me about self-optimisation culture is that it is self-absorbed. It's all about you. In contrast, a big part of self-actualisation, at least as I'll articulate it in this book, is how you are with others. Self-actualisation requires you to identify where you belong, how you can be useful to the people you care about and how you can contribute to your collective goals. It is a very social endeavour. Self-optimisation culture, whether it's in podcasts, blogs, popular books, YouTube channels, TikToks or even academic articles, so rarely ventures into this social domain. In fact, it often turns fundamentally social practices, like gratitude, into individual practices to improve your personal outcomes. This feels instrumental, mercenary and grubby. I can't help but feel like it ultimately leads to social alienation; a world where we're all trying to one-up each other, monetise each other and get a little more for ourselves.

One place where I already see this dystopia is people offering advice on how to *optimise your mental health*. Ugh, gross. Your wellbeing is not a resource to be exploited so that you can get ahead. If the circumstances of your life make you feel like an egg about to crack, the solution is not to reinforce your psychology with steel bars, but to change your circumstances so that they are less stressful, toxic, demoralising, depressing or whatever it might be. Optimising your mental health sounds like some toxic management jargon invented by an overpaid, workaholic consultant to squeeze a bit more product from a strung-out workforce. Anyone advising you to optimise your mental health is not your friend. They are misguided at best and out to make a buck from your misery at worst.

Your 'best' self is not 'optimised' in the sense of being a winner, being 'better' than others or being a success according to social standards. Your best self is the person you feel most at peace being. Your best life is one that you find pleasant, fulfilling and meaningful, not a competition you must win.

There will be things about yourself that you want to improve, but this will often be de-optimisation. For example, I'd like to be able to care less about how fast my rock climbing is improving, and just enjoy the experience. Resist this incessant drive to be a little bit more perfect and think instead about how you can be a little more your authentic self. If you don't know where to begin, start by listening to yourself...

## 1.5. Look inwards

> When she is alone in the rooms I hear her humming to keep herself from thinking.
>
> Jean-Paul Sartre, *Nausea*

In 2014, a team of psychologists from the University of Virginia led by Timothy Wilson published a disturbing if amusing study.[11] When left alone in a room with nothing to do for fifteen minutes, 67 per cent of male participants and 25 per cent of female participants chose to electrocute themselves rather than sit with their thoughts. Pain was at least something to do. Anything to escape the boredom. Wilson offered disappointed reflections on the results to a journalist at *Science* magazine:

> We went into this thinking it wouldn't be hard for people to entertain themselves. We have this huge brain and its stuffed full of pleasant memories, and we have the ability to construct fantasies and stories. We really thought this thinking time was something people would like.[12]

Obviously, a huge part of the story here is boredom, attention span and the 'attention economy' we find ourselves in today. But another part is that people are so uncomfortable being alone with their thoughts. People are so uncomfortable turning inwards.

Unfortunately, turning inwards is typically the first step in becoming well. Listening to ourselves, understanding ourselves and being comfortable with ourselves was always the first plank of psychoanalysis. Creating quiet for the subconscious to speak is one objective of silent meditation retreats. Conversation, devices, entertainment – all are prohibited. Besides eating, sleeping and bathing, most of your time is taken up with directing attention inward. Such retreats aren't for me, personally, but something I like to do every year is go away on a multi-day camping trip where I take no books, no devices and no company so that I must also be alone with my thoughts and embark on inner dialogue.

This is the opposite of what contemporary society conditions you for. Everyone wants your attention, so there is none left for yourself. You think you don't know what to do to be well, so you queue up forty podcasts with titles like '5 Tips From the Stoics on How to Live a Better Life'. Reading this book might be part of this potentially unhelpful pattern, but at least I am telling you here, up front, that you aren't going to make progress on much at all to do with your wellbeing if you don't put down the books, take off your headphones and disconnect from the 'advice' people are giving long enough to *hear your own advice.*

Oddly, even a lot of contemporary psychological counselling discourages people from going inwards. Classic psychoanalysts frequently noted that people take a long time to be 'ready' for deep therapy. They're scared of what they'll discover inside. Afraid of their daemons and their inconvenient, uncomfortable, disappointing truths. They'd rather electrocute themselves. They'd certainly rather get a 10-step plan of cognitive behavioural therapies (CBT) than 'do the work' of self-reflection and self-renovation. Well-executed CBT is about separating constructive and accurate thoughts from destructive, false and ruminative ones. It thereby creates the foundations for a helpful inner dialogue. Bad CBT, which is sadly very common, just applies a cookie-cutter list of workbook exercises in no way tailored to the unique life narrative and complex subjective experiences of a particular patient. It is just another means by which society imposes its structures, in this case its idea of 'normal', on individuals. It encourages people to conform to something that arrives from outside, instead of developing themselves from within.

We arrive into adulthood heavily preconditioned by our families, our experiences and our societies. It's important to be able to get past all that conditioning to something like your authentic self. It may be unformed, confused and volatile, but at least it's genuine. In dialogue with this authentic self, you can determine values, goals, perspectives and behaviours that feel true to you and that will undergird intrinsic motivation and self-actualisation.

So regardless of how extroverted you might be, make sure you spend time with yourself. Be comfortable with boredom. Take it as an opportunity for quiet reflection. Make space for that voice from deep within. For your intuition to articulate itself you will probably have to listen very *carefully*, at least at first. You are likely to mishear your intuition. You're likely to misinterpret your intuitions through the lens of your outer world – the conditioning you receive every day from the environment around you. Nurture that inner dialogue to develop its own language, one likely to come in feelings more than words or ideas, and give it time to grow courageous, honest and authentic. It takes practice to hear your own advice with precision. Then turn to the world again and figure out what you want to do with that advice.

## 1.6. The desire for tranquillity

> The way I see it, if you want the rainbow, you've got to put up with the rain.
>
> Dolly Parton[13]

Learning to love the treadmill requires turning towards personal growth. This runs counter to a human tendency to want tranquillity, predictability and a steady worldview. We want to feel that we understand the world and can make sense of new phenomena with our existing frameworks and theories. There are good evolutionary reasons why we like predictability, but these reasons might not be suitable for today's world. Two concepts are especially relevant: the free energy principle and worldview defence theory.

The free energy principle is an arguably inappropriate name for the idea that the human brain, and its associated motor system and behavioural tendencies, works to minimise surprises.

In evolutionary settings, surprises are often life threatening. Didn't expect that landslide? Now you're dead. Didn't expect this region to be periodically affected by drought? Now you're dead. Didn't expect a bear to be sleeping in that cave? Dead again.

This evolutionary pressure encouraged our brain to become good at prediction. Indeed, there is an increasingly dominant view in neuroscience that 'prediction' can explain a vast amount of brain activity.[14] For example, the intuitive way of understanding perception is that light arrives on your retina and your brain translates this light into an image. In fact, this would be prohibitively energy intensive. Instead, your eyes feed clues to your brain about the world and then your brain uses its predictive powers to fill in the detail. Imagine you're looking at the ceiling of an Art Deco room. It's mostly a flat white expanse. As your eyes scan along it, there is nothing to suggest any change. Then all of a sudden you hit some embossed detail. Now your brain predicts what that embossed detail looks like based on prior experience. *Prior experience* is key. If your brain has never seen that detail before, it might move you to look closely at it in case there is something to be concerned about. Otherwise, it will make a prediction and move on. Readers who have travelled in new cities might recall how exhausted they are at the end of a day in which they did little but walk around and sit in cafes. Parents might note how much their newborns and young children sleep. In both cases, the mind is processing huge amounts of novel information. It can't make predictions as effortlessly as usual, and so it fatigues.

Prediction reduces the amount of energy that is needed by our brain to process information, but prediction is averse to surprises. So we tend to abhor surprises. This has obvious advantages and we shouldn't put our brain into distress by always bombarding it with novel experiences. But it also makes us averse to new ways of thinking, living and being, and discourages us from expanding our worlds, including the people in those worlds, once we have found something we can settle into.

This is fine if we only settle once we've developed a rich, broad and detailed life. But our tendency to seek tranquillity can terminate the process of self-actualisation prematurely, and that's disastrous.

Research on worldview defence leads to similar conclusions. The basic idea behind it is that certain forms of threat or anxiety cause people to become more zealous about the systems of meaning and value that they use to make sense of the world. One example is that humans have constructed elaborate cultural practices around death – perhaps our most primitive anxiety. The contention of terror management theory is that humans are unusual among animals in that our ability to prospect – to ponder the future – makes us aware of our impending death.[15] This triggers a deep terror in us that we can only deal with by plugging into some structure that we think will persist beyond our death, like a national identity or a religious cosmic order. In laboratory experiments, participants who are primed to think about death display textbook worldview defence, such as exaggerated displays of loyalty to their race, nation or religion. They also administer more hot sauce to other participants who question their values – a way of testing hostility that passes ethical review.

Terror management theory isn't the only hypothesised driver of worldview defence. There are three others: uncertainty management, unconscious vigilance and coalition threat.[16] The first two of these are, arguably, more generalised versions of terror management theory. Rather than death phobia, uncertainty management explains worldview defence as a response to ambiguity. Similarly, rather than fear of death, unconscious vigilance argues that worldview defence is a reaction to all sources of fear and anxiety. For example, worldview defence appears to be more common in places of economic decline and community disintegration like the de-industrialised regions of the United Kingdom and United States.

Coalition threat picks up a theme common to all theories

of worldview defence, which is that we seek social support when we are threatened. In evolutionary environments, the principal determinant of our survival was whether others cared for us. The human capacity for cooperation, as we will discuss in detail later, is grounded in cultural practices that bond individuals into a group around shared values and meanings. As such, when we want to rally social support to our side, we loudly proclaim and defend those values: this is worldview defence.

How all this interacts with tranquillity is that when we come across challenges to our worldview, we react by doubling down on that worldview and associate with people who reinforce it. This can make us close-minded and limit our personal growth.

That's not to say that we should go hard in the opposite direction. As with the free energy principle, it is in a sense good for us to have a stable worldview. It helps us to feel close to our friends, peers and community. It helps us to feel like the world is a safe and predictable place. It helps us to find meaning and purpose in life and to live with a conscience.

What we need is to *balance growth and stability*. This is reminiscent of what I said about the treadmill: you want a safe and rejuvenating steady state that facilitates a dynamic engagement with life. Terror management theorists Tom Pyszczynski, Jeff Greenberg and Jamie Arndt provide a succinct description of this sweet spot:

> Ironically then, a secure worldview and sense of self-worth allows us to venture forth to uncharted mental territories where discoveries can emerge that question those very security-providing structures, requiring us to revise those structures to accommodate our self expansions… Unfortunately, we often fail to allow this dialectic process to continue its forward momentum; rather, we give up the potential pleasures of intrinsically motivated growth-promoting activity in exchange for the comfort and security

that clinging to existing forms of psychological organisation of self and world provides.[17]

So the key is to develop a worldview that affords you some peace of mind and gives you a rudimentary framework for making sense of the world, but to leave that worldview open to growth and revision. We must be particularly attentive to only defend that worldview in good faith. That is, to defend it with reason and wisdom and not just because attacks on it are scary. If we deploy the powers of hypocrisy, dissonance and fallacy to retain our worldview despite incisive critiques, then that worldview is not a sanctuary but a sandcastle. We should welcome those critiques and use them to reform and improve our worldview until it is a fortress. Then it really does provide stability in our life, and we can venture forth from it to chart new territory.

There's an often-overlooked character trait, one might call it a virtue, that helps us to maintain this robust but open worldview – fallibilism. It's our first port of call in the next chapter, but before that, a small thought...

## 1.7. Wellbeing stocks

> When you see a good person, think of becoming like them. When you see someone not so good, reflect on your own weak points.
>
> Confucius

The way I spoke of the treadmill above might have given you the impression that wellbeing is about always looking for your next goal or activity. While there is some truth to that, I want to push back against that idea.

Most of us are wired in a way that means we need to learn to enjoy running on the treadmill, which means having projects. You don't necessarily need to be getting better at anything, you just need to explore the world and yourself, and stay occupied. There is no standing still in wellbeing. However, wellbeing is not like financial income where you need to keep it coming in by generating more. It is more like a stock portfolio that you build over time. As your portfolio matures, it pays more and more dividends passively – that is, without active effort.

Perhaps the easiest way of illustrating this idea is to think about your relationships. As relationships mature you unlock new possibilities that come with intimacy, trust and shared memories. You have someone you can turn to in times of need – good friends will drop everything to fetch you in an emergency, and a long-term lover will offer you an emotionally wise shoulder to cry on. Mutual trust leads to reciprocity and sharing that can make things like multi-family holidays feasible. And shared memories are one of the most amusing and comforting ways to spend an evening. Such wellbeing depends on having done the work to form deep relationships. But once you have those relationships, they pay out well beyond the effort required to maintain them. The above applies to many of the 'projects' you pursue in self-actualisation, such as hobbies, physical and mental self-improvement, wise investments of time and money, and your career.

While wellbeing stocks tend to accrue organically during your self-actualisation, it can be valuable to actively pursue them. Some activities might help you to self-actualise without producing wellbeing stocks, but a small adjustment could achieve both outcomes. Jogging three times a week will keep you healthy, for example, but jogging three times a week as part of a running club that occasionally participates in fun runs will also give you warm memories, help you build friendships and potentially open you to new experiences and perspectives on the world. Keep an eye out for ways to increase your wellbeing stocks.

## Chapter 1 summary

> Your time is limited, so don't waste it living someone else's life. Don't be trapped by dogma – which is living the result of other people's thinking. Don't let the noise of others' opinions drown out your own inner voice. And most important, have the courage to follow your heart and intuition.
>
> Steve Jobs, founder of Apple,
> Stanford commencement address, 2005

One of the few frustrations I had in writing this book was that I couldn't quite organise it as a linear narrative around a big central metaphor. That's because wellbeing is just not like that. It's multidimensional and has a lot to do with how many disparate things, from personal character traits to the city in which you live, fit together into a coherent whole (indeed, I very nearly titled this book *Wholeness*). So wellbeing is less a narrative and more a landscape painting, with each chapter here filling in that picture a bit more. These chapter summaries are meant to help bring the image into focus.

They will also give me an opportunity to offer some practical advice or exercises, however, I'm wary of that. I know people want activities, but these feel to me like 'one weird trick for happiness' type things, which often act as a *distraction* from deep work rather than a catalyst for it. In my experience, you need ideas more than activities, and you just need to let those ideas digest in your mind and spirit for a while. Once internalised, you'll start to notice situations where they are relevant, and your behaviour will shift. You don't need to keep a daily gratitude journal, for example. You just need to know that focusing on the negative in your life is not conducive to happiness. Then when you're making yourself miserable this idea will pop out of your unconscious and you'll realise, 'Oh, I'm focusing on the negative here instead of all the things I could be grateful for.'

With that disclaimer out of the way, here are some practical tips for implementing Chapter 1. Lead an examined life. To begin that process, shut off the noise from outside you. Turn off the 'influencers' (me included), forget about what's 'cool' and try to tune out from society for a bit. Create some peace and quiet for yourself to think about what's authentic to you. Think about your childhood through to today, and what and who brought you joy, fulfilment and purpose. Make a list and think about how you could invest more time, energy and resources into those things and people. A journal can be a helpful device for this reflective activity and I'd encourage you to write in one whenever big thoughts or feelings come to you, or when none come at all and you need to stimulate them.

# 2
# Character

> Be more concerned with your character than your reputation, because character is what you really are, while your reputation is merely what others think you are.
> John Wooden, arguably the most decorated coach of American college basketball

One of the main themes of ancient Greek and Roman philosophy is virtue. In contrast to the emphasis during the eighteenth-century European Enlightenment on duties, consequences and moral acts, ancient moral philosophy put much more emphasis on moral *character*. The virtues are character traits that the ancients considered 'good'; things like a sense of humour, honesty and an even temperament. For the ancient European philosophers, being a good person and living a good life were inextricable. Compare this to enlightenment thinking wherein you were supposed to do good because it was right, not because it would make you well. The link between righteousness and self-interest was lost. Indeed, 'modern' ethical philosophy often places moral conduct and self-interested conduct in explicit opposition. I think this is wrong, very wrong, but we can leave that issue aside until Part III. What we should do now is revive the ancient emphasis on character and look at some of the most important candidates for virtues that promote wellbeing. We'll start with fallibilism.

## 2.1. Fallibilism

> Uncertainty is an uncomfortable position, but certainty is an absurd one.
>
> Voltaire

Fallibilism is the attitude that 'I could be wrong'. It is a foundational part of the growth mindset. Fallibilism keeps you seeking new insights, perspectives and experiences. It prevents you from becoming reliant on a too simple worldview, a too narrow circle of friends and too few sources of new information. It also makes you a delightful conversation partner because you're genuinely interested in people and the different perspectives that they might offer you on the world and yourself.

Fallibilism as an idea is usually credited to the philosopher of science Karl Popper, who played a decisive role in codifying the scientific method in the second half of the twentieth century.[1] At that time, much effort was being expended on understanding how science could *confirm* factual claims and thereby arrive at The Truth. Popper's innovation was to focus instead on science's power to *falsify*. Very succinctly and crudely, the argument goes something like this. Reality is something we experience with our senses. As such we can only test claims about reality with induction. This is where we rely on evidential support for a claim, and that evidence always comes from our senses. This is distinct from deduction where conclusions follow from premises, that is, where the basis for a claim is pure logic. Mathematics uses deduction to prove that certain propositions are true. However, mathematics operates in an abstract space, not reality. Maths can therefore only be used to derive *hypotheses* about reality that must then be tested empirically – with our senses – before we know whether they're reasonable. So you're back at induction.

Now the problem with induction is that it is inherently statistical. Say I'm an Englishman in the eighteenth century and I only ever observe white swans. I've seen thousands of swans in my life, and they were always white. I might reasonably conclude that all swans are white. If told that Bertie is a swan, I might reasonably deduce that Bertie is white. Is this The Truth? Well, I can never be sure because it's possible that I simply haven't seen enough swans. As it turns out, if I take a trip to the newly colonised lands of Australia, I will discover the existence of black swans. This will disprove my belief that all swans are white.

Popper's view was that we can treat as fact (not truth) any claim that has stood up to rigorous tests, like controlled experiments, until such time as new evidence comes along to contradict those claims. Until then, we can build upon our factual knowledge with new conjectures and refutations to expand our knowledge and deepen our understanding of the world. Sometimes we have to junk an enormous amount of supposed factual knowledge on the basis of new evidence. This has been called a 'paradigm shift' since the work of the American historian and philosopher of science Thomas Kuhn's work on the subject.[2] Perhaps the most famous such shift is the move away from Newtonian physics after experiments started to confirm Einstein's postulates of quantum mechanics.

What does this digression into the theory of knowledge have to do with wellbeing? It's about being comfortable with ambiguity. As we discussed in section 1.6, humans like certainty. One manifestation of this in our present nihilistic moment is that there are many people on the hunt for The Truth and they're convinced that science is supplying it. But that's not right. Science supplies falsification, not truth. Maths provides truth, but not about reality. And neither maths nor science can provide *normative* truth; that is, truth about what's valuable, good and right. So when you set about searching for the truth and put your trust in science, you're really just setting yourself up for a painful failure. The best we can do is to be less wrong. Ambiguity will always remain.

I'm not saying you shouldn't be fond of science or reasoned argument. I love science and rationality. But I love them mostly because they help me get rid of my crappy ideas, not because they bring me more certainty. *Let go of the need for certainty*. That's what fallibilism is about.

Popper's most important book on the theory of knowledge is *The Logic of Scientific Discovery*, but many of the themes of fallibilism and falsification carried over into his acclaimed works on social and political theory, notably *The Open Society and its Enemies*, a gigantic two-volume critique of totalitarian thinking. The first volume takes on right-wing fascism via a critique of Plato and Hegel, and the second volume takes on left-wing communism via a critique of Marx. Popper's targets are political theories that claim to know what the good society looks like and how to get there. These ideologies lay claim to moral truth and Popper comes down on them with the logic of falsification. He argues that it is much easier for people to agree on what's bad than what's good. Fixing these problems as consensus emerges leads to an incrementally better world, whereas revolutions to achieve vaguely specified paradises always end in tragedy. There is too much that is unknown and unknowable about the good to get there in one jump, but moral crusaders will always cover up this insecurity with tyrannous zealotry.

Ironically, many of the most ideological people believe they have taken Popper's lessons to heart. They have understood his logic of *scientific* discovery and think it's the only way for us to develop useful knowledge. I confess that I used to be a bit like this. I resented the phrase 'other ways of knowing', which is popular among anthropologists and sociologists. I thought that there is one way of knowing and that's *science*.

I've mellowed. I still think science is the only way of getting Knowledge with a capital K, but such knowledge is often much less useful to our wellbeing than other understandings. I'll tell you the example that changed my mind. During the Middle Ages, the Celts supposedly had a story. Sometimes a new mother has her spirit whisked away by the fairies to the fairy kingdom and she becomes listless and neglectful of her baby as a result. Her spirit must be coaxed and guided back from the fairies by spending time with the mother and looking after her baby. Everyone in her family and the village must visit the mother and her child, sit with them, speak to them and offer them good cheer so that the baby is looked after and the mother's spirit remembers how much love there is for her back home. This is a story of postnatal depression that communicates an effective cure for the condition in a way that is much more meaningful, actionable and social than a scientific explanation like 'childbirth can destabilise serotonin levels in the brain; take these pills'. This story is a 'way of knowing' about the world that benefits individual and community wellbeing.[3]

If you are only able or willing to learn from people who communicate their understandings to you in scientific terms (or any narrowly specified terms, for that matter), then you are going to miss out on a lot of wisdom. Popper's *Open Society* was one of free discourse about how society should be organised. Take a leaf from his book and be an *Open Person*. Be ready to meet people where they are at and try to inhabit their ways of thinking about, interpreting and knowing about the world. Obviously, you are going to encounter a lot of disordered thinking, conspiracy theorising and just general bullshit. Keep your rational wits about you. As my friend Katie likes to say: 'Don't get lost in the wu.' But try to adopt the attitude of the first great rationalist, Socrates, who was fond of saying: 'The only thing I know is how little I know.' Adopt a Bayesian attitude: 'I've only seen part of the statistical distribution.' And adopt a fallibilist attitude: 'I will stick with this while trying to prove it wrong.' These attitudes are fundamental to your wellbeing.

## 2.2. Self-improvement by negation

> Well then get your shit together, get it all together and put it in a backpack, all your shit, so it's together. And if you gotta take it somewhere, take it somewhere, you know. Take it to the shit store and sell it, or put it in the shit museum.

> I don't care what you do, you just gotta get it together. Get your shit together.
>
> *Rick and Morty*, 'Big Trouble in Little Sanchez'

The emphasis in most self-help literature (especially the business kind) is on leveraging your strengths and improving by *expanding* your self – acquiring new skills, learning new knowledge, integrating with new social groups. There's nothing inherently wrong with that, but it overlooks that a tremendous amount of self-improvement, and I daresay the most important self-improvements, comes about through *negation* – by getting rid of bad parts of yourself.

Things that we would like to gain tend to dominate our goals – I would like to be stronger, prettier, more knowledgeable, more qualified, more awarded, richer, etc. Make a conscious effort to also develop goals of negation: I will stop being late, I will stop telling white lies, I will reduce my consumption of single-use plastics, I will stop drinking to excess, I will resist peer pressure, I will be less greedy, I will be less irritatingly competitive, I won't use my introversion as an excuse to skip chores and be moody. That sort of thing.

This is Popperian falsification applied to the self. Identify the things in your life that aren't working for you and excise them. Identify the things that aren't working as you would expect and investigate them. Identify the things that are actively making your life miserable, especially your own personality traits, and reform them. Get rid of the bad.

Our negative qualities are more pernicious to our interpersonal relationships than our good qualities. Fame, talent, success, status and wealth are dazzling and undeniably attractive, but they are not enough for a relationship to persist if a dazzling individual is also self-absorbed, ungrateful, vain, unreliable, mercurial, needy, cynical, perpetually unsatisfied and jealous. Indeed, it is easier, at least in my experience, to sustain wholesome, nourishing relationships with people who are in most ways mundane but possess qualities that make them easy to hang around with. Think about the people in your life who you like, but also consider people who you never dread spending time with. These are the sort of people that when you bump into them at a reunion or you're stuck with them at a family event enable the day to pass pleasantly. I bet these people *lack* the following qualities: tardiness, stinginess, self-absorption, self-righteousness, arrogance, pretence and insecurity, and they're probably not too busy for others nor judgemental of them. These are qualities you can remove from yourself as well.

One of the best things about self-improvement by negation is that it is relatively easy to identify errors. You know what aspects of yourself make you cringe, make you embarrassed, make you feel guilt or shame. These are all social emotions – signals that your behaviour makes you less appealing to your peers. Direct your attention to these qualities and try to remove them. You'll feel less of these negative emotions, and you might strengthen your interpersonal relationships in the process. If you never experience these emotions, do check whether you're a sociopath – ask your friends if you have any behaviours or habits (especially habits) that make them annoyed, grossed out, frustrated, angry or hurt. I'm sure you'll get something if you're genuinely interested.

## 2.3. Self-serving biases

> Man naturally desires not only to be loved, but to be lovely; or to be that thing which is the natural and proper object of love.
>
> Adam Smith, *The Theory of Moral Sentiments*

So-called 'cognitive and behavioural biases' are one of the hottest topics of twenty-first-century research. For a primer that is oriented towards helping you live a better life, see Daniel Kahneman's *Thinking, Fast and Slow*.[4] There are many aspects of this literature that bear on wellbeing but, owing to space constraints, I'm going to restrict myself to just two: self-serving bias and positivity bias. These are two character traits that you should be working to remove.

Self-serving bias has two manifestations. First, we attribute good outcomes to our own efforts and bad behaviours to external factors. For example, when we get promoted, we think it is because we are productive and well-suited to the job. When we get passed over for a promotion, we assume it is because management are idiots or chummy with our rival. This self-serving bias also inclines us to see things that benefit us as fair.

Second, we think we are more excellent than we are – this is sometimes called illusory superiority.[5] The clearest and often funniest examples of illusory superiority come from surveys where people are asked to indicate whether they are 'better than average' at a task. For example, in a study from the early 1980s, 93 per cent of American drivers said they were better than average (i.e. in the top 50 per cent of drivers).[6] In a more recent survey of Stanford Business School students, 87 per cent thought their test scores were above the class median.[7] In 1976, the College Board of the United States attached a survey to the SAT exam in which 25 per cent of students rated themselves in the top 1 per cent for 'ability to get along well with others' (everyone *else* is a bitch, it seems).[8] My favourite is a survey of university teachers where nearly 70 per cent of lecturers rated themselves in the top 25 per cent in terms of teaching quality, and a full 90 per cent thought they were above average.[9] This is funny because students almost universally complain about the quality of teaching. Maybe the professors know that they are bad but think everyone else is worse?

The relationship between self-serving bias and wellbeing is complicated. On the one hand, this bias is important for the maintenance of self-esteem. You are more inclined to see yourself in a positive way if you give yourself responsibility for good things and others responsibility for bad things. Tellingly, self-serving bias is often reversed in depressed people: they attribute bad things to themselves and good things to external factors. Such behaviour can be associated with rumination, where fixating on the bad things that you've done becomes a habit, and learned helplessness, where you develop a belief that you are powerless to change your life because you think everything happens *to you* rather than as a result of your own agency. Both rumination and learned helplessness are associated with sustained depression.

On the other hand, self-serving bias gives us a distorted sense of what we are responsible for and deserve, which can have a range of negative consequences. A straightforward indicator of a shit person is that they don't take responsibility for the bad things that they do. This is poisonous to interpersonal relationships, which are critical to wellbeing, and a hallmark of narcissism. Illusory superiority can make us think we deserve to get ahead when in fact we aren't worthy. The consequences of this can include an irritating sense of entitlement mixed with laziness, frequent unpleasant feelings of disappointment and, in extreme cases, a persecution complex (a form of paranoia where you think everyone is scheming to marginalise you). More broadly, wellbeing requires sometimes accepting that something is a bad fit for you, while at other times recognising that you just aren't trying hard enough.

Which hand do we favour? If I can be permitted a simplification, I suggest cautiously eradicating your self-serving bias and replacing it with self-compassion. Wellbeing requires that you perceive reality accurately. But this is associated with depression – there are many studies observing that depressed people are more likely to have correct views of reality than mentally healthy people. The world is often bleak. Life is fantastic and the standard of living is improving so fast it makes my head spin, but this doesn't change the fact that there is no cosmic justice, we don't matter in a transcendental sense, death is coming, people are disappointing for the most part, childhood leukaemia exists and shit happens. Humans have developed a range of defence mechanisms like self-serving bias to keep us sane and productive, even as an awareness of these dreary facts percolate in our subconscious. Depression has an annoying habit of plugging you into this awareness. That's why we need self-compassion.

Compassion is about constructive sympathy. Its formal components are: 1) the ability to recognise suffering; 2) understanding the universality of suffering in human experience; 3) feeling empathy for the person suffering; 4) tolerating uncomfortable feelings that might be aroused in response to the suffering person and thereby remaining open to accepting the person (non-judgement); and 5) motivation to act to alleviate the suffering.[10] The big one for self-compassion is no. 4. When you're suffering because of guilt over having done something immoral, or shame because you think you're a failure, you must engage with those feelings in a non-judgemental way. This can be particularly hard when these feelings are tied into major aspects of your identity, like career goals and close relationships, and fundamental structures of your psychological life, such as your relationship with your family. In those cases, compassion is even more important. You need to keep in mind that we are all flawed creatures who make mistakes.

You will get better at compassion if you genuinely work at it. You need to recognise that circumstances are sometimes outside of your control. Even when you are responsible for something bad, consider whether the roots of your actions lie in things that were done to you, like childhood bullying making you cold and introverted. Do not use these things as an excuse but do be patient with your self-improvement when they are at play. Compassion doesn't mean be soft, it means be constructively sympathetic – understand the challenges and constraints at play and try to work past them.

It is critical that we practise compassionate regard for our self-image – how we see ourselves in our mind's eye. Be honest about your deficiencies and weaknesses, *including your ability to change them*. There is a risk in this attitude that you become lazy about changing those aspects of yourself that you don't like. Such an outcome should be avoided. But equally, hating yourself for things that you cannot change is a toxic and counterproductive attitude. Compassionate self-regard is fundamentally about being reasonable with yourself.

## 2.4. No pretending business

> I think doing something well is a form of respect for humanity in general. I have found that all incompetence comes from not paying attention, which comes from people doing something that they don't want to do.
>
> Hal Hartley, American film director and screenwriter

Don't do things pretentiously. It is common for people seeking depth, meaning or identity to reach for the cosmetic indicators of these things. Visit any tennis club and you will come across someone who can't hit a backhand but owns multiple top line racquets, a wardrobe full of quick dry gear and a huge six-racquet bag for all their kit. This person *looks* like a tennis player but isn't one. You need to focus on substance. An identity can only support your wellbeing if it's real. Fake identities don't fool anyone, especially yourself.

As we'll discuss in Part II, you want to achieve a state where your actions and the assessments of others confirm that you are the kind of person you want to be and believe you ought to be. If your identity is a charade, then you'll constantly receive confirmation that you are not that person. Those posers at the tennis club might feel chuffed looking at themselves decked out in all their Federer gear, but that confidence evaporates as they double fault their opening service game. Nothing drives home that you aren't a tennis player quite like losing games of tennis.

When you're trying to become something, focus on becoming the essence of that thing. It's typically a skill or a way of being, not a look or a vibe. You can't confect essences, only cultivate them. It takes effort to be real.

A challenge to my view is that we often don't know whether we want to make the investment in something that is required to be identified with it. People change jobs, degrees, partners, hobbies, habitats and many other things throughout life after discovering that they're not quite the right fit. This is particularly true for young people, who furiously try on new identities while they search for something that suits them. There's nothing wrong with that. But when trying new things, you should still give them a *proper* go, otherwise you aren't going to learn whether they are in fact suitable for you. This means that even when experimenting, dabbling or just dipping your toe into something, you should focus on sampling its essence, not its cosmetics.

I'm reminded of a visit my partner and I made to a café in Byron Bay, Australia, that served food grown on its own farm. The farm gave introductory courses on permaculture, sustainable gardening and organic farming. As we were sipping our coffees and enjoying the view of a huge, almost mythical pig that occupied the grounds, students for one of these courses started streaming in. Almost without exception they were wearing brand new, fashionable gardening gear, including various fine leather holsters for artisan (probably hand forged) trowels and other tools. Few of them looked like they'd spent a day in the dirt.

Now to be fair, they were here to learn some gardening – the essence of the identity they wanted. Good on 'em. But why invest in all this flashy kit? The most sustainable way to acquire gardening gear is to reuse existing items second hand. And your clothes are going to get dirty anyway – why buy brand new ones when you can just repurpose your old jeans? The reason is that Byron Bay is the Instagram capital of Australia – a place where young bourgeois folk flock to try and get a slice of a wholesome, sun-drenched life they've seen on social media. What they copy first is the image they've seen, not its substance.

Focusing on the essence of things reduces the costs of experimentation, both in terms of money and time. You only buy the things that are absolutely necessary to make a start and you allocate your time to the activity that will give you the clearest sense of what that thing is like. If it turns out not to suit you, you cut your minimal losses and try something else.

I've only talked about pretence in terms of cosmetics and in the context of experimentation, but the rule 'no pretending business' is broader than that. Pretending includes doing the essence of things in a half-arsed way, like when people do the bare minimum at the gym and then complain that they can't get the body they want. I'm not talking here about doing things casually because you genuinely prefer that level of intensity – that's fine. The issue here is one of dishonesty with yourself. You have to understand, intimately, what level of investment an identity requires in order for you to step into it and then give it that level of investment. Otherwise, you will never step into any identity and always be a touch disappointed in yourself. Repeatedly doing things in a half-arsed way leads to a half-arsed life.

Let me finish with a caveat. Most people need things in their life that aren't part of the project of their life. These are things that you're not trying to get better at. They are something you want in your life, but you don't want them to define your life. For me this is cooking. I buy cookbooks occasionally and work my way through them very slowly, and I try to give over an afternoon a week to cooking something a bit elaborate, especially if I have guests over. I want to be known as someone who 'can cook', but not as a foodie or someone for whom cooking is 'a passion'. It's nice to have this low-stakes thing in my life that sparks joy when it goes well but doesn't send me spiralling when it goes badly. In contrast, when I get bad news on the professional front, like one of my papers getting rejected from a journal, it can often spin me out for days. This is because my identity is bound up with success in my academic goals. When I get negative feedback, it makes me question whether I am in fact a good academic. My sense of self is riding on that feedback, which is why I am very attentive to doing academic things properly. With cooking, I don't care if I'm a good cook, so half arsing it isn't a big deal.

So be mindful of the things that are central to your identity and do them properly. No pretending business. But it's probably also a good idea to have something in your life that's casual. The key thing is never lie to yourself about something being casual when it is in fact central. That can only end in self-loathing.

## 2.5. Radical honesty

> Above all, don't lie to yourself. The man who lies to himself and listens to his own lie comes to a point that he cannot distinguish the truth within him, or around him, and so loses all respect for himself and for others. And having no respect, he ceases to love.
>
> Fyodor Dostoevsky, *The Brothers Karamazov*

In the previous section on pretending, I spoke a lot about dishonesty. Let's do a deep dive on that. Try to avoid lying, especially to yourself, and when you do engage in falsehood, be very honest with yourself about what you are doing and why. I think it is best to interpret this rule quite strictly. Omissions count as lies. Anytime your intent is to deceive, mislead, misdirect, obfuscate or do anything less than be fully frank, you're lying. White lies are lies. Little embellishments can be harmless, especially when they're charming or characterful, but that's lucky. More often they are pernicious because they reflect an insecurity or sense of inadequacy in you. Just don't lie.

A particularly seductive form of lying is where you interpret ambiguities in ways that suit your interests instead of being explicit or seeking clarification. When the truth is difficult, we are liable to say the easy part of it and leave the hard part unsaid. We can then fool ourselves into thinking that we have been honest when in fact we skipped over the important part. I have been guilty of this on multiple occasions in my life, typically when relationships have been delightful and valuable but also obviously doomed, and it has always led to grief for myself and others. When you cannot bear to engage with something because you are worried you will ruin the lovely thing it is associated with, that is precisely when you must engage most of all. The thing is already ruined. You must clean it now to salvage what good is there.

Going where the truth hurts is a general rule for life. It is fundamental to many forms of psychotherapy, especially those associated with trauma. Whenever you discover a scenario that your spirit refuses to think about, a feeling that your heart refuses to process or a fact that your mind refuses to accept, you've discovered a bomb. You need to deal with that bomb now, even if it means detonating it, because it's only going to get bigger over time. This is the essence of honesty: facing pain, discomfort, loss, tragedy, trade-offs, whatever bad thing it might be now, courageously.

Besides turning people off you, lying has three negative consequences. The first is that it distracts you from dealing with your insecurities. Many lies, especially white lies, are a manifestation of something you feel inadequate about. We exaggerate stories because we wish our life was cooler, more interesting or more exciting. We overstate our abilities because we find our actual abilities embarrassing. And we cover up our errors, indiscretions and misdeeds because we are ashamed of them. All of these must be confronted head on and dealt with, either by improving, or by making peace with ourselves, or by offering a genuine apology. If your life bores you, then takes steps to make it more compelling. If you are insecure about something then fix it, don't hide from it. And if you've done something wrong, own up to it, make amends and help everyone heal, including yourself. Lies are a pretence – they are a seemingly light way to avoid the hard work of being the person you'd rather be.

The second harm of lying is that it makes space in your mind for dissonance, hypocrisy and compartmentalisation. These are all ways of holding inconsistent things in your psyche simultaneously, which is pernicious to wellbeing. As we will discuss in Part II, the human psyche has a natural tendency to growth and integration. Children start to notice inconsistencies in themselves from early adolescence and seek to resolve them. Trauma and other sources of neuroses often block this natural process of psychological harmonisation, leading to mental illness. They create a sort of immovable object in the psyche that can't be jettisoned but also can't be integrated; it just sits there blocking integration until it is dealt with. Don't invite the same forces into your life by lying. Dishonesty creates a little pocket of space in your mind and fertilises it so that inconsistencies can grow from little white lies into big dark problems.

The third harm of lying is that it generates cognitive load. You must remember whom you told what lies to. You must keep all your stories straight. You must make sure that your fabrications are believable. And you must be on guard that you are not discovered. All that takes effort that could be better spent on achieving real growth in yourself rather than concocting fake stories.

Honesty has benefits too, the most important of which is that it typically improves your relationships with other people. Consider all these 'virtues' that we respect, admire and appreciate in people: trustworthy, tells it like it is, straightforward. These are all virtues you can have today if you just stop lying. Note that these qualities are distinct from being blunt or abrasive. Honesty doesn't mean you have to be rude.

I think you should default to *radical honesty*. You should be open about who you are and what you're about. People are often scared to present themselves so candidly. They're worried that there are things they should be ashamed of. But as we've discussed, you should try to change or make peace with anything that you're insecure about. Once that work is done, presenting yourself honestly is a great way to get social verification – see whether other people see you the same way you see yourself. It might turn out that you're still lying to yourself. Or that what you thought was good is actually problematic in the eyes of somebody else. That sort of social feedback is something for introspection, as we'll discuss in Part II. But even if you get critiqued, that's valuable. It's information you can use for growth. What if people just don't like you as you are? Well then f**k those people. They aren't worth your care and attention. The great thing about radical honesty is that it sweeps aside all the people, places and groups you're not compatible with and steers you towards communities where you'll belong.

Now some very important caveats. I have written this section assuming the best in other people, but this isn't always the case. If you're part of a persecuted minority, as many LGBTQ+ people are, for example, then it is often necessary to be secretive about aspects of yourself to avoid harm. Find people with whom you can be honest and try to move away from people with whom you can't, but your situation is probably more complicated than 'just let it all hang out'. Similarly, many neurodivergent people, especially those on the autism spectrum, will benefit from learning to play along with social conventions of tact or subtext that occur in neurotypical discourse. I think the key thing here is to do this out of an earnest desire to make friends and help others to enjoy your company, rather than out of a cynical desire to manipulate them.

This brings us to the second caveat, which is that there are a lot of psychopathic people and dishonest situations out there, like corrupt bureaucracies or mercenary workplace cultures, that will cynically take advantage of your honesty. You don't need to play by the rules here. These are not cases where if you are honest, it will encourage more honesty in return. Psychopaths are incapable of caring about anything other than their self-interest, and organisational cultures are set from within and high up rather than influenced by the little people like you.

The strategy of tit for tat can be useful here. This is where you are honest, cooperative and generous by default, but if someone takes advantage of that you stop cooperating with them until they do something generous. Even then, be wary of manipulation. Psychopaths know how to push your buttons. If we are generous by default, we encourage the world to be a kind place, while tit for tat limits the extent to which people can take advantage of us. That protects our kind hearts to express love where it is better appreciated.

## 2.6. Generosity

> The only wealth that you will keep forever is the wealth you have given away.
>
> Widely attributed to Marcus Aurelius, though perhaps apocryphal.[11]

Society is built on generosity. This is one of the main lessons of the take a hit game, which I play with my public policy undergraduates every year. I ask eight of them to form an orderly queue so that they cannot see the chest of the person in front of them. I ask them to each hold a hand to their chest either clenched as a fist for 0, or with a finger up to indicate that they want chocolate. I walk down the queue noting who wants chocolate. They all get a piece as long as at least three people in the group asked for 0. They 'took a hit' so that the other members of the group might prosper.

There are so many aspects of social life that are characterised by take a hit dynamics. Perhaps the biggest one is child rearing. Months of sleep deprivation, years of temper tantrums and a lifetime of provision so that humanity can perpetuate itself. Child rearing is obviously often a pleasant, fulfilling and meaningful endeavour, but I doubt even those who gush about parenthood would deny that there's a lot of unreciprocated generosity involved.

More broadly, generosity is the foundation of social insurance. We help people in need. When they get on their feet, they pay it forward and take their turn to help someone in need. Eventually the circle comes all the way back around when someone helps us out when we're in need. Social insurance is very cognitively efficient. We don't need to think about all the bad stuff that can happen and take out financial insurance against it. We can rely on our neighbours, peers, friends and family to be there for us when something unexpected occurs. Social insurance is also heartwarming. It's emotionally comforting, even joyful, to see people taking care of each other with no regard for compensation or even reciprocity.

Generosity has benefits for the giver too. It builds your relationships because everyone likes a generous friend; just be careful of parasites. Being able to give things away, whether it's time, money or care, helps you to appreciate what you have, avoid avarice and stay grounded in what matters to you and what's superfluous. Securing those core needs and being generous with what else you have enables other people to secure their own core needs and be capable of generosity in turn. Putting our own house in order helps others in our community to do the same. It creates a virtuous circle that results in us living among people who are at ease materially, psychologically and emotionally.

There's now quite a large scientific literature on prosocial behaviours and happiness (both in terms of mood and life satisfaction). It is very well summarised by Lara Aknin, Ashley Whillans, Michael Norton and Elizabeth Dunn, all academic psychologists, in their chapter from the 2019 World Happiness Report.[12] I'll give you the CliffsNotes. The first and most important point is that while there are hundreds of studies in this space most of them use unconvincing methods, so we have to be careful about our claims. For example, there are many studies showing a positive statistical relationship between volunteering and positive affect (i.e. feelings), life satisfaction and reduced depression, but this might be reverse causation. It could be that happier people volunteer more. The few experimental studies that existed in 2019 showed no positive benefit of volunteering on affect, life satisfaction or reduced depression. There has since been at least one paper that I know of – a quasi-experimental study of volunteering for the UK National Health Service during the Covid-19 pandemic – that found large improvements in life satisfaction and feelings of worthwhileness, social connectedness and belonging among volunteers.[13] So it's complicated.

Experimental evidence for financial generosity is both more abundant and clearer in its conclusions. Charity makes you happy. The positive relationship between mood and giving away money holds across cultures, even if you don't know or see the person who receives the money. Evidence of a similar quality and clarity exists for a variety of prosocial gestures like holding the door open for a stranger, paying someone a compliment, caring for a sick relative, comforting a spouse or returning a lost wallet.

In their chapter of the World Happiness Report, Aknin, Whillans, Norton and Dunn provide a summary of the factors that are most likely to affect the strength of the relationship between charitable acts and happiness. The first is autonomy: being able to choose who, when and how to help. Giving in a way that is consistent with your values seems especially important. The second factor is a sense of connection to the people you are helping. Charity seems to be more effective at generating happiness when you know and interact with the people you are helping, and when the charitable act itself is social, like volunteering at a food bank, in part because you interact with other volunteers. Being around good people makes you feel good. The third and final factor is being able to see how your help is making a difference. People seem to derive more joy from concrete acts like donating a mosquito net to prevent the spread of malaria than from donating to a more amorphous crusade like the multifaceted work of UNICEF.

What's the upshot of this scientific evidence for you? Get involved locally, with people you care about, and do good collectively. Look for opportunities to turn your social networks into sites of altruism and generosity. In doing good locally in this way, you become a healthy node in a social network. You radiate good vibes outwards and these help other people to become similarly healthy nodes that radiate good vibes.

## 2.7. Being pleasant to hang around with

> You can make more friends in two months by becoming interested in other people than you can in two years by trying to get other people interested in you.
>
> Dale Carnegie,
> *How to Win Friends and Influence People*

I want to conclude this section on character with some virtues that are too often overlooked in the search for grand ideas about wellbeing – virtues that make you pleasant to hang around with. I've touched upon this theme a few times throughout Part I, but it deserves its own section. These virtues have two principal benefits. First, they are likely to improve the quality of your social interactions and make it easier for you to find friends. As a sense of relatedness to others and of belonging to a group is a basic psychological need, this is liable to improve your wellbeing. Second, as most of these virtues are about taking things less seriously, less personally and less combatively, they're likely to make you more *chill*. They will reduce the stress and anxiety in your life and help you direct your limited cognitive and emotional bandwidth to things that actually matter.

So what are these virtues? Let's start with one that I don't think I've seen discussed anywhere – the ability to capitulate *immediately* when confronted by superior reasoning. When we get into a debate, we typically get defensive, especially if the argument touches on our fundamental values or self-beliefs. This makes us liable to straw man our interlocutor's arguments, which means to interpret them or represent them in as flimsy a way as possible (as opposed to 'steel manning'). This inhibits our ability to see the truth in their words and learn from their perspective. Defensiveness also makes us liable to fortify our own views. We skip over weaknesses in our logic and pretend that holes in our arguments aren't there. This inhibits growth in our understanding. Finally, defensiveness makes us reluctant to admit that we are wrong. When cornered, we tend to throw a rhetorical smoke bomb and find some way to exit the conversation rather than accept defeat and be forced to change our ways. This is interpersonally unpleasant. I'm sure we are all familiar with the frustrating feeling of someone retreating into dissonance when confronted with their irrationality.

There is virtue in not expecting someone to capitulate in these circumstances. Admitting you are wrong and plugging the gaps in your reasoning is hard, painful and takes time. Be patient and compassionate. People will appreciate your sensitivity. They will increasingly trust you going forward and be more willing to capitulate in the future. At the same time, there is virtue in capitulating as soon as it is clear that you are wrong. It is a show of respect to your conversation partner, which ingratiates you. It distinguishes you as an honourable person worthy of trust and honesty. And it implies that the systems of meaning, values and reasoning you use to understand the world and your life are flexible and adroit enough to handle ambiguity and synthesise new information. As we'll see in Part III, this is critical for well-being, especially in our complex, contemporary world.

Another virtue: don't be a 'debater' (and ignore the lame people who are). Discuss instead. Debate culture is toxic and I've never understood why we celebrate and promote it. The purpose of a debate is to win, not increase wisdom. The medium rewards rhetoric at your opponent's expense, which encourages sophistry, witty but cheap point-scoring, ad hominem and the obfuscation of weaknesses in your own position. Advocates of the traditional Cambridge debating format of three speakers for and against argue that it requires people to express their arguments logically and respond to counter-arguments promptly. But there's no reason why a discussion can't achieve this same goal. At a minimum, debaters should always debate on behalf of the view that they disagree with. If you treat disagreements as an opportunity for discussion rather than debate, then you're less likely to get defensive and more likely to steel man points of view, root out errors, address gaps in logic, admit it when things are irresolvable, respect impasses and try to learn from your interlocutors. Overall, discussion is much more likely to result in everyone becoming wiser, and much less likely to result in hurt feelings.

Capitulating easily and preferring discourse over debate are examples of a larger class of virtues I think of in terms of being a 'low-stakes interactions' person. The idea is that interacting with you shouldn't be a risky affair. If you forgive easily, give the benefit of the doubt and assume incompetence rather than malice in people (or that they are overburdened rather than negligent), then people are more likely to socialise with you. This includes inviting you to parties and group outings, suggesting cool collaborations and introducing you to their networks. In contrast, if you get angry or offended easily, interpret clerical errors and the like as an egregious personal failure or even a deliberate slight against you, and generally hold grudges, then people will avoid you. It's just not worth the hassle of interacting with people like that regardless of how brilliant they might be.

If you want to be a low-stakes interaction person, it helps to not take yourself too seriously. You should be able to laugh, even celebrate, good jokes that you are the butt of. A mature person is aware of the 'bad' aspects of their personality that they can't change and has hopefully even been able to transform them into something characterful. It's a sure sign that you've made peace with yourself if you can laugh at your shortcomings. Not taking yourself too seriously also means cutting the pretence. Few things are as comical and pathetic as dictators and aristocrats decking themselves out in military medals they've never earnt for parade days. Don't be like that. If you like dressing up, then just be frank about that. Never pretend that you're more than you are, and especially don't come down on people who point out your pretentions. Finally, don't overcompensate. That's what the dictators and aristocrats are doing – an elaborate pantomime to obscure the fact that they're craven and effete. It is so cringeworthy when people play-act the qualities that they so obviously do not have. Be real, and when someone points out that you're being fake, thank them for it. Good people value genuine interactions.

Another broad class of low-stakes interactions virtues is being able to admit your mistakes. I'm not talking about capitulating here. I'm talking about owning errors and apologising. So many dramas have been written off the simple premise of someone failing to admit their mistakes or covering up the fact that they made them. Just front up and take the L. Obviously, the best quality is not to make errors in the first place because you're attentive, organised and considerate. But all of us fall far short of perfection, and most of us fall very far short. It is important to the health of your interpersonal relationships to confess and show contrition when your actions have harmed them in some way, even when chance is to blame rather than incompetence or negligence. People will understand, and if they don't, they're probably not someone you want to be interacting with.

We discussed self-improvement by negation earlier in this chapter. Some of the qualities you might want to remove are things that make you unpleasant to hang around with: untrustworthy, mercurial, flaky, tardy, cruel, hysterical, explosive, etc. Now think about their inverse: qualities that make you pleasant to hang around with: reliable, punctual, kind, peaceful – try to cultivate these in yourself. Think about the people whom you want to spend time with and work to make yourself more like them.

## Chapter 2 summary

> Resolve to be honest at all events; and if in your own judgement you cannot be an honest lawyer, resolve to be honest without being a lawyer. Choose some other occupation,

rather than one in the choosing of which you do, in advance, consent to be a knave.

     Abraham Lincoln. *Notes for a Law Lecture* in
       *Collected Works of Abraham Lincoln*

This chapter has explored what *character traits* are conducive to wellbeing, building on the exploration in Chapter 1 of the right *attitude* for wellbeing. We're laying good foundations that the rest of the book can build on. Let's recap. First, be real. Strive for authenticity, avoid dishonesty and pretentiousness, and be mindful of your self-serving biases and other weaknesses. Second, be pleasant. Keep an open mind and an open heart, work on the things you don't like about yourself, and try to make it easy for people to interact with you. And third, be generous, but don't let people take advantage of you. Play tit for tat – be kind to people who are kind to you but expect people who wrong you to demonstrate contrition before you forgive them. Play tit for tat munificently. Offer to cooperate first, with no expectations of reward. Expect the best in people, and don't take it badly if they're less magnanimous than you. As German philosopher Friedrich Nietzsche said: 'What are my parasites to me? Let them grow and prosper – I am strong enough for that!'

What about a practical exercise? It may sound corny, but set New Year's resolutions, except focus on the negative. What do you want to be rid of? Don't make it about doing more of something, like going to the gym or reading novels. Resolve to do less of something. I'm going to do less impulse buying. I'm going to do less aimless scrolling on my phone. I'm going to stop cutting people off mid-sentence and be a better active listener. These sorts of resolutions require less willpower than positive affirmations because you only need to pay attention to them when you're already doing something. And the neat thing about New Year's resolutions is that you get a year before you check your success. That's a good amount of time to make small but steady progress towards improvement by self-negation.

# 3
## Emotion

> Though nothing can bring back the hour
> Of splendour in the grass, of glory in the flower;
> We will grieve not, rather find
> Strength in what remains behind;
> In the primal sympathy
> Which having been must ever be...
>         William Wordsworth, *Splendour in the Grass*

This chapter is about 'happiness', by which I mean pleasant moods, smiling, laughing and joy. I used to be down on 'happiness'. I remember listening to a TED talk on the subject by the Buddhist monk Matthieu Ricard where he lamented how disinterested French intellectuals were in the subject; they would say, 'don't talk to us about happiness, we like our ups and downs'.[1] I was sympathetic. It seemed to me that the meat of life was in meaning, purpose, virtue, all that existential stuff. But I mellowed for two reasons.

The first was that I started to think that there was too much conflict between ways of thinking about happiness and well-being and that we should try to integrate instead. Some people were arguing that the good life was about happiness and pleasure, and the absence of sadness and pain. Other people were arguing that sadness and pain were necessary to achieve the outcomes that make life worthwhile, whether that's something relatively mundane like raising a family or quite dramatic such as changing the world. Why not both? I'm still mostly sympathetic to the second view. I certainly don't think it is right to talk about 'negative' moods or emotions. Being sad, bored or angry is often perfectly normal and well adjusted, as is grieving or feeling anxious about something consequential on the horizon. These emotions give us information and help us to process, physiologically and psychologically, the effects the world has on us. We shouldn't seek to rid ourselves of these feelings. But it's also the case that pleasant feelings are, well, pleasant, and life does seem better when we have a preponderance of 'good' moods rather than 'bad' ones. There is certainly little harm in finding ways to stimulate, intensify and extend our good moods.

The second reason why I came around to happiness is that in pursuing my own grand existential ambitions I often found myself beleaguered. I was not just emotionally exhausted, but sometimes even unhappy in a debilitating way, like when you're so demoralised you stop trying. I realised that I needed a bit more joy in my life to maintain motivation for the hard stuff. I needed more emotional payoff. I realised that in steeling myself for the hard slog of achieving challenging goals, which inevitably involves a lot of bad moods like frustration and disappointment, I had made myself numb not only to difficult emotions but also to pleasant ones. When good things happened, they didn't register much emotionally, even if I capitalised on them by having a party or something to celebrate. So I became much more interested in the science of happiness and put more effort into integrating it with the thinking I had done on the broader notion of wellbeing. This chapter reviews the top ideas I've come across on happiness, from ancient philosophy to modern economics and psychological science.

## 3.1. Sleep, exercise, diet and mood

> I've missed more than nine thousand shots in my career. I've lost almost three hundred games. Twenty-six times I've been trusted to take the game winning shot and missed. I've failed over and over and over again in my life. And that is why I succeed.
>
> Michael Jordan, arguably the greatest basketball player of all time

I don't want to dwell on these things, because they're not what this book is about nor my area of expertise, but the point must be made, at least in passing: *your wellbeing depends substantially on your diet, exercise and sleep.* If I don't sleep right for a week, I will become depressed, irritable and cynical, and no amount of mind training is going to prevent it. Make sure you sleep enough. If you're getting eight hours a night and still feeling off, then sleep for ten. Don't use an alarm clock – go to bed earlier. Follow simple rules like not using screens in the two hours before bed, avoid having dessert late and lay off caffeine.

That brings us to diet. If you're eating shit, you will feel like shit. Crank the vegetables and fruits, avoid processed foods and trans-fats and be mindful of fat in general, go easy on the carbs, drink in moderation and remember sugar is the devil.

And finally, exercise. Vigorous exercise helps your brain to balance its stress hormones, like adrenalin and cortisol, which are a key ingredient in bad wellbeing associated with (common) job pressures. It also releases endorphins, which make you feel good. You don't need to be athletic to engage in vigorous exercise, and you don't need all that much of it either. There are so many books, vlogs and scientific articles on healthy exercise that I am going to say no more except that exercise is something you should make time for.

Now I appreciate that for many people, sleep, diet and exercise aren't easy. I feel particularly for people who constitutionally hate exercise. What can be done? My only suggestion is to associate exercise with something that you like doing; the most obvious thing being hanging with friends. If you exercise with a group of people you like meeting, it makes exercise less of a chore. Lean into this. Go for dinner/lunch after exercising. Organise social events around exercise, like watching basketball so you get pumped to play a game together. Get team jerseys so you bond as a group.

What if you hate people? There might still be some way to associate exercise with something you like. Let me give you an imperfect example. I hate lifting weights, but I need to do it for my health. Fortunately, I love rock climbing because it is cerebral (bouldering problems are puzzling), feels vaguely practical and the community is super wholesome. So I can motivate myself to climb even if I can't get myself to do chin ups. After climbing for a few months, I could even summon the willpower to lift because it made me a better climber. The moral of the story is that you should try and *find something you value that exercise makes you better at*, like carrying your dog down the escalators or being able to keep up with your kids. If you can find something that you have some intrinsic motivation for and then attach exercise to that, you will find it easier to make exercise part of your life.

My one tip with dieting (this holds for exercise and life in general) is to go slow if you can't go all in. My diet sucked for most of my youth, but I made up for it with huge amounts of exercise. When making changes, I didn't go whole hog. I tried to take one step forward every 3–6 months. Small steps. I removed the chocolate from my office drawer. I stopped buying dessert as part of my grocery run. I grilled chicken fillets instead of deep-frying schnitzels. I bought Greek yoghurt and put fruit in it to make it palatable instead of buying sugary flavoured yoghurts. I halved the carbohydrates in my meals and doubled the vegetables. I drank my beers a bit slower so that I wouldn't drink as much. I took fruit and nuts to work instead of muesli bars, which are a sugar bomb. All this happened sequentially, months or even years apart.

This sort of incremental change is part of self-compassion — you can't expect yourself to go from zero to hero in a week. But you can expect yourself to stodge through some change. *Break your big goal into small and manageable goals* and take them down one at a time. You will succeed, and you will feel encouraged every time you do. Then after years of small triumphs, you'll look at your grocery list and be struck by how healthy it is. When did I start eating chia seeds?

All right, that's enough on diet, sleep and exercise. There are a million books and blogs on these things and some of them are even OK, so go ask them for advice if you want more. I'm only good for the psychology. In that regard, we should revisit the very first concept I introduced in Part I — homeostatically protected mood — and the profound insights the ancient philosophers had on related themes.

## 3.2. Epicureanism

There are moments in moist love
when heaven itself is jealous of what we on earth can do.
*A Year with Hafiz,* poems by Daniel Ladinsky[2]

Part I of this book opened with a quote from the OG (original gangsta) of the pleasant life, Epicurus, a Greek philosopher who lived from 341–270 BC. It seems appropriate that his thinking get its own section. In the popular imagination, both of today and of his contemporaries, Epicurus was a hedonist dedicated to a life of pleasure: gluttony, debauchery and sumptuousness. Ironically though, his philosophy is quite different from that ideal. He certainly put more stock in pleasure than a lot of classical philosophers do, but he shared his peers' sympathy for the idea that wellbeing requires more than hedonism: 'It is impossible to live a pleasant life without living wisely and well and justly. And it is impossible to live wisely and well and justly without leading a pleasant life.' Epicurus' notion of pleasure is also meaningfully distinct from the classical utilitarian one that emphasises sensations or some phenomenon in the brain that we can isolate as 'pleasure'.[3] His philosophy is more about establishing a tranquil existence that allows the pursuit of intrinsic motivations. As the Stanford encyclopaedia of philosophy puts it:[4]

> The elimination of fears and corresponding desires would leave people free to pursue the pleasures, both physical and mental, to which they are naturally drawn, and to enjoy the peace of mind that is consequent upon their regularly expected and achieved satisfaction.

You might recognise these sentiments from section 1.6 on the desire for tranquillity. Epicurus was surprisingly sceptical of sex as fundamental to the good life, discouraged excessive drinking and arguably placed his highest value on friendship. He was famously content with little, and there are times when his philosophy sounds quite Buddhist and ascetic. He writes, for example, that, 'Not what we have but what we enjoy constitutes our abundance', and, 'If thou wilt make a man happy, add not unto his riches but take away from his desires', and finally, 'Nothing is enough to the man for whom enough is too little'. Hardly becoming statements for a philosopher of hedonism as it is commonly conceived.

It's fair to say that Epicurus was anti-materialism, and a central plank of the path to a good life that he outlined was being satisfied with modest living. Many of his ideas foreshadowed what economists who study happiness now call reference points: our tendency to gauge our situation relative to some external standard. If that standard keeps shifting upwards as our life improves then we will never feel satisfied. Consider the following passage from Epicurus: 'Do not spoil what you have by desiring what you have not; remember that what you now have was once among the things you only hoped for.'

Epicurus' philosophy is a powerful tonic against some of the self-destructive behaviours that materialistic culture encourages us to engage in. Notably, focusing on what you have, what you enjoy doing and relational rather than material wealth inoculates you against the pernicious status anxiety and FOMO (fear of missing out) that social media perpetuates. Limiting your desires, avoiding excess and being wary of accumulating possessions disinclines you from participating in the rat race and thereby doing work that you hate just for the money, leaving you open to exploitation by unscrupulous bosses and toxic workplace cultures.

Speaking of work, Epicurus was strongly in favour of self-sufficiency and counselled against working for others. He writes, for example, that 'A free life cannot acquire many possessions, because that is not easy to do without servility to mobs or monarchs.' We see a strong emphasis here on autonomy. More broadly, Epicureanism – the school of thought Epicurus founded – was against what we would nowadays call extrinsic motivation and extrinsic pursuits of fame, status, power and wealth, which I will discuss in great detail in Part II. Succinctly, the Epicureans thought that you should be active and engaged in your life, not idle. However, unlike Calvinism and twenty-first-century American capitalism, they distinguished this activity and engagement from paid employment. Paid employment often results in what Marx called 'alienated labour' – doing work owing to physical need rather than out of self-expressive agency. Instead, people should, as mentioned earlier, 'pursue the pleasures, both physical and mental, to which they are naturally drawn'. This is intrinsic motivation. We need to work for money (or to grow our own food) insofar as it frees us to follow these intrinsic motivations.

Epicurus lived in a rural house, growing his own food with his friends and students, who lived there with him. He thereby avoided one of the more prominent grinds of modern life: the commute. While recent studies have not found a negative relationship between commuting and overall life satisfaction, long travel times to work are consistently found to reduce satisfaction with leisure and family time, and to contribute to feelings of stress. In early time-use studies, the commute to work was found to be one of the most miserable times of the day.[5]

A final point that I take away from Epicurus is that while a materially pleasant and secure situation is important to wellbeing, it is merely a precursor. A necessary but not sufficient condition. The real work begins once you have pleasure. This insight seems to pass over a huge number of people today. At the risk of seeming like a grouch, I am bemused by the number of people on online dating apps whose interests consist only of food, travel and exercise. These are great things but they're not a personality. Epicurus talks about securing the means to 'pursue the pleasures, both physical and mental, to which they are naturally drawn'. Food, travel and exercise are these means, not the pleasures themselves. The pleasures Epicurus is on about have some connection to living 'wisely, and well, and justly'. They're about *values*. What do you *care* about? What sort of changes do you want to bring about in the world and in yourself? These changes might pertain to food, travel and exercise, as they do for many chefs, anthropologists and athletes, but most people aren't pursuing these professions. Food, travel and exercise are just tranquil ways to pass the time for them. Again, that's fine. You need a pleasant life. But we also need a fulfilling and valuable life.

## 3.3. The economics of happiness

> Jacob Moore: What's your number…? The amount of money you would need to just walk away from it and live. See I find that everybody has a number and it's usually an exact number. So what is yours?
> Bretton James: More.
> *Wall Street 2: Money never sleeps*

The economics of happiness has a lot more to say about wellbeing than just being mindful of reference points, so let's take a deeper look. There are some insights worth unpacking about money, unemployment, security, loss and how we use our time. Let's start with money. Unsurprisingly, the relationship between money and wellbeing is what happiness economics has thought about the most.

Happiness economics got started in the mid-1970s with an observation from Richard Easterlin that has become known as the Easterlin Paradox.[6] He found that income explained a lot of the variation in people's satisfaction with life both between nations and especially within them, but that growth in income over time didn't seem to have a noticeable effect. Richer people were relatively happier than poorer people, and richer nations were relatively happier than poorer nations, but getting richer didn't seem to matter a whole lot. This observation ran counter to much economic analysis, which assumes that wellbeing rises with income as greater purchasing power allows individuals to satisfy more of their preferences.

Easterlin posited two explanations for his paradox. The first was adaptation: we seem to acclimatise to changes in our circumstances much like we acclimatise to a hot bath. As our wealth increases, so too can our desires, such that the wealth doesn't seem to have much of an effect over time. The second was social comparisons, status anxiety, envy and other similar phenomena. If we are getting richer but so is everybody around us, we won't evaluate our lives as getting better. Or if we're getting richer but moving as a result into wealthier circles wherein we don't feel special, then that wealth might not translate into greater happiness. In a 2020 paper using survey data from forty countries published in the *European Journal of Political Economy*, Markus Knell and Helmut Stix found that the more income someone earns, the higher they think average incomes in their country are, and that relatively rich people underestimate how rich they are relative to the population.[7] If I was a left-leaning government I would pay to have the national income distribution advertised on a regular basis to encourage more progressivity in public policy. It's not uncommon for people in the top 1 per cent of income earners to regard themselves as 'middle class'. I guess it's because they don't have a private jet?

An enormous literature has debated Easterlin's paradox since he first started publishing on it in 1974 (he's still going today at 97 years of age!) Many economists are sceptical of the paradox, arguing that it was a product of bad data. Early waves of the World Values Survey used by Easterlin relied on sampling methods that gave a distorted impression of people in developing countries. There have been papers in lots of top journals with sample sizes of several million arguing over various minutiae in the paradox.[8] Nobody really disputes the existence of adaptation or social comparisons. What they mostly argue about is at what level of wealth does money stop having *any* effect on life satisfaction.

I find this literature incredibly boring and even nauseating at times. Recall from section 1.3 that money is a *medium of exchange* – having more of it doesn't mean much if you don't know how to spend it. So there isn't a direct causal relationship between income and happiness anyway. It's also the case that earning a lot of money usually requires spending a lot of time at work, rather than a lot of time enjoying your wealth. Work stress isn't good for wellbeing. As a boss or investor, you might also be tempted to exploit labour, pollute the environment or hurt animals to increase your yields to get rich. This sort of thing puts you out of harmony with others and the world around you, which I doubt will lead to wellbeing in the long run. At the national level, markedly increasing the wealth of an advanced economy like the United States or Australia is likely to require, at least with current technology, massive environmental damage and a commitment on the part of its population to work longer hours (American salaries are higher than European ones, but European leave entitlements dwarf those available to Americans). So this fixation among economists with income just strikes me as a bit glib. My main takeaway from the Easterlin Paradox literature is that advanced nations have got enough money to live a good life, and now we need to get on with that good life.

One body of research from the economics of happiness that is relevant to good living is the study of time use and what activities are associated with good moods. By way of an introduction to this research, let me regale you with the parable of the fisherman. The story goes that a businessman meets a fisherman selling some fish. He asks him how long they took to catch, to which the fisherman replies, 'Not very long.' The businessman inquires what the fisherman does with the rest of his time. The reply: 'I sleep late, play with my children, cuddle with my wife, spend time with friends, play the guitar, sing a few songs.' The businessman sees an opportunity to help: 'You should spend a bit more time fishing every day, then you can make more money and buy a bigger boat.' The fisherman, bemused, asks, 'And why would I want to do that?' The businessman holds forth, 'Well, then you could catch even more fish, and if you sold those you could afford a crew, and a third boat, why eventually you could have a whole fleet!' The fisherman remains unconvinced: 'And then what?' The businessman is visibly excited, 'Well, then comes the best part – you could retire from work, live by the coast, sleep late, play with your children, cuddle with your wife, visit friends, spend time on your hobbies...'

Now the thing is, I don't like this parable; it's too simple. The businessman's problem is the one we discussed in section 1.3 – he's only thinking about how to get money, not what to do with it. He's missing the *why*. So is the fisherman! His life is pleasant, but I suspect that many people would not find it fulfilling nor valuable, and eventually this would undermine their wellbeing. The fisherman has tranquillity and a secure steady state; but he's missing a journey. The journey the businessman is suggesting is a lame one because it's all about money, not making the world a better place, and what personal growth there is has little to do with personality and everything to do with stuff and status.

But let's stop dumping on this parable and zero in on what it gets right, which is how the fisherman spends his time to make life pleasant: sex, relationships, hobbies. This is entirely in line with the results of time-use studies that focus on what activities people enjoy the most.[9] These studies involve giving people beepers or, more recently, smart phones, that ping them at random times and ask them what they are doing and how they feel at that moment. The best things in life were sex, socialising, relaxing, eating, exercising, practising religion and watching television. The best things in life aren't all free but they're pretty cheap! The worst things were talking on the telephone, chores, cooking, shopping, computer tasks, housework, childcare, commuting and working. That fisherman sure was onto something.

Paul Dolan at the London School of Economics has extended these time-use studies to examine activities that promote pleasure and/or *purpose*.[10] His research suggests that some relatively less pleasurable activities like household chores and working are high in purpose, while some pleasurable activities like watching television are low in purpose. Two items that were relatively high in both pleasure and purpose were spending time with kids and volunteering activities. We see again the centrality of relationships and generating value for others in wellbeing.

One thing I left hanging from the discussion of the Easterlin Paradox was where the science stands on adaptation and social comparisons. These topics are much more interesting than the income–satisfaction relationship, but similarly uncomplicated. Just don't make social comparisons and try to be grateful for what you have! These are tendencies of our psychology but they're not immutable. In fact, psychologists have developed a range of techniques for stymying these bad habits of mind, and we will discuss them in the next two sections.

## 3.4. Hedonic psychology

Be happy for this moment. This moment is your life.
Omar Khayyam, *The Rubaiyat*

Recall from the beginning of Part I that mood seems to be homeostatic, which means that it is drawn back to a steady state after being disrupted. Both your good and bad moods tend not to last and your baseline is a mild level of positive affect.

Of course, if there is some continuous pressure in your environment then you might find yourself in some moods frequently and for longer durations. Prison, poverty or an oppressive manager, for example, will have such an effect. I spent most of 2022 waiting for immigration authorities to approve visas so that I could visit my girlfriend and start a new job overseas. There were severe delays owing to Covid and no way to get an explanation. This was very stressful and while my mood would come back to baseline for a few hours at a time, I was generally irritable and anxious because the source of these moods was not resolved. If you find that you are frequently in bad moods, recognise them as a *symptom* and try to ascertain their deep and constant cause.

Along with environmental pressures, there are certain experiences that we don't seem to adapt to, at least not fully.[11] These include long-term unemployment, disability, bereavement and, on the positive side, plastic surgery (I confess that I was surprised by this last one). People who have gone through these experiences seem to bear scars, with their life satisfaction remaining depressed for many years. In the case of the unemployed, this is true even if they eventually become re-employed, which suggests social stigma is involved.[12]

Ideally, we want to organise our life in such a way that our environment exerts continuous positive pressure on our life. If we fill our days with activities we enjoy, people we love and delightful places, then our mood will frequently be pushed into the positive ranges. How to do this is the subject of Part II.

But there are also particular habits of mind that we can use to increase the duration of positive moods and decrease the duration of negative ones. I call them 'methods of mood management'. Many of these are summarised into what positive psychologists Christina Armenta, Katherine Jacobs Bao, Sonya

Lyubomirsky and Kennon Sheldon call the 'hedonic adaptation prevention model' (HAP).[13] They include savouring, basking, capitalisation, gratitude and mindfulness. We will discuss each in turn, with gratitude and mindfulness getting their own sections.

Before getting into this literature, a brief word on the science. The study of adaptation, especially of satisfaction with life rather than just transitory moods, is riven with measurement concerns. The fields of positive psychology and happiness economics have done extensive work over the last few decades to assuage these concerns – enough at least to make me comfortable sharing these 'mood management' techniques with you as facts – but a great deal of uncertainty remains.

Succinctly, many of the associated empirical studies rely on 'life satisfaction scales'. A common form for such a scale is to ask survey respondents: 'All things considered, how happy are you with your life at this time on a scale from 1–10?' If someone gives a higher number after an intervention, like training in the techniques of gratitude, then researchers conclude that the intervention has increased happiness. While I think this conclusion is often reasonable, it is not necessarily the case. A voluminous literature in quality of life studies demonstrates that people change the qualitative meaning of the points on their scales over time, such that a 6/10 before an intervention might mean something quite different from a 6/10 after an intervention.[14]

I'll give you a quick example. In our research interviewing people about what determines their life satisfaction and how they communicate this on scales, we had one respondent suffering quite badly from long Covid.[15] She said that she was 7/10. Why? Well because she had been able to return to work part time and walk her dog for twenty minutes. She thought of 8/10 as working full time and walking her dog up a hill, 9/10 as being able to run again and 10/10 as being able to run a local half marathon. I asked her what the points on her scale would have meant in 2019 before the Covid pandemic began.

She said that she was also a 7 or 8 then, but she was regularly running half marathons and her 9 and 10 out of 10 related to finishing her PhD, which had been on hold for several years due to Covid. Now my colleagues tend to see these sorts of numbers and say, 'She adapted to Covid.' They think my interviewee's 7/10 in 2019 and her 7/10 today correspond to the same level of satisfaction with life, even though the qualitative experiences that they are associated with are completely different. My interviewee didn't see it like that. I asked her directly: 'Is your scale from 2019 in any way comparable to your scale today?' Her response: 'Totally different, because I would not have started from a point of extreme illness...' The numbers on the scales over the two time points correspond to different feelings and evaluations.

Understanding differences in how people use their scales is one of the main areas of my academic research. I don't want to bore you with the technical details in this book; suffice to say that we don't have a precise understanding of the speed, strength or nature of adaptation, and a lot of what we think is adaptation might actually be changes in the way people use their scales over time. Additionally, we can't be confident that we have accurately measured the size of the effect of interventions to improve happiness because we can't tell what is a change in feelings or judgements, and what is a change in the way people use the scale. In any case, the effects for the interventions below (as for most things in positive psychology) tend to be very small.

The central idea in the HAP is to focus attention on the emotional valence of positive experiences so that they can be sustained and turn attention away from negative experiences so that they fade from consciousness. Stay 'in the moment' when you're having a positive experience, but when you're not, try to reflect on what's good in your life. This strategic use of your attention will bring positive emotions to the fore, reducing cognitive space for negative emotions. Focusing your attention on positive experiences as they are happening, rather than getting distracted by the future, will deepen those experiences and prevent the associated emotions from fading. So when you get promoted at work, for example, do not indulge the temptation to think 'what comes next?'; just *savour* the feeling of achievement you are experiencing right now. *Basking* is this same technique applied to the positive experiences of other people.

*Marvelling* and *awe* are the same again, but applied to things that amaze or stagger you, like a beautiful sunset or sublime athleticism. It's a good idea to seek out such experiences and to encourage anybody who is capable of producing them, but you will often find them in mundane places. I have tried, for example, to make a habit of pausing when I see a lovely flower (a somewhat rare occurrence in grimy London where I live) and taking the time to observe it closely and fully. This practice started when I got a new pair of sunglasses that partially corrected my colour blindness. I could properly see purple for the first time. It was *awe*some to see the vibrant and striking colours of some flowers that I'd previously thought were just an odd shade of blue. I realised that there were probably many such cool things that I didn't appreciate because I simply wasn't looking closely enough, with my mind always on my work or my plans.

When something pops into your thoughts as beautiful, nice, heartwarming, exciting or otherwise 'good', try to *stop* and appreciate it. Don't let anything distract you from that positive experience.

When something good happens, try to *capitalise* on it. This involves doing something extra to extend or enhance that good thing. For example, when you get promoted, go out with your partner to celebrate. Or when you move somewhere new, have people over for a housewarming. Basking and capitalising really go together like burgers and fries. Care about people, help them succeed, and when they do, throw a party so you can all have a great time together.

A corollary insight of the HAP is that experiences that generate a variety of positive thoughts and feelings have a more substantial effect on your life than those that generate only a single positive effect. For example, the effect of most material goods, like a new car, tends to fade because they provide only one sensation. By contrast, a new and enjoyable job can provide a plethora of positive things to reflect on, such as colleagues, location, the work itself, pay and a meaningful mission. In general, experiences have been found to produce longer lasting positive emotions than goods.

It is worth noting that two behavioural tendencies that are in a sense the opposite of the HAP are rumination and living for the future. Rumination is basically just focusing on negative things, especially in a repetitive or cyclical way, without active problem-solving. It is a hallmark of depression and anxiety disorders. Living for the future is the opposite of living in the moment. It is a tendency to focus on the next step or what remains to be maximised rather than what you have just achieved. It encourages you to be dissatisfied with your current circumstances, even if they have just recently improved markedly.

There's one technique from hedonic psychology that I want to mention, even though it isn't related to adaptation, and that's *satisficing not maximising*.[16] Studies in positive psychology have found that happy people tend to look for and quickly take 'good enough' options when making decisions rather than investing time and resources to find the best possible option. In contrast, maximising is negatively correlated with happiness. This isn't because maximisers make worse decisions. They actually make better decisions, as you might expect given the research they're liable to undertake. It's because they agonise over those decisions, even after they have been made. By looking for perfection, you're inviting a whole bunch of psychological sludge into your life and leaving less time, brain power and emotional space for you to enjoy the good things you have. Speaking of appreciating the good things, that's our next big insight from hedonic psychology – the power of gratitude.

## 3.5. Gratitude

> And even though the drunkenness of love
> Has ruined me,
> My being's built upon those ruins for
> Eternity.
> *A Year with Hafiz*, poems by Daniel Ladinsky

In its simplest form, gratitude is about being thankful for the positive things in your life. This helps you to manage your reference points by keeping you focused on what you have rather than what you lack. It's a great antidote to desire. As a regular practice, it can also dampen hedonic adaptation and induce positive moods by bringing good stuff to mind.

That's the small picture on gratitude; there's a bigger picture too, one that Christianity and other religions that emphasise divine grace have long been clued into, but it is much harder to get at convincingly with science. It revolves around appreciating where the things that you are thankful for often come from, namely others, or even the universe more broadly.

Robert Emmons is an emeritus professor of psychology at the University of California at Davis and editor of the *Journal of Positive Psychology*. The scientific study of gratitude was his life's work. He puts the big and small picture together in a succinct summary of what gratitude is about:[17]

- Affirm that there are good things in your life.
- Give thanks to where those good things come from.

It is especially powerful to be grateful for things that we could not get on our own. In so doing, we recognise our dependence on external forces, whether fate, nature or other people. By thanking those forces, especially when they are other people or an environment that we can nourish, we show respect and encourage more generosity in the future. In turn, we might perceive our own contribution to the good things that happen to other people. We start to recognise the great karmic web of giving and thanking that holds the world in harmony. So give thanks – when someone does something nice for you, acknowledge it and show appreciation. A simple thank you goes a long way. It rewards generous behaviour and encourages more of it. Conversely, if you see an opportunity to be generous, even if it's just a small compliment, take that opportunity.

One of my favourite things about Emmons' gratitude paradigm is his emphasis on gratitude as a trait and not just a state. A state of gratitude is something you enter into transitorily when you give thanks for something. There are ways to induce it, like making a list of things you are grateful for (gratitude journaling) or taking turns to say what we are grateful for at an annual thanksgiving dinner. One of my favourite traditional gratitude practices, even as an atheist, is the ritual prayer of gratitude before dinner. In my extended Catholic family, the prayer goes something like this (translated from Hungarian): 'We thank you, Lord, for this food that we are about to eat and ask you to please spare a thought for those who have less.' What a remarkable cognitive technology for stimulating gratitude and grounding our reference points.

Trait gratitude is deeper; it is an orientation or attitude towards life. Emmons speaks of 'grateful people'. They tend to be more satisfied with life and say that they're happy more often than less grateful people. They perceive their life as abundant, blessed and full of love, in contrast to the opposite, often self-centred and toxic sentiments of scarcity, resentment and persecution. Sometimes your life really is like that, and you need to use negative sentiment as fuel, like if you're a freedom fighter battling oppression and injustice. But even then, it bears saying that many of the most successful freedom fighters like Mandela, Gandhi and King, started from a place of love and returned to that positive sentiment when their successes bore fruit. And most of us aren't freedom fighters nor are our lives all that bleak, and it's going to be more beneficial to our wellbeing to pay attention to the good things we have.

I like Emmons' emphasis on trait gratitude in part because it makes gratitude a continuous practice, rather than something you do periodically, probably on your own, in order to be happier. When you're a grateful person, attuned to what you receive from others and eager to thank them for it, you become a healthy node in a social network. You compound altruistic forces that flow around and through you, and you do so organically, easily, subconsciously. In contrast, a lot of gratitude practices feel like a disingenuous trick that you play on your own psychology to be happier. Recalling the story of when someone was generous to you might make you feel better, but it doesn't do much for that person. Maybe it encourages you to be more thankful in the future, but that's not the motivation. Ultimately, the practice seems grounded in selfishness. Trait gratitude, on the other hand, seems to require transfiguring yourself, perhaps through individual gratitude practices, into the sort of person who gives freely and receives graciously, and this transformation is motivated by a desire to be a generous and social member of society. The motivation is altruistic and collective, and happiness is a by-product.

## 3.6. Stoicism

> To try to be happy is to try to build a machine with no other specification than that it shall run noiselessly.
>
> J. Robert Oppenheimer, physicist and director of the Manhattan Project

Stoicism was a Greek and Roman school of philosophy operating around the third century BC that finds many adherents to this day, especially among Manly Men™. Ironically, it is precisely the aspects of stoicism that appeal to machismo that are incorrect, but teasing them apart from all the 24-carat gold in stoicism is a hard analytical exercise. I mean, just look at this small sampling of bangers from the thought leaders of the Stoic school:

'The best revenge is not to be like that.' Marcus Aurelius

'Life is long if you know how to use it.' Seneca

'We have two ears and one mouth so that we can listen twice as much as we speak.' Epictetus

Sublime. There are other quotes from the Stoics scattered throughout this book. I encourage everyone to read stoicism in some detail. Ideally the works of its major thinkers: the Roman emperor Marcus Aurelius, the Roman statesman Seneca, the Greek philosopher Epictetus, born a slave, and Zeno, the founder of the Stoic school. If you have an abundance of time, you can also read some of the works of Diogenes, who wrote biographies of these key thinkers. If you have less time, Massimo Pigliucci, professor of Philosophy at City College of New York, has written a cracking summary of stoicism's main ideas for a popular audience in *How to be a Stoic*, and given many podcasts on the topic. And finally, if you want something very accessible, the bestseller *The Daily Stoic* won't lead you astray.

I can't possibly give a full accounting of stoicism here, so I want to focus on only two big lines of thought in the school that relate to emotion, the subject of this chapter. One line is a collection of good ideas and aphorisms that revolve around the idea that you should focus on things you can control and try to worry less about everything else. The other line is mostly bad, and it revolves around hyper rationality.

The Stoics hit upon many of positive psychology's methods of mood management back before the birth of Christ. In particular, they were aware of the power of attention. When we dwell on the negative, especially on negatives that *might* happen, we feel bad for reasons that are entirely in our power to change. By simply thinking about something else, or not dwelling on a future that hasn't happened yet, we can improve our mood. As Seneca noted: 'We suffer more in imagination than in reality.' The Stoics were also early proponents of gratitude. Focus on the positives in your life, especially the positives you are in the midst of right now. Here's Marcus Aurelius: 'Each day provides its own gifts.'

There is an element of mood management in stoicism that I haven't come across in positive psychology, well summarised by William R. Connolly: 'To avoid unhappiness, frustration, and disappointment, we need to do two things – control those things that are within our power, and be apathetic towards those things which are not in our power.'[18] Epictetus has perhaps the pithiest quote in this regard: 'Make the best use of what is in your power, and take the rest as it happens.' And Marcus Aurelius says something very similar: 'The more we value things outside of our control, the less control we have.' The sentiment here is remarkably similar to that expressed by the serenity prayer of Christianity: 'Lord, grant me the serenity to accept the things I cannot change, the courage to change the things I can and the wisdom to know the difference.' It is also very similar to ideas in Buddhism and mindfulness practice, namely that we have much more control over our reaction to things than we do over those things themselves.

Forces out of our control alludes to another theme of ancient thought that has been lost of late – fate, represented in Greek mythology by the Morai, three sisters who wove the threads of destiny. Their names were Clotho (the spinner), Lachesis (the allotter) and Atropos (the inevitable, especially death). A lot of life comes down to luck, both good and bad, including the circumstances of our birth, which still have a strong role in predetermining people's life outcomes. Pagan mythologies like that of the Hellenic period tend to emphasise predestination. In a world where you can be born into slavery, die suddenly from a fever, have your crops fail due to an unpredictable plague of locusts or be killed by a rampaging army, it's very sensible to cultivate a solemn attitude to random events. While not quite so vicious, luck remains a potent force today. Indeed, one of the most common methods for determining the causal effect of getting into elite schools, college programmes and certain jobs is to compare people just above and below the cut-off for these opportunities. These people are statistically indistinguishable except that some of them were lucky enough to clear the threshold on the entrance exam by 0.01 per cent. If you don't want the vagaries of chance to turn your life into an emotional rollercoaster, you'd be wise to cultivate a Stoic attitude.

You can often create what seems like luck with persistent effort. Good football strikers always seem to be in the right place to take advantage of a spillage and score amidst the chaos. It's not because they're lucky; it's because they consistently position themselves to take advantage of random events. You cannot predict when they will occur, but you do know that they occur occasionally. The same principle is even more pronounced in poker. You don't know when you are going to be dealt a strong hand, but the laws of probability dictate you will be dealt a strong hand occasionally. So you need to play your other hands in a way that will maximise your advantage when a good hand comes along. This carries over to life in general. People who build skills and connections, keep their ear to the ground for opportunities and maintain some energy in reserve can cash out by following through on opportunities when they do arrive.

Let's get back to stoicism and turn to its weaker side. The fundamental error of stoicism, or at least in many interpretations of stoicism, is defining wellbeing as living in accordance with one's nature but then arguing that this requires the elimination of emotion in favour of reason. Here are a few quotes. First, from Epictetus: 'It is the nature of the wise to resist pleasures, but the foolish to be a slave to them.' Credit it where it is due, Epictetus is dissing people who focus on the pleasant life at the expense of the fulfilling and valuable one. But we also shouldn't resist the pleasurable life – Epicurus was right about that. The Stoic who really gets it wrong is Zeno. He counselled, 'Steel your sensibilities so that life will hurt you as little as possible', and argued that, 'A bad feeling is a commotion of the mind repugnant to reason, and against nature.' Yet how could it be 'natural' to excise from our ourselves something so central to the human organism as emotion, whether positive or negative? This error continues through to Christian scholasticism, which similarly resents the passions and exalts the mind over the body, as though they weren't all part of the same nature. The perfection of our nature requires the cultivation of harmony between our reason and our feelings.[19]

This harmony will be a central theme of Part II, but I will mention the key issue in passing here: emotion, mood, affect and intuition are ways that we communicate with ourselves. They are *information*. Fear, for example, tells us that we need to leave a dangerous situation, and if we stop to interrogate that feeling rationally then we'll often die. These feelings can of course be in excess. Temper tantrums, wailing despair and other forms of hysteria are a situation where feeling has so overwhelmed the other aspects of our mind and body that we lose ourselves. They are often an efficient way to vent our emotions, especially stress, evacuating our mind, heart and spirit, and thereby allowing us to think more clearly. But they can also inhibit our agency and overwhelm our ability to think in situations where level-headedness is required. This is disharmony, and stoicism is often wise in its treatment of these issues. However, *reason* can also be in excess and here stoicism is naive. A failure to grieve death, process a breakup or acknowledge callousness out of contempt for or fear of emotion leads to neurosis in the long run. Psychotherapists have long known that supressing and repressing your emotions is not healthy.

There is a similar idea in Nietzsche: 'become cold, hard, and tough in the realization that the way of this world is anything but divine; even by human standards it is not rational, merciful or just'.[20] I love Nietzsche, but this teaching definitely led me astray. Life is tragic, often relentlessly so. But if we dull our senses to the associated pain, sadness, anger and grief, then we also dull our senses to joy, delight, wonder and excitement. As above, so below. You can't have the rainbow without the rain. You can't have the happiness without the pain. My sensitivity to tragedy and my associated tendency to repress my feelings was exacerbated by a lot of bullying when I was a small boy and the common but misguided advice to never react to a bully because they're just trying to get a rise out of you. I retreated inward. Cut off my emotional range. Became a rock. Rocks are stable and tough, but they're also callous. It took me a lot of very expensive therapy to uncork my emotions, and I had to feel decades of bottled-up bad stuff before I could turn my face to the sun. Don't make the same mistake.

A subtler concern I have with the Stoics is that sublimating your feelings so that 'reason' might guide your decisions will lead you to overlook critical information about your own *individual* nature. Philosophy has until very recently sought, foolishly, to find logical reasons that justify certain values or actions that are true for *everyone*. But when it comes to putting values into action it is critical that our values suit us *personally*, otherwise we will ultimately lack the motivation to consistently follow through on them. Now the only guide to whether a value is a good fit for you is the feelings you receive when living in accordance with that value. This includes the feeling of coherence that attends coming across compelling reasons for a value. But it also includes feelings like joy, achievement, disquiet, boredom, revulsion and other positive and negative sentiments. If you have hardened yourself to feeling in the name of reason these signals won't reach you. Perhaps I am being a little unfair to the Stoics here. In some passages, they seem cognizant of these traps of privileging reasoning over anything else, at least insofar as personal character is concerned. Here's Marcus Aurelius again: 'Waste no more time arguing about what a good man should be. Be one.'

A charitable reading of stoicism is that they did not counsel emotional repression, but rather mindful awareness of your feelings so that you could engage with them more effectively. This links stoicism to Buddhism, another body of thought that originated at a time when life was characterised by endemic dysentery, famine and war. The horrors of life are not quite so relentless these days, and we have the space to heal from the traumas we experience. We do not need to *cope* quite so hard. But mindfulness practices can still be very useful, both for dealing with hard things and healing from them.

## 3.7. Mindfulness

> Worrying is like a rocking chair; it gives you something to do, but it doesn't get you anywhere.
>
> Old English proverb

Mindfulness is a concept in Buddhist philosophy and practice that has been adapted in secular forms for use in psychological therapy, especially for stress, anxiety and depressive relapse. One of the most influential Western adapters of mindfulness was Jon Kabat-Zinn, who defined it as 'paying attention in a particular way: on purpose, in the present moment, and non-judgementally'.[21] Meditation coaches James Baraz and Shoshana Alexander give a bit more detail about what being 'non-judgemental' means: 'Mindfulness is simply being aware of what is happening right now without wishing it were any different; enjoying the pleasant without holding on when it changes (which it will); being with the unpleasant without fearing it will always be this way (which it won't).'[22] The definition used by the Philadelphia Mindfulness Scale, a commonly employed tool for measuring mindfulness, gives a bit more detail about how we should understand 'what is happening right now': mindfulness is 'the tendency to be highly aware of one's internal and external experiences in the context of an accepting, non-judgemental stance towards those experiences'.[23]

So mindfulness is about paying attention not just to what is going on around you but also to how your thoughts and physiology are responding.

The therapeutic effects of mindfulness derive in large part from its ability to grant patients control over their thoughts, especially the ability to recognise emotions as not existing independently of mind. As we exercise some control over our minds, we can choose to let go of negative thoughts. In the words of Vipassana teacher Joseph Goldstein: 'One of the most freeing insights of meditation practice is realising that the only power thoughts have is the power we give them.'[24] This is referred to in Buddhist doctrine as renunciation. It can help individuals to avoid ruminative thoughts and control stress. The non-judgemental aspect of mindfulness allows people afflicted with stress and depression to manage these emotions without them provoking feelings of self-hate ('Why am I so incompetent?') or hopelessness ('Why am I always depressed?'). Mindfulness practices, notably meditation, can help people with chronic emotional afflictions – like anxiety or emotion regulation difficulties such as anger management issues – to be less affected by their feelings. In the words of Jon Kabat-Zinn: 'You can't stop the waves but you can learn to surf.'[25] The practice of mindfulness makes us aware of our thoughts, emotions and body sensations, and this awareness helps us to manage difficult experiences and savour pleasant ones.

In addition to emotional regulation, mindful awareness underlies kindness and compassion towards ourself and others. We need to notice struggle or suffering before acting to alleviate or prevent it. Acting with kindness and compassion acknowledges our own and others' vulnerability and common humanity, and leads to greater acceptance, understanding and cooperation between individuals and between groups, focusing on what we have in common rather than what divides us. Self-compassion has been shown to increase intrinsic motivation to change for the better,[26] and a one-week self-compassion programme boosted happiness for up to six months.[27] Patients with recurrent depression who learned to be self-compassionate were less likely to have a depression relapse over the next sixty weeks.[28] Extending kindness and compassion to the natural world increases the chance that we will value and nurture it, which will benefit us all in the short term as well as future generations.

A word of caution is in order. Be careful that when you're mindful of your negative emotions you aren't just repressing them. You have to *feel* your negative emotions, not just observe them. Your psyche needs to cleanse itself. You might just be putting aside some bad shit instead of dealing with it. Observation aids reflection and composure but should not result in distance and detachment from our feelings.

I don't face big challenges from unwanted thoughts or feelings, but I'm still very interested in mindfulness because being able to control your attention is fundamental to self-awareness, which is in turn critical for self-actualisation, the subject of Part II. To understand who you are, you must be aware of your actions and decisions as they take place. When we act or react, the person that we are is revealed for a moment. The French existentialists referred to this as 'the disclosure of being' and it's an important source of information about our identity. If you are unable to regulate your behaviour in line with your values, or if you are incapable of recognising when you are acting in or out of line with your values, you cannot self-actualise.

Non-judgement in the moment is important here as judgement will cause you to remove things from your conscious awareness that you're uncomfortable with. Being judgemental will essentially encourage your self-serving biases, especially confirmation bias and motivated reasoning. This can be a hindrance to self-actualisation if you avoid confronting the fact that you are behaving out of line with who you want to be and claim to be. You especially want to be non-judgemental in the discovery phase of self-actualisation when you are still trying to figure out who you are and who you want to be. You will often discover that you're much less than who you would ideally like to be and may even be incapable of becoming that person. That can be very painful, but only if we're judgemental. If we treat these insights as learnings instead, and recalibrate appropriately, they can be positive experiences.

In the affirmation stage of self-actualisation, when you set about becoming who you would like to be and acting in accordance with that idealised identity, *compassionate* judgement becomes increasingly necessary. Judgement allows you to regulate your behaviours, which often emerge instinctively or from some other subconscious domain over which you have less decisive control, so that they are in line with your avowed self. If we avoid judging behaviours that are out of line with who we want to be then we won't excise those behaviours, and this will impede us becoming that ideal self. To take a small but not trivial example, if I want to be a better listener then I need to be mindful of my tendency to enthusiastically interrupt people when what they are saying triggers various word associations in my mind. This kind of mindfulness is more general and trait-like than the techniques developed for therapeutic applications. It's about being aware and conscious of yourself in the world, not being hyper attentive.

This way of using mindfulness is somewhat antithetical to the way Buddhism applies the technique.[29] In Buddhism, mindfulness allows the practitioner to 'recognise the emotion at the very moment that it forms, understand that it is but a thought, devoid of intrinsic existence, and allow it to dissipate spontaneously so as to avoid the chain reaction it would normally unleash'.[30] I am here quoting Matthieu Ricard, the French Buddhist monk who I mentioned in the introduction to this chapter on emotion. Mindfulness in Buddhist practice, or at least in some Buddhist practice, is grounded in metaphysical propositions about the nature of mind and existence. In particular, that life is characterised by suffering, and that the ego and its desires are the root of this suffering. If we can dissolve these desires and simply 'be', in harmony with others and the natural world, then we will achieve happiness. Consistent application of mindfulness in Buddhism allows the user to gain control of the mind and, through it, the substance of conscious experience. The end goal is to completely empty the consciousness of self:

> If we want to be free of inner suffering once and for all, it is not enough to rid ourselves of the emotions themselves; we must eliminate our attachment to the ego. Is that possible? It is, because as we've seen, the ego exists merely as mental imputation. A concept can be dispelled, but only by the wisdom that perceives the ego is devoid of intrinsic existence.[31]

I'm really not into these metaphysical commitments in Buddhism. I don't think life is suffering, I don't think desire is bad and I absolutely do not want to be rid of the self. In fact, the philosophy of wellbeing that I put forward in this book, especially the material on self-actualisation in Part II, is in some ways the opposite of (Tibetan) Buddhism. Where Buddhism seeks to dissolve the ego, which is merely 'mental imputation', I encourage you to build, multiply and thicken the ephemeral strands of self until it is no longer ephemeral, but deep, dense, precisely articulated, aware of itself and its nature over time and consistent in that nature. The purpose here is not to become free of 'suffering', which I think is impossible, but rather to become able to make sense of suffering and transfigure it into a source of meaning in life. Mindfulness is a technique that can be used to bring about either the dissolution or consolidation of the self. This book argues for the latter.

I also don't vibe with the at times obsessive emphasis on the present in much mindfulness and meditation material, like this quote from Ekhardt Tolle: 'Wherever you are, be there, totally.'[32] The present is great, sure, but you also need to think about the future. Pondering the future can be a very pleasant mental exercise. As Albert Einstein is supposed to have said: 'Imagination is the preview of life's coming attractions.'[33] And planning for the future typically makes it better when it arrives in the present.

What's key is not to become obsessive about the future such that you're always living for the next thing and never enjoying what you already have, nor to be ruminative over the past such that you're always crying over spilt milk and other mistakes you can't correct. The same is true for the present. We should pay attention to it, experience it deeply, viscerally, and enjoy it, but not obsess over it. We are a temporal entity – we can feel our growth, maturation and development over time, and it feels good.

## Chapter 3 summary

> If you have good thoughts, they will shine out of your face like sunbeams and you will always look lovely.
>
> Roald Dahl, *The Twits*

This chapter has drawn on ancient wisdom from the Stoics, Epicureans and Buddhists, and very recent wisdom from hedonic psychology and happiness economics. Let me try to summarise this 2000-year sweep in three points.

First, be reasonable about your emotions, but don't become so rational that you lose touch with your feelings. Ancient wisdom provides us with the powerful insight that while we can't control our feelings, we do have a measure of control about how we respond to them. We must respect our feelings, but we should not be ruled by them, especially those that are destructive of our relationships, like anger, spite and envy.

Second, stay grounded. Be aware of your reference points and set them to emphasise what you have in your life to be grateful for. Happiness is often a choice. Have goals and ambitions, but don't let them distract you from all the good things that are happening in your life right now. You've probably achieved things you used to only dream about, so stop long enough to savour the experience.

And finally, pay attention. So many significant, wonderful, heartwarming and inspiring things are happening all the time. Be mindful of them. Enjoy them and reflect on them. Think about what's so good about these experiences, and how you can create more of them for yourself and others. When good things happen to people you love, help them capitalise with a party or just a well-timed 'Congratulations!', and bask with them in the good vibes.

A technique you could use to practise these things is to generalise the sort of thanks we have traditionally given before meals. The Japanese say *'itadakimasu'* (thank you for the food) to the universe and the cook before eating. It's a small cognitive technology to help us be mindful of the good things, appreciate those who make them possible and stay in the moment. Try it whenever you experience something you value, whether it's a friendly dog, entertaining athletic prowess or a helpful colleague. Acknowledge what's good in your life.

We've come to the end of Part I and you're hopefully equipped for a pleasant life. You understand that you're on a treadmill that you can't get off, so make it an enjoyable place to be. That requires shutting off outside noise so that you can turn inwards and figure out what treadmill – what life – is right for you. It also requires some character traits like fallibilism and generosity that make you an open and gregarious person. This allows you to find values and friends that fit you. And finally, it requires methods of mood management so that you can learn from your emotions and relish life when it feels good. All this sets up for self-actualisation, the subject of Part II.

# PART II
## A Fulfilling Life

Follow that will and that way which experience confirms to be your own.

                                      Carl Jung, *Letters: Volume 2*

# 4
## Self-actualisation

No one can construct for you the bridge upon which precisely you must cross the stream of life, no one but you yourself alone.
Friedrich Nietzsche, *Untimely Meditations*

For most of human history, and still today in developing countries, a lack of resources has constrained our self-actualisation. The vast majority simply haven't had enough money, health, education and political enfranchisement to live the life that was best suited to them. But as access to these resources has increased over recent decades, the major barrier to most people's self-actualisation has become *information*. Specifically, information about what sort of life we are individually best suited to – what values, hobbies, occupation, friends and activities should we engage with if we want to be well? This will obviously differ by individual, yet our society generally promotes a one-size-fits-all solution to this big question.

It is still common for a person's family and community to mould them from birth into the person that their family and community want them to be, rather than who that person is authentically. Society bombards us with messages about what is desirable and confers high-status. But desire and status are things granted by *others*. For wellbeing, we must look to ourselves as well as our communities, and we must often look to ourselves before looking for communities that might suit us. Relatedly, our education systems remain focused on preparing people for work rather than life in general, so we come into adulthood without the tools we need for self-discovery or self-creation. Part II focuses on discovering and living in accordance with your authentic values, and its first chapter covers the basic principles of self-actualisation, so that you can overcome the information shortfall. Its points are grounded almost entirely in research in psychology and psychotherapy from the last hundred years.

## 4.1. Self-discrepancy theory

> A person is a process.
> Carl Rogers, *Becoming A Person: A therapist's view of psychotherapy*

Self-discrepancy theory is the brainchild of Tory Higgins, a professor of psychology at Columbia University. His theory neatly characterises the core of self-actualisation, which is goal pursuit. It posits that people act to harmonise their actual, ideal and ought selves:[1]

- *Your actual self* is who you are right now.
- *Your ideal self* is who you would like to be.
- *Your ought self* is who you feel a responsibility to be.

Each of these self-concepts contains multitudes. For example, you probably don't have a single 'ideal' self that informs all of your goals. Rather, your ideal self is made up of several identities – bodybuilder, father, Texan, Christian, democrat, vegan, etc. – that manifest with varying force in different parts of your life. When you're voting or watching the news, you're more of a democrat than a bodybuilder. When you're interacting with your neighbours, your Christian identity comes to the fore. And when you're alone reflecting on how you'd like to spend your spare time, it's your bodybuilding goals that are salient.

These multitudes mean that you will need to harmonise both *within* each of the self-concepts and *across* them. For example, it has been important to me to optimise my time, and so I typically shopped at one grocery store that sold everything. But recently I've wanted to commit more intensively to a low-waste lifestyle, especially when it comes to single-use plastic. Most supermarkets nowadays sell everything wrapped in plastic, so I've swapped to doing my shopping at multiple venues – a bulk store for staples and household items, a small greengrocer who abhors plastic as much as I do for fruit and veg, and the local ethical butcher for meat who is willing to pack stuff into Tupperware for me. It takes more time, but I feel better about my consumption habits. This is a case of harmonising *across* my ideal and ought selves.

In comparison, I've always enjoyed exercise and wanted to be able to identify as someone who is genuinely athletic. In 2009, I took a year off from university to pursue my passion for tennis. Putting my time coaching, training, weightlifting or groundskeeping together, I was doing something related to tennis around seventy hours a week. That number slowly came down over the subsequent years as I started my PhD, which is something that is not really achievable when you're dog tired all the time. This is an example of optimising *within* the ideal self – I had to balance my desire to be athletic with my desire to finish a doctorate.

Harmonisation is typically a matter of finding an acceptable synthesis – a bringing together of the three in a way that intermingles them. Imagine, for example, an ambitious young woman who aspires to be a judge. She loves the law, cares deeply about the justice system and pursues her objective with her eyes open to the demands of this career path. Her parents though, are making noises about wanting grandchildren and, truth be told, this young woman would like to start a family too, she's just worried about the impact this might have on her career. How can she harmonise these conflicting goals? As Australian journalist Annabel Crabb explores in her entertaining book, *The Wife Drought*, one solution is to find a father who doesn't mind taking on the bulk of the household tasks that make family life possible.[2]

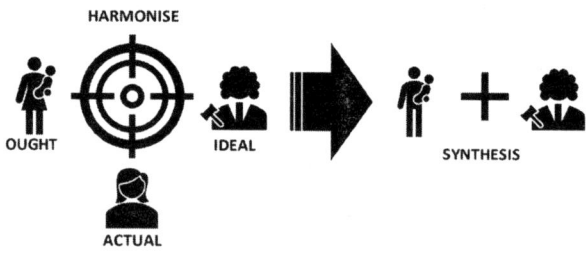

The process of harmonising discrepant self-concepts

Sometimes there is no synthesis to be found, and you'll need to abandon one goal to foster another. Both Roger Federer and Rafael Nadal were outstanding football players in their youth who had to cut that sport out of their lives to pursue their tennis careers. But how can you know which goals to cut and which ones to double down on? Self-discrepancy theory provides some insight here with its theory of how our affective signals can provide information to guide our self-actualisation.

## 4.2. Affective signals

> This process of the good life is not, I am convinced, a life for the faint-hearted. It involves the stretching and growing of becoming more and more of one's potentialities. It involves the courage to be. It means launching oneself fully into the stream of life. Yet the deeply exciting thing about human beings is that when the individual is inwardly free, he chooses as the good life this process of becoming.
>
> Carl Rogers, A Philosophy of Persons

Affective signals are a critical guide to harmonisation. Affect is basically a technical term for our 'feelings', including emotions, moods and more subtle things like a sense of 'clicking' with a group. Self-discrepancy theorists have paid attention to how negative affect in the form of anxiety and depression, and positive affect like joy and pride, interact with our actual, ought and ideal selves. They have found that discrepancies between your actual and ideal selves is associated with depression – to put it crudely, when you fail to achieve your dreams it makes you sad. Discrepancies between the actual and ought selves is associated with anxiety – when we feel we have behaved badly, we worry about the consequences from our community. However, alignment between our actual and ideal or ought selves is associated with positive affect. The exact type depends on the specifics of the alignment, but a sense of accomplishment is a common affective signal. In comparison, when you succeed at something you don't especially care about, your psyche won't give much of a reaction.

A neat illustration of how affective feedback, goal pursuit and identity are intertwined comes to us from a study of so-called 'contingencies of self-worth' by the psychologists Jennifer Crocker and Lora Park.[3] Their central proposition is that our self-esteem – a form of affect – fluctuates when we receive information about who we are only when that information pertains to some aspect of ourselves that we really care about.

Consider this graph of US students applying for graduate schools. For some, graduate school is just a means to an end, and getting in, while important, is not an existential matter. For others, graduate school is a critical step on their path to a particular ideal self. These differences show up in the study. The self-esteem of the student with little ego involvement in academic goals barely reacts when they receive acceptance and rejection letters from graduate schools. Compare that to the graph for the student with a lot of ego involvement in their academic goals: you can see that those letters send them spinning. They're euphoric after acceptances, and off to the underworld after rejections, even if they've already been accepted elsewhere.

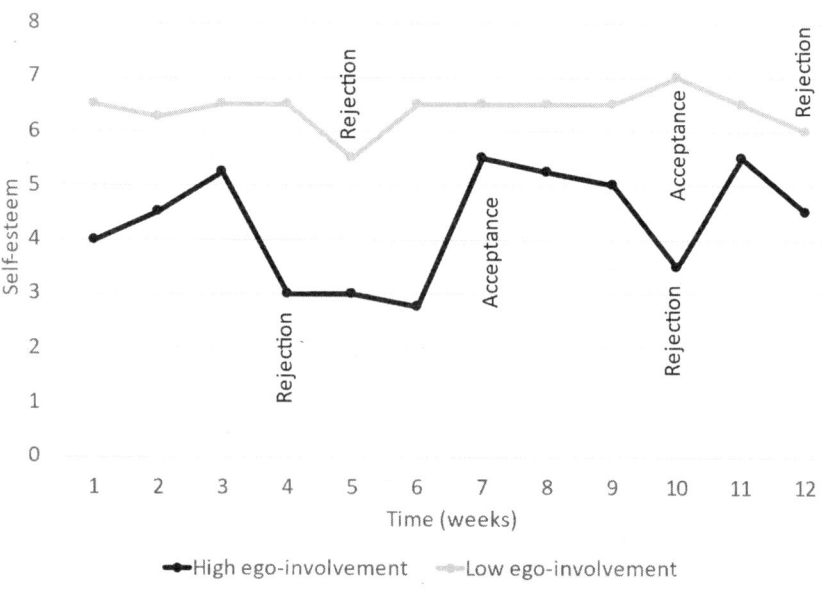

Contingencies of self-worth

Affective signals will tell you what matters to you. They aren't always your friend – remember all that talk of self-compassion in Part I. Sometimes our affective signals are merely passing on unhelpful lessons we've internalised from the likes of our parents or society. But putting this aside, affective signals are often your best guide to what values are right for you to pursue. If it feels good, double down. If you feel bad for not doing something, try harder next time. If it's just relief you feel when you succeed, then you've probably internalised something from others, and the value or goal isn't authentically yours. But if you get a genuine sense of achievement, then you can be confident that this is something you really care about and should continue with.

The role of affective and other forms of feedback in fostering wellbeing is a rich vein that we'll explore steadily over the course of this chapter. To move to the next layer of insights we first have to explore motivation, as that is what connects our goals and values to our behaviour. This brings us to self-determination theory.

## 4.3. Self-determination theory

> [Goethe] adapted himself to resolutely closed horizons; he did not remove himself from life, he put himself squarely in the middle of it; he did not despair, and he took as much as he could on himself, to himself, in himself. What he wanted was *totality*; he fought against the separation of reason, sensibility, feeling, will... he disciplined himself to wholeness, he *created* himself.
>
> Friedrich Nietzsche, *Beyond Good and Evil*

Self-determination theory (SDT) was created by Richard Ryan and Ed Deci, two American psychologists with backgrounds in counselling, who developed the theory while working together at the University of Rochester, New York, in the 1980s.[4] It is principally a theory of motivation and has several component parts. Perhaps the most important of these is the motivation spectrum.

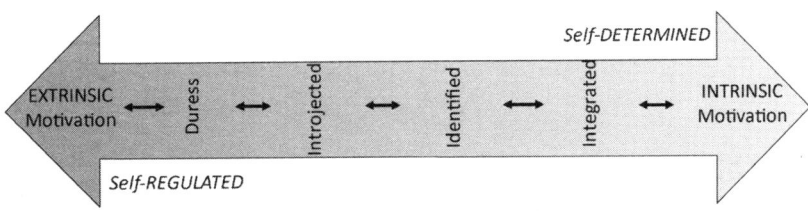

The motivation spectrum runs from extrinsic at one end to intrinsic at the other. Extrinsically motivated behaviours are performed under *duress*. They are behaviours you have no desire to do, but you undertake them to avoid some external threat, like abandoning your home to escape a bushfire, or towing the party line to avoid being disappeared by the secret police. Such behaviours require a great deal of self-regulation. You need to use your willpower to overcome the parts of your motivational system that are resisting the action. As such, extrinsically motivated actions tend to be exhausting, and can lead to mental illness if sustained.

Individuals also hold little fondness for behaviours that are *introjected*. These are behaviours that are undertaken for some contingent reason. They're instrumental. A classic example is behaviour done purely for parental approval. We don't want to play piano, we want to play video games, but as much as we tell our parents that they're the same skill set (i.e. finger coordination) they just won't listen. Sometimes parents may resort to duress to motivate their children to play the piano, but more often the threat of disappointment is enough. We want our parents to be pleased with us, or to stop hassling us to practise. So we slog through the chords. This is introjected motivation.

The *identified* behaviours in the motivation spectrum are not inherently enjoyable to us, but we value them intrinsically, which means that they involve a greater degree of autonomy and self-determination than introjected behaviours. Exercise is an example. Many of us identify the benefits of stamina, flexibility and strength, but not all of us will earnestly enjoy early morning swimming, running or repetitive weightlifting at the gym.

*Integrated* motivation is where identified activities become bundled up with intrinsically motivated activities. As an example, we might join a social sports team to force ourselves to do some regular exercise. We don't really enjoy playing the sport, but we identify its health benefits. What we do like is catching up with our friends every week. As we do this when we play the sport, some of the intrinsic motivation we have for the socialisation rubs off on the sport and it becomes easier to sustain our motivation. (A tip for sticking with any difficult New Year's resolution is to find ways to integrate it with your intrinsically motivated activities.)

So what is *intrinsic* motivation? These are activities that we engage in for their own sake, typically spontaneously, and without much mental fatigue. I daresay that all of us, at some point in our lives, have come across something that fascinates us. We want to spend time on it. Maybe it's a hobby that we enjoy, a skill we want to master, a place we like to hang out, people whose company we relish, a task we feel proud performing or a habit we always keep up. Such intrinsic motivations are a fundamental part of our actual selves. They are often innate, and it takes a lot for us to move away from them, like an injury that stops you from pursuing your favourite sport. Identifying and cultivating your intrinsic motivations is a critical step in achieving wellbeing and is the principal component of self-discovery in self-actualisation.

So, how can you cultivate your intrinsic motivations and grow your authentic self? The answer is through a process known as internalisation, by which our motivations move along the spectrum from extrinsic to intrinsic. Here's a simple example.

Imagine you stick with mathematics through the final years of high school only because your parents impress upon you to do so. This might be an autonomous decision on your part, as you respect the wisdom of your elders, but this can only ever produce introjected motivation. You find maths a grind, and you need to factor this into your routines – you might, for example, always need to prioritise your maths studies when you're fresh and full of willpower. This effort pays off when it's time to apply to university and you discover that you're qualified to study software engineering, which you value because it seems to open up a lot of cool jobs, like designing video games. Now your mathematics study is identified in motivation. Soon you've graduated and you're working with great colleagues creating ambitious computing projects. Maths has now helped you to realise your intrinsically motivated goals, and it has become integrated.

If we think back to Tory Higgins' self-discrepancy theory, our actual self is principally made up of intrinsically motivated behaviours, and behaviours that have become integrated over time. It is characterised by behaviours we undertake largely on autopilot, and for this reason intrinsically motivated behaviours tend to be the bulk of what we do because they don't require much willpower or deliberate attention. However, we might not be proud of many of our intrinsically motivated behaviours. We might lament our fondness for the wrong type of partner, resent how easily we acquiesce to bossy colleagues and dislike our tendency to take the lift instead of the stairs. Oftentimes, transitioning away from the intrinsically motivated behaviours of our actual self to become our *ideal* self will involve eliminating intrinsic motivations. This may require us to identify some replacement value that we then internalise. This sort of self-renovation is typically arduous because intrinsic motivations come so naturally to us. But it can also be the most satisfying and defining form of self-renovation because it gives us a strong sense that we can control our destiny and reshape ourselves in a desired image. Understanding this project of self-renovation and trying to figure out why I found some aspects of it easy and others hard, was one of my main motivations for developing a general theory of self-actualisation that I call the coalescence of being.

## 4.4. The coalescence of being

> My soul is like a hidden orchestra; I do not know which instruments grind and play away inside me, strings and harps, timbales and drums. I can only recognise myself as symphony.
> 
> Fernando Pessoa, *The Book of Disquiet*

The next step in developing our understanding of self-actualisation is to extend our model to include not just growth, internalisation and purposeful action but also destruction, externalisation (getting rid of aspects of our self) and exogenous shocks. We also need a clearer delineation between what is core to the self and what is periphery. This leads to the coalescence of being, where 'coalescence' evokes the formation of a star or planet.

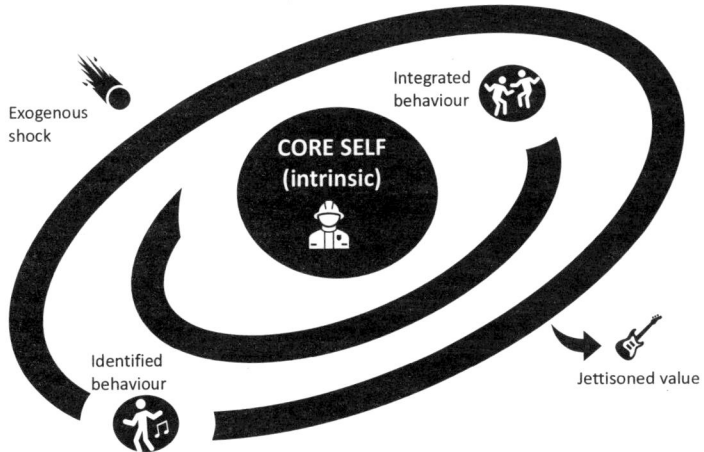

The coalescence of being

The image above illustrates the coalescence of being for a hypothetical individual; let's call her Aretha. Her core self is defined by her identity as a firefighter. In her youth, she also loved playing music, but she struggled to reconcile this with the demands of a firefighting career. To find some harmony amidst this incompatibility, Aretha chose to relegate music to hobby status. She identified dance as the optimal way to engage with music in her limited time, because it enhanced her fitness for firefighting. This meant that Aretha had to give up on playing the guitar, something she enjoyed and had invested a lot of time in practising. Over time, Aretha made many friends in the dance community, enjoyed participating in competitions and festivals, and even met her life partner at a dance class. Thanks to these social experiences, and their compatibility with firefighting, dance has become an increasingly integrated behaviour for Aretha and is now almost a part of her core self.

Sadly, an exogenous shock strikes: Aretha has an injury that will limit her ability to dance and requires that she change to a more administrative role at work. This shock will dislodge several aspects of her core self and send them rocketing out into space. Doubtless, this will be a painful experience, with major negative implications for Aretha's mood, life satisfaction and sense of self. The effectiveness of her adaptation will depend on whether she can find ways to integrate her new job tasks and alternate hobbies into her existing value system – in order to stay the same, she will need to find ways to change. This transformation will be guided, like all self-renovation and self-actualisation, by affective signals.

## *Affective feedback*

Affect and its constituent parts – moods, emotions and 'feelings' in general – carry information. We need to learn to listen to these signals and interpret their messages, which can often be highly complex. For example, positive affective signals like joy, camaraderie, pride in a job well done and a sense of achievement, should encourage us to invest further in a value or behaviour. Negative affective feedback in the form of anxiety, dread, irritation and boredom should encourage us to change our values or behaviour. So, if your job is demanding and leaves you feeling burnt out and stressed, but with little compensation in feelings of satisfaction, triumph or self-expression, then it's time for a career change. In contrast, if you are spending all your time at work, but find it engaging, enjoyable and rewarding, then those long hours indicate your passion – they are themselves a positive signal.

In many cases, negative emotions will encourage you to try harder. We feel bad because our ideal self is something we really want, and are disappointed by not having it. So a rule of thumb is, in the first instance, redouble your efforts and see if a positive affective signal results. If it does not, then maybe your ideal self is not authentically yours, but rather something you have internalised from the culture around you. For example, it's a common trope of teen dramas like *Mean Girls* that the protagonist really wants to be one of the cool kids. However, once they are accepted they realise the values of the cool kids don't suit them. How do they realise this? Through the absence of positive affective signals, and the preponderance of signals suggesting they were happier with their old clique, such as feelings of nostalgia and yearning.

Sometimes your depressive feelings are accompanied by other feelings that suggest your failure to achieve your ideal self is out of your control. In such cases, trying harder is likely to make things worse. Perhaps you cannot achieve your ideal self because it is too out of step with the constraints imposed by your actual self. It's hard to be a pro-basketballer if you're short, for example. Other times it is because the identity you pursue requires social endorsement, and the people you seek endorsement from are intractable. The *nouveau riche* mercantile classes of the industrial revolution, for example, often struggled to find acceptance among the old money aristocratic families of Europe. This had little to do with the merchants, and everything to do with the aristocrats. In either case, trying harder will not lead to success, only more frustration. You will therefore need to adjust your ideal self to something achievable. Motivation plays a critical role here, because it isn't possible to achieve something if you can't bring your sustained attention towards it. Motivation thus offers clues with respect to our self-actualisation – a whole other set of affective information.

## *Motivational feedback*

Motivation contains its own set of signals. Two particularly important signals are disillusionment and disenchantment. These feelings emerge when something we previously valued loses its lustre. For example, in the superhero spoof *The Boys*, Annie

January has always wanted to be a superhero and dreams of working with 'The Seven', a high-profile cadre of exceptionally powerful superheroes. Her dream comes true, but then she discovers that The Seven are terrible people pursuing egomaniacal goals and corporate profit. Such discoveries are extremely jarring – many behaviours that were internalised over time might now suddenly be associated with things we don't value. We might find ourselves aligning with what self-discrepancy theory calls the 'feared self' – the person we do not want to be. In Annie's case, she is filled with self-loathing, distrusts everyone around her and lacks motivation for her daily tasks. She does a smart thing and tries to find satisfaction in incognito acts of super heroism but is chastised by the corporation behind The Seven for messing with their public relations campaigns. Annie struggles with her disillusionment, pondering how to use her profile for good while remaining uncorrupted by The Sevens' culture. Eventually, she becomes a kind of double agent, acting out her intrinsic superhero motivations by undermining the corrupt institution in which she finds herself.

Disenchantment is not quite as devastating as disillusionment but it is psychologically painful nonetheless. It occurs when a value or behaviour loses its sense of meaning and purpose. The key difference from disillusionment is that we aren't accidentally aligning with our feared self, we merely don't find value in something any more. I used to play a tabletop strategy game called *Infinity* competitively. I was mad for it, ploughing at least a dozen hours a week into the hobby. Unfortunately, this intensity meant that after a few years *Infinity* had lost its mystery. I found games highly predictable, despite the fact that random number generation is built into the game in the form of frequent dice rolls. I started deliberately employing strategies I knew were suboptimal to keep the game challenging and novel, but this didn't sit well with my intrinsic desire to win. While I continued to occasionally hang out with my gaming buddies, I stopped investing as much time in the hobby.

I eventually made the difficult decision to retire from *Infinity*. It was difficult because I had mixed feelings. I liked the community a lot but found it difficult to interact with if I wasn't actively playing the game. Sorting through these feelings required a lot of introspection, a process by which your feelings become an object of mindful contemplation so that you can interpret the information they carry effectively.

## *Introspection*

So far in this chapter we have discussed relatively blunt emotional signals, but what about when the signals are more nuanced? Signals can be subtle, like a faint intuition at the edge of consciousness, and they can be complex, combining multiple feelings and sometimes conflicting messages. This is when introspection becomes indispensable. Nuanced signals can only be understood through careful consideration, deep thought and emotional sensitivity. We need to be alert for affective signals and make them an object of conscious contemplation. If we can grasp them and dwell on them, then we can interpret them. This introspection is a lost art in our hyper connected online world.

Nuanced signals are typically context specific, so it's hard to give a concise example. It's easier to illustrate the various ways people fail to take them on board. We receive affective signals all the time, but often brush them aside to 'get on with things' or some such. We may also repress our emotional signals when they contradict the conventions of the culture or groups around us, or don't immediately seem rational. This is usually a mistake. Our affective system has evolved over a much longer time span than our rational faculties. It contains immense wisdom developed through pattern recognition and natural selection over millennia. If its messages seem irrational, consider whether you have simply rationalised something foolish, and your emotions are now trying to make this apparent to you. In other words, your affective system is a remarkable bullshit detector.

It is better to digest these affective signals as they arrive. Repressed emotions tend to blow up, at which point we are overwhelmed by feelings that are hard to shake and can be debilitating. Instead, maintain an open dialogue with your unconscious mind and your intuition. This isn't the same as being easily overcome with emotion; it means being open to emotional signals, aware of them, present for them and ready to contemplate them. Rather than moodiness and other strong feelings, the result is more often serenity and steadiness.

Remember that the actual, ideal and ought selves contain multitudes – Aretha the firefighter we discussed previously, for example, has an ideal self that contains both her professional identity and a hobby identity of musicality. Introspection on complex affective signals can allow these seemingly divergent aspects of our selves to be blended together. The next section explains how.

## 4.5. Multiple selves

> They say that to know oneself is to know all there is that is human. But of course no one can ever know himself. Nothing human is calculable; even to ourselves we are strange.
> Gore Vidal, *Julian*

Our ideal self is rarely so dominant that it subsumes all our values and behaviour within it (exceptions tend to be highly demanding careers, like being a Supreme Court Justice). Instead, it often spreads in many incompatible directions. We may want a career and also to be a stay-at-home parent, or to look svelte while also indulging in triple chocolate fudge brownies. Our ought self, too, is often a battleground between competing principles. When Russia invaded the Ukraine in 2022, for example, many people simultaneously wanted Europe to ban imports of Russian fossil fuels in retaliation, while being concerned about the impact on the energy bills of low-income households.

These sorts of conflicts can often be reasoned through, and compromise solutions found. But an open dialogue across our psyche is required. Let's take an example; we have two hobbies and only limited time to devote to them. In order to get the balance right, we need to be sensitive to our emotions week to week. As we allocate a bit more time to one hobby, do we feel a distinct lack of the other hobby in our life? Then maybe we should change our allocations. If we split our time 50/50, do we feel like we aren't putting enough time into either hobby to gain satisfaction? Then perhaps we need to make the painful choice to stop one.

In this example, we are sorting through emotional signals that we are sensitive enough to recognise. A more complex case is where emotional intuitions and rational arguments need to be reconciled. Imagine you have a strong attachment to the place where you grew up, and always planned to return there to raise your own children. Yet when the time comes, you realise that there is no work for people of your occupation there, and so it would be an economically unwise decision. One way to sort through this impasse is to think about what aspects of that place emotionally resonate with you that can be replicated elsewhere. Part of you may feel nostalgia for the halcyon days of your family life before your parents divorced, but that's not coming back. Another part of you might value the opportunities you had as a child to roam the neighbourhood and go on adventures, but this could be done in any safe suburb, especially one with some access to nature. A further part of you might place a high value on the network of families and community that you were embedded in growing up. Upon reflection, though, you realise that this network emerged after your family moved to where you grew up, rather than being something that was already there when you were born. Perhaps you could create such a network elsewhere, provided that place attracted the right sort of people.

If we can communicate our emotions in an articulate way with ourselves then we can hit upon these solutions. If instead our affective signals come at us in a vague wave – say, you get a sense that you should move back to where you grew up, but you don't know what values, people or activities you associate with your birthplace – then we might find ourselves unable to harmonise our multiple selves. Let's turn now to two ideas that can facilitate this sort of rational analysis of our affective signals and help us work through complex clashes between multiple selves: evaluative integration and internally consistent patterns of behaviour.

## Tips for harmonisation

We can sometimes maintain clashing values provided we restrict each of them to certain settings only. For example, psychologists Carolin Showers and Virgil Zeigler-Hill at Oakland University give the example of a 'superdad' who wants to be a hard-arsed executive breadwinner in the office, but a gentle and nurturing dad at home.[5] These identities would be incompatible if exercised simultaneously but are perfectly fine when employed only in their appropriate domain. If the superdad ever got them mixed up, his affective feedback would let him know – his children would probably recoil from his corporate persona, and this would reach him as a negative affective signal.

Showers and Zeigler-Hill have generalised this notion into their theory of evaluative compartmentalisation vs evaluative integration. Evaluative compartmentalisation places positive and negative beliefs about the self into separate mental constructs. For example, a mother of young children might have two self-concepts organised around her parenting and her interpersonal relationships. The former contains mostly positive self-concepts like her being attentive, nurturing and patient. She is proud of these qualities because they make her a good mother. The latter contains mostly negative self-concepts like distracted, one-dimensional and dishevelled. These self-perceptions arise when she is with old friends and struggles to hold conversations because her children demand her attention, which she provides. She has little to talk about besides her children, and she is often a mess from cleaning up after them. When compartmentalised individuals are in their negative identity they tend to experience low mood and self-esteem, which makes that identity unstable. They are prone to flee from it, often discarding aspects of their personality that they value in other contexts and should therefore retain.

In contrast, evaluative integration produces self-concepts that blend positive and negative categories together. In the case of the mother, part of the reason she is 'one-dimensional' is the sophisticated philosophy she employs in parenting, which is very time-consuming but interesting and multidimensional. If her friends asked her about parenting, the mother could talk their ear off, which would validate her sense of self and enhance her wellbeing. While it would be ideal if her existing friends engaged with this aspect of the mother's identity, it could also benefit her wellbeing to find new friends attuned to her current way of life.

Another way of harmonising the self is to seek consistent patterns of behaviour, rather than uniform behaviour. An example often cited by economists when discussing this issue is indulging in junk food. Our ideal self might involve eating healthily while also being open to gastronomical adventures. If we never order cake with our coffee then we aren't going to be able to harmonise these values, and only affirm one over the other. In contrast, if we generally avoid treats but then occasionally make an event of travelling across town to try some delicacy, then we are cleaving to both values. Not simultaneously, mind you – but consistently over a period of time. This constitutes a pattern of behaviour, and one that we can stick to with integrity.

So far we've focused exclusively on affective information from within our inner empire, but there's another important sort of information that comes from without – social feedback.

## 4.6. Social feedback

> Hell is other people.
>
> Jean-Paul Sartre, *No Exit*

Thinking about our affective feedback is a great way of working through self-actualisation, but there's a problem: research in behavioural psychology makes it clear that we often lie to ourselves. We discussed perhaps the most glaring example in Part I: self-serving bias, in which we tend to see ourselves through rose-tinted glasses. If we are unreliable judges of ourselves, that means it is important to get an outside opinion. This is where social feedback comes in. This is information we gather from peers, family, random strangers, respected individuals, colleagues, social media, our boss and so on. If you want to be confident that your self-assessment is accurate, it is important to check that other people see you in the same way. You might think that you're a good person because you work in activism, but this self-image won't last long if your friends point out that you're unreliable, overbearing and self-righteous.

Social feedback can reveal things about you that you'd never considered. You might be going about your life thinking of yourself as a free spirit, only to discover that your friends get annoyed by your lack of punctuality.

Social feedback can be especially important for confirming that we have achieved a goal. Affective feedback tells us when our competence is growing – we'll get a sense of achievement at something we've accomplished, like lifting more weight at the gym or painting a still life noticeably better than last time – but it isn't so good for confirmation of achievement because of our self-serving biases. In some cases, we can test ourselves against objective criteria. In many other cases we need the appraisal of peers. Art is an obvious example, because much of the 'quality' of art is in the eye of the beholder. But the point generalises beyond purely subjective domains. You might think you are a 'good' tennis player because you are the champion of your local club, but when you venture out to a city-wide tournament you get destroyed in the first round.

Of course, social feedback is not always accurate. Your peers might give you the impression that you're ugly, but actually it's just that your curls and pale skin don't conform with the local fashion for suntans and chemically straightened hair. Maybe you're a phenomenal artist, but your family members can't understand your abstract works.

As with affective signals, we need to introspect on social signals to understand their meaning. People's opinions can wound us, and we should be careful and exercise self-compassion when exposing ourselves to negative feedback. But such suffering can be the affective signal to disconnect from inappropriate or unachievable goals, and may help us move towards healthier social groups (such as those with tastes closer to our own). How can we mediate between our own feelings and those of others when considering the right course of action? Self-verification theory provides some answers.

The theory posits that the views we have of ourself guide social interaction and, provided they are stable, make an individual's behaviour more predictable to others, creating a self-reinforcing cycle. A simple example is if you're vegetarian you will tend to hang out with people who endorse vegetarianism. This in turn makes it predictable to others that if they share a meal with you, it will be vegetarian. This predictability stabilises the way others respond to you, which makes it easier to verify your identity through social interaction. Stable self-views thus encourage a stable and coherent social environment, leading to a virtuous cycle wherein both your identity and social environment become clearer and better fitted to each other.

An important, empirically validated hypothesis that emerges from this theory is that people prefer social appraisals that align with their self-view, even when these appraisals are negative. Someone who regards themselves as the emotional rock of their household, for example, won't necessarily mind being criticised as emotionally inert. Broadly speaking though, people move away from both incorrect and correct-but-negative appraisals over time, towards groups that are both accurate *and* affirming in their social appraisals.

## 4.7. Becoming who you are

> *Caminante no hay camino: Se hace camino al andar.*
> (There is no path: The path is made by walking.)
> Antonio Machado, *Proverbios y cantares XXIX*

The following illustration integrates all the ideas we have covered in this chapter so far. It begins with a girl who has an ideal self of being an astronaut. (Remember, ideal selves do not need to be ambitious – such ideal selves are just easier to illustrate.) However, she notes a discrepancy between her actual self and her ideal astronaut self: she's not athletic enough to be an astronaut, nor does she know enough science. So she identifies a behaviour, gymnastics, that will help to resolve this discrepancy. She proceeds to join a gymnastics club and starts training three days a week, receiving affective and social feedback while doing so.

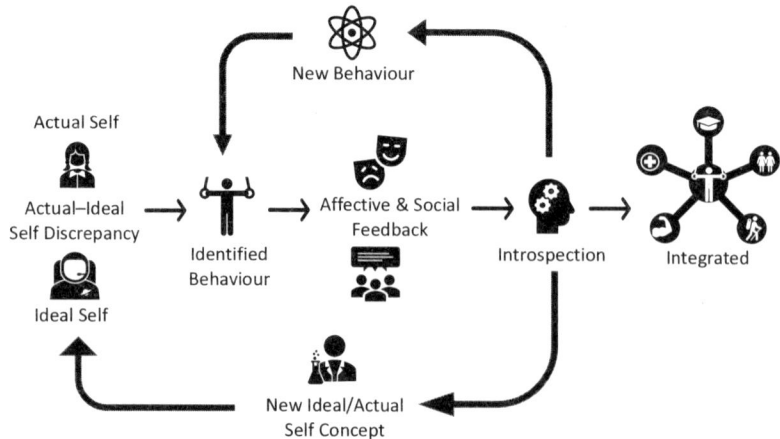

Integrating social and affective feedback into the coalescence of being

From here, the flowchart can go a few different ways. The feedback might be overwhelmingly positive. Her club mates are encouraging, she enjoys her time exercising and the motivation to persist with her new behaviour is abundant. Introspecting on these positive social and affective signals, she doubles down on gymnastics. She increases her training to four days a week, hires a private coach, starts watching gymnastics events and eventually competes in them herself. Over time, gymnastics becomes integrated into various other intrinsically motivated values and behaviours. She likes the strong physique she is sculpting through gymnastics. She likes how the fitness it imparts unlocks other activities she enjoys, like mountaineering. She finds that exercising hard helps her study in her science classes. Maybe she meets an intimate partner through gymnastics. And the health benefits of regular exercise are wonderful. In all these ways, gymnastics becomes a central feature of the girl's life, and her actual self comes to be defined by 'gymnast'.

However, the situation could be a lot more complicated. Perhaps there are some positive affective signals associated with gymnastics, but also negative social ones. The girl likes the feeling of having worked out. She likes getting stronger and more flexible. She likes the uneven bars, but not the more delicate exercises like the balance beam. What she really doesn't like is everyone else at the club. They've all been doing gymnastics since they were very young, and the club is cliquey. They look down on her for being a newbie, and don't make her feel welcome. How should the girl interpret these signals? One way to start is to note that strength-based physical exercise seems to be positively coded. Maybe a different club that specialises in that would be a better fit. The girl could join a cross-fit gym, for example. This gym puts a stronger emphasis on raw power than gymnastics and is well-known for welcoming newcomers.

A third possibility is that the social feedback is positive but the affective feedback is negative. The girl really likes the other gymnasts at the club. She admires their perseverance, enjoys watching their routines and gets along with them. But she has no love for practising gymnastics herself. Aside from a general lack of motivation for it, she gets dizzy when tumbling and a physiological issue with her shoulder joints makes them prone to dislocate due to the exercises. These things suggest that gymnastics is incompatible with her actual self, but that there are some things to salvage. She enjoys watching gymnastics, which is something to remember when the Olympics is on television, and she likes gymnasts, perhaps even enough to consider helping with the administrative side of running the club or other gymnastics events so that she can hang around with them more.

What of her astronaut ideal self? Well, while athletic pursuits are out, she is enjoying her science classes a lot. Perhaps she should adjust her ideal self. Rather than being an astronaut, which combines science and athletics, perhaps she should just focus on the former. Instead of gymnastics, she could enrol in physics classes, and instead of trying to be an astronaut she should target being a terrestrial scientist – maybe the astronauts can send her data and samples for study. This recalibration starts the process off again. The overarching goal of 'scientist' informs new behaviours and values from which more feedback will need to be drawn. This process of recalibrating the actual, ideal and ought selves over time, based on choice and feedback, continues until the integrated self at the right-hand end of the graphic emerges. That's self-actualisation in a nutshell.

## Chapter 4 summary

> Wholeness is not achieved by cutting off a portion of one's being, but by the integration of the contraries.
> Carl Jung, *Memories, Dreams, Reflections*

It's a cliché that therapists do little more than ask you, 'And how did that make you feel?' This question is so common in therapy because it's so powerful for self-actualisation. Your feelings are very honest, but their meaning is often not immediately clear. They can have layers, and you need to give yourself time, space and focus to understand them.

So my advice for putting Chapter 4 into practice is to set up a personal reflection habit in which you go through the things that have happened of late and ask yourself, 'How did that make me feel?' You should also go through the big feelings you've had and ask, 'Where did that come from?' You're trying to foster a constructive dialogue with yourself, and an open communication channel between your thoughts and your feelings. Be especially mindful of motivational signals and social environments, as these will be key determinants of the sustainability of your lifestyle and whether you persist with your values.

A journal can be helpful for this. I would suggest making quick notes in it when you have big feelings, noting what those feelings are (e.g. anger, frustration, joy, relief, etc.) and their likely triggers. Then block out some time once a week or so to revisit these short notes and engage in a more thorough reflective practice about their meaning and the environments, behaviours and people that give rise to them.

Personal reflection requires a conducive environment. That will be different for each of us, but it will always be free of intrusive distractions, help us turn inwards and put us at ease. I like to take walks in nature. Some people prefer a gallery. Others light a few candles, spray a bit of lavender and take a bath. Many people meditate to clear their mind and create space for insights to surface from within themselves. Experiment with what helps you feel present. The best coach on your self-actualisation journey is you, so get acquainted and make time for regular conversation.

# 5

## The Inner Empire

The words spoken to Socrates in dream are the only hint of any scruples in him about the limits of logical nature; perhaps, he must have told himself, things which I do not understand are not automatically unreasonable. Perhaps there is a kingdom of wisdom from which the logician is banished? Perhaps art may even be a necessary correlative and supplement to science?

                    Friedrich Nietzsche, *The Birth of Tragedy*

This chapter deepens the model of self-actualisation from Chapter 4 by picking up two themes. The first concerns common 'traps for young players' in the process of self-actualisation – wrong ways of going about self-actualisation that are easy to fall into. A key idea that we need to appreciate here is the notion of 'basic psychological needs' for autonomy, competence and relatedness from self-determination theory. Going about your life in a way that doesn't nourish your basic psychological needs is going to undermine your wellbeing. A second wrong way to go about self-actualisation is to turn inwards ineffectively and thereby miss your deepest intrinsic motivations. To lessen the risk of this happening, we will discuss where our intrinsic motivations come from and how we might identify them.

The second theme in this chapter is the balance between

reason and intuition in self-actualisation. Western culture has an almost morbid obsession with reason. This is true of the Judeo-Christian reification of the pure mind over the earthly body (sins of the flesh and all that), and the Hellenic and Enlightenment emphasis on rationality among academic types. As I said in Chapter 3, our intuition evolved over millions of years and got us to the point where our frontal lobe and higher order reasoning could develop. It is very wise and very astute. We need to cultivate a harmonious relationship between intuition and reason, and between the means by which they compel us, namely emotion and logic. Achieving this harmony promotes three things that are very important to wellbeing: automatisation, zest and flow. Automatisation sees our authentic values and behaviours practised on autopilot. They're not something we have to think about, which frees us to live our lives more experientially 'in the now'. Zest is engagement in life with a healthy appetite; partaking of all the things we enjoy without overindulging and thereby ruining the experience. And flow is the feeling of being 'in the moment'. It can be extended across all domains of our life.

## 5.1. Basic psychological needs

> Happiness is when what you think, what you say and what you do are in harmony.
>
> Mahatma Gandhi

Self-determination theory posits that all humans have three basic psychological needs: autonomy, competence and relatedness. Understanding these can help us to improve our wellbeing, orient our self-actualisation and diagnose the causes of our illbeing.

Autonomy is the need to self-regulate one's experiences and actions. An autonomous individual is not externally controlled. However, autonomy in self-determination theory is not about independence, self-reliance, freedom from all social influences, detachment from others or individualism. An individual can autonomously be group-minded and care foremost about their friends, family and community. Many people who work in social jobs, like social workers and priests, would fit this mould.

Competence is about being good at the things you want to be good at. It is a need for effectiveness and in some cases even mastery. Renowned cellist Yo-Yo Ma obviously needs to master his instrument, but all of us need to feel effective at feeding ourselves, raising our children, preventing the weeds in the backyard from getting out of control, that sort of thing. Don't master things you only care about being sufficient at. Competence can be easily thwarted by excessive challenge, pervasive negative feedback and overwhelming social comparisons to people like professional athletes.

Relatedness concerns having healthy and satisfying relationships with people you care about. More generally, it is about social connectedness and a sense of belonging. It is nourished both by being cared for by others and by being valuable to others, typically because of contributions to the group. Love is the ultimate expression of relatedness, and nothing destroys relatedness (and wellbeing with it) quite like love spurned, perverted or betrayed.

A basic need is defined by its direct causal relationship with optimal development, psychological integrity, health and wellbeing. If your needs are unmet, you will start to show symptoms of illbeing: low mood, depression, anxiety, loneliness, etc. If your needs are abundantly met, then you will likely show the symptoms of wellbeing: good moods, life satisfaction, vitality and so forth.

Self-determination theory argues that if your basic psychological needs are met, then your basic physical needs (food, water, shelter, sex, etc.) will be too, barring a hostile environment. Your autonomy ensures that you have the freedom to take action to improve your situation; your competence ensures that you have the necessary skills; and your relatedness ensures that you have the necessary support. An oppressive political regime, tsunami or global financial crisis might interfere with your behaviour, but that is out of your control.

Basic psychological needs are a powerful diagnostic framework. If you are mentally or existentially unwell, think about which of your needs is being thwarted. What was hard about Covid lockdowns for many people was how they challenged all three basic needs. It's obviously hard to feel autonomous when you're not allowed by law to move about as usual. Relationships were hard to maintain for those of us not living with our besties nor used to socialising online. And many of us were incompetent at entertaining ourselves at home. The mood state that worsened the most during Covid was boredom![1] The people who flourished were often able to find new things to love in life that were enabled by lockdown, like baking bread at home.

## 5.2. Goals that fit

> The curious paradox is that when I accept myself just as I am, then I can change.
> Carl Rogers, *On Becoming a Person: A Psychotherapist's View of Psychotherapy*

One of the most common reasons why people are unwell is that instead of nourishing their basic psychological needs they are instead looking for poor substitutes. The most common of these are power and wealth instead of autonomy; popularity and status instead of relatedness; and validation instead of competence. These are what psychologists Kennon Sheldon and Tim Kasser dubbed 'extrinsic pursuits'.[2]

Extrinsic pursuits only provide counterfeit satisfaction of basic needs. This is clearest with popularity and status. People who are attracted to you because of your social clout are only interested in you instrumentally – they want to use you in some way. It's your status that is valuable to them and if you ever lose that status, they'll fall off like parasites to find someone with richer blood to suck. You'll be left feeling used and lonely.

A similar pattern of contingency infects all extrinsic pursuits. Power does grant you influence and control, but it must be constantly protected. Challengers will come for your throne and you'll spend time fending them off. This will affect your sense of autonomy – 'Why won't these bastards leave me alone!?' Better to find freedom from oppression than to become the oppressor yourself.

The problem with validation is that you're always measuring up to someone else's yardstick. Competence is about feeling skilful at the things *you* care about to the extent that *you* want to be good at them. Contrast this with the approach of big management consulting companies. They're explicit that they hire 'anxious overachievers'. Why? Because they do good work and need constant validation, so the firms can work them to the bone in exchange for little more than occasional praise.

I mention big consulting firms deliberately because you might think that the poor association between extrinsic pursuits and wellbeing depends on the individual and their environment. But research has found a negative statistical relationship between self-reported extrinsic pursuits and self-reported wellbeing, even in social contexts like business schools and corporate law firms that espouse such values and celebrate their achievement.[3]

I don't deny that some people thrive in these sorts of organisations. What's critical is whether the values, behaviours and lifestyles associated with these environments are *self-concordant*, i.e. they 'fit' us in terms of our personalities, innate dispositions and authentic values. They are intrinsically motivated and nourish our basic needs directly. There are undoubtedly people who are intrinsically motivated to do corporate legal work for eighty hours a week. Some of them are even my friends. They aren't doing this work for contingent reasons like money, prestige or validation, but because they care about it and enjoy it. They're aiming at intrinsic pursuits like mastery, affiliation with people one admires and personal growth.

## 5.3. Where do intrinsic motivations come from?

> Why do you never find anything written about that idiosyncratic thought you advert to, about your fascination with something no one else understands? Because it is up to you. There is something you find interesting, for a reason hard to explain. It is hard to explain because you have never read it on any page: there you begin. You were made and set here to give voice to this, your own astonishment.
>
> Annie Dillard, *Write Till You Drop*

Presumably part of the reason people take life cues from their surrounding culture, and why they persist with 'prestigious' jobs they hate, is because they don't know what to do instead. They don't know how to turn inwards and 'do the work'. The previous chapter on self-actualisation talked a lot about the self-*creation* side of that work, but there's also a very large self-*discovery* piece. To set our sights on a self-concordant ideal and ought self we first need some sense of who we are authentically, especially with respect to our intrinsic motivations. Where can we look for clues?

The first thing to appreciate is that we don't have a 'true' self that is just waiting to blossom. What is innate to us are some talents, dispositions and biological parameters like good eyesight. Even much of this is malleable with a strong enough environment or effort. We also have a nascent 'self' – an inherent organismic tendency to grow, engage in the world and build our mental image of it and our place within it. The rest is mostly a matter of self-creation. But this limited innate self can be extremely important, nonetheless.

Therapists have a practice they undertake with some clients

where they ask them to imagine themselves at different ages. I'll quote the induction given by Maureen Murdock in her *Heroine's Journey Workbook*:[4]

> Close your eyes... and imagine, if you will, that you are moving back in time to sometime in your early childhood, perhaps the time when you were five years old... look down at your five-year-old feet. Notice the colour and style of your shoes. Notice whether you are wearing lace up shoes, sandals, Mary Janes, or whether you are barefeet. Now, become aware of your five-year-old body, your legs, buttocks, pelvis, belly, chest, back, shoulders, arms and hands, your neck, face, and hair. How are you wearing your hair as a young child? Is it short, curly, straight? What colour is it? Do you have braids or a ponytail? Become as aware of yourself at five as possible.
>
> Now become aware of the environment around you. Are you at home, in nature, in the city, by the seashore? Notice the colours, shapes, smells, tastes, and sounds in your environment. Perhaps you are with your family. Who are the important people in your life at this time? Do you have a sibling, a pet, a grandparent? Who are the people who appreciate you for who you are? What are you learning about yourself from how people respond to you?
>
> Now become aware of your skills at this time in your life. What are you learning to do? How are you being challenged mentally, artistically, and physically? What are you curious about? What do you appreciate about yourself? What do others appreciate about you? How do you feel about yourself?

The induction goes on for different age groups and asks different questions, but the idea is the same: to get in touch with yourself. Some of the questions also ask you to consider important influences on your development – other people, for example, or the places you grew up. If you're engaging in such an exercise to discover authentic values and motivations, it's worth reflecting as well on some of the following questions, and considering them right up until early adulthood – say, your mid-twenties:

- What things did you care about?
- What aroused your curiosity?
- What things engrossed you, holding your attention and fascination?
- What things did you persist with without external encouragement?
- What could you do for hours, barely noticing time pass?
- What sort of people did you want to be friends with? Why?
- What sort of people did you try to avoid? Why?
- What upset you as a child? I don't mean in terms of trauma, but rather in terms of morality – what made you indignant? What seems like an injustice?
- Did you ever do anything that made you feel guilty or ashamed? It is especially useful to identify guilt and shame that came only from you, rather than other people.
- Did anything happen, or did you come across something, that you thought was very 'good', like the world was better for that thing being in it?
- Were there any people or organisations that you looked up to? Why?

There are two themes to these questions: intrinsic motivations and moral instincts that you've had since childhood. You might genuinely have grown out of them – I used to spend a lot of time playing with action figures but have zero interest in that today – but you might also have been misdirected from them by society, peers and your parents. These aspects of your innate self might be buried under layers of socialisation but easy to uncover if you revisit them.

The second place to look for clues after childhood is your confused teenage years. Adolescence is characterised by multiple selves that are inevitably incompatible and compartmentalised. It is also characterised by a rapid improvement in our ability to take the perspective of other people, a rapid increase in social awareness and a heightened concern with how others perceive us.

The natural consequence of these characteristics is identity chaos. Teenagers rapidly try on identities, typically cosmetically through clothes rather than deeply through values. They worry both about who they are authentically and what other people care about, and often struggle to tell the difference. They discard identities that don't fit either themselves or what's fashionable, and display what seems like a remarkable lack of commitment.

Revisiting memories from this tumultuous time with a more mature mind can prove a goldmine for discovering intrinsic motivations and moral instincts. With hindsight and the wisdom of age we can see through what was authentic in our teenage fumbling and what was awkward, insecure or a desperate seeking for social approval. I have quite a few painful memories from my youth of trying to dress like the cool kids and both feeling like a goof in my fashionable threads and ultimately being rejected by those kids. These days I realise that I just fundamentally don't care about dressing stylishly. This helps me to prioritise only shopping for well-made, timeless men's clothes, and this dovetails delightfully with my sustainability ethics. A small insight maybe, but a thorough excavation of your past self might yield a bounty of many such insights.

I want to stress that this introspection is not about discovering your 'calling'. That might happen, and if it does that's wonderful. But many people, perhaps most people, don't have a 'calling'. They have a wide variety of things they care about to a greater or lesser extent. Becoming familiar with your innate self is probably not going to reveal to you the one big thing that you're supposed to dedicate yourself to. But it might remind you that you liked the warm yellow feature wall in your childhood bedroom, that you got irritated by people who didn't bag their dog poo in the local park and that you were so excited every time you helped your grandad in the garden. These are all valuable clues for how to organise your life today.

This little section has extended one of the earliest themes of this book – turn inwards. Wellbeing begins in the inner empire. As Pythagoras said, 'Nobody is free who has not obtained the empire of himself.' We'll return to this quote, and the importance of integrity, in Part III. Right now, I want to explore how looking for direction 'outside' oneself can lead you astray. We'll start with the error of trying to optimise your life according to some overarching 'reason'.

## 5.4. 80,000 hours

> Use what talents you possess; the woods would be very silent if no birds sang there except those that sang best.
> Henry Van Dyke, American author, educator, diplomat and clergyman

There is a global movement that I admire, and operate at the fringes of, called Effective Altruism (EA). One of its slogans is 'Do the most good'. Figuring out how to achieve this *maximisation* of the good occupies a lot of the movement's analytical capabilities. Having grown out of Ivy League Universities, EA has substantial expertise in this area. But the movement also tends to have large blind spots because of the extreme dominance of reason over intuition and emotion in the way they approach knowing and understanding.

One example is 80,000 Hours, an early branch of the EA movement concerned with how to maximise the good you do through your job, which picked up on the yearning among the young people that make up the EA movement for direction. Many of EA's grassroots members are extremely talented, enthusiastic, hard-working and even altruistic, but they don't know what to do with all those blessings. Enter 80,000 Hours.

The idea is that you work for approximately 80,000 hours of your life, and so there is massive scope to inefficiently contribute to the good through your occupation. A lot of 80,000 Hours discourse is highly sophisticated, but in its crudest forms it often advocates for 'earning to give'. This basically involves identifying what in your talents and skills would allow you to make the most money. You then pursue that work path so that you can donate most of what you earn to effective charities.

I think earning to give is dumb. It's not the sentiment – generosity is great. It is instead two things. First, the idea that you should pick a job based on earning potential rather than motivational fit is naive. And second, fixating on money as the means to do good is excessively narrow and misses much of what makes life great. Both errors share a common root in the attitude that you can and should rationally optimise your life to maximise one thing (*the* good), but let's analyse each of them separately.

You've probably heard the phrase: 'Do what you love and you'll never have to work a day in your life'. The point is that 'work' sucks, but things that are intrinsically motivated don't feel like work. They are engrossing, fun and rewarding. Earning to give misses this elementary insight. It encourages introjected motivation – *working* in something you don't care for so that you can contribute financially (not in any visceral way) to charitable causes you care about. I find it very unlikely that someone can sustain this introjected motivation for 80,000 hours. Maybe with the leftover money you're buying yourself lots of nice things. But this is a purely pleasurable rather than a fulfilling payoff. And it's again disconnected from motivation.

Why not just contribute directly to the charitable cause you care about? *Get involved.* The rebuttal from 80,000 Hours is that if your earning potential is much higher elsewhere, then you can do more good by doing that other thing than by applying your suboptimal talents in charitable ventures.

My response is that you then need to figure out how to apply your comparative advantage charitably. Write software for charities, help them with their finances, do pro-bono legal work, set up a B Corp providing services people need at less than profit maximising rates... If we were all involved in the world in ways that maximised collective value rather than profit then the world would be a much better place.

This leads into the second problem with earning to give – it's impoverished understanding of value. How could you contribute to 'the good' other than through money? Consider the Korean pop singer Xooos. She had a brief music and acting career out of high school that didn't quite take off, so she went to university to study sociology and find a different path. After graduating, she wanted some way to keep singing – something she was intrinsically motivated to do – so she set up a YouTube channel featuring her cover songs. This thought process isn't inspired by 'How can I do the most good?' or 'How can I make money?' It's inspired by 'How can I do the things I enjoy doing and share that energy with people?' Xooos now has over 1.6 million YouTube subscribers and a thriving career as a singer. My point isn't that she's a 'success'; it's that she's now generating huge amounts of value for people who enjoy her music, which she makes available largely for free. She is certainly generating much more value than if she had gone to work at a bank and made donations to Give Well, and the variety of that value – her style of music – is unique to her.

Sustained motivation typically allows you to get good at something, and this skill allows you to generate often quite special or niche types of value to humanity. 'Quality of life' in modernity depends substantially on the vibrancy and pluralism of our existence. We need a variety of good things in life. People value excellent music, food, clothes and so forth. They also value very mundane things, like a well-built, affordable apartment, skinny fries at the pub, good biscuits and green tea. And they value sentimental or unique things, like the sweater their nan knitted for them or the ambiance at their local café. Whatever your passion is, even if it's just baking excellent biscuits, if you do it well and share it with people, you will generate value for them and joy for yourself. We need to recognise and respect the particular ways that we each contribute to the many things humanity values. Narrowing our understanding of 'the good' to making lots of money, even if we mean to give it away, impoverishes the soul.

You should avoid doing things with your life that are obviously not doing good, like being a lobbyist for the gambling industry. But broadly speaking, the best way to do the most good sustainably is to be your best self.

Each of us is unique in our way, so you're not going to find a plan for *your* life 'out there'. This isn't because such plans aren't on offer, mind you. The world is littered with influencers trying to convince you that they have found the one true way to live. Whether they're worked out through science and logic, revelation and scripture, tradition and received wisdom, or by optimising within the incentives contemporary culture presents, what these plans all have in common is universality. This way of living true is for everyone, always; it's written in the firmament. There are often kernels of truth, titbits of wisdom and flashes of insight in these dogmas, but they're ultimately false. Living well is something you are going to need to feel and think your way into. Often you need to make time and space for the magic to happen.

## 5.5. Let the magic happen

> My life has been one long descent into respectability.
> Mandy Rice Davies, model and showgirl

There are some people who are what I call 'dialled in' to their life. Just about everything they do is dedicated towards some goal, activity or role and they ruthlessly avoid distractions from it. Most political leaders and CEOs of large firms are of this sort – their jobs are too demanding to permit wayward attention. Cass Sunstein, author of *Nudge*, is an example from my own field of academia. He seems to write a book and more than a dozen articles annually. For reference, the expectation at high-ranked research universities is typically for around two articles per year and no books ever. Western culture, especially American culture, celebrates this sort of productivity. But most of us are not so dialled in, nor should we try to be, and the worship of productivity around us is often actively harmful to our ability to find wellbeing.

So much of life and so much of wellbeing happens when you are open to possibility; when you have spare capacity in terms of time, cognition and emotional space to take up something that falls in your lap. It could be a new acquaintance that blossoms into a friendship. It could be a poster you see in the street for a new exhibition that turns into an adventurous and memorable day out. It could be something as simple as noticing a babbling brook as you walk by, stopping to appreciate how serene it is and feeling yourself cleansed an hour later when you finally move on. This is what I mean by letting the magic happen.

The magic is a big part of why childhood and youth are such wonderous times. You have abundant capacity. You can be whimsical, adventurous, spontaneous. Delightful things happen randomly because you can pull on every thread that comes your way. I think in hindsight many of us think we 'wasted' time in our youth. We were a little bit too aimless perhaps as we sampled all the delicacies random chance can offer. But I would affirm the philosopher Bertrand Russell's statement from *In Praise of Idleness*: 'time you enjoy wasting is not wasted time'.[5]

The magic comes to us in different ways at different moments in life. I will pick up on three themes in particular: drifting, the descent and leaving time to think.

Sometimes in life you're drifting. It's especially common in youth when you don't know what to do with yourself. There's nothing wrong with drifting so long as you're drifting purposefully. Bad drifting is basically the sin of sloth – sitting in your mum's basement masturbating and playing video games. You're going nowhere and you're not doing anything about it. Of course, some people are disabled, have mental health challenges and are surrounded by structures that reinforce these hopeless, lonely situations. That's obviously not what I'm talking about. I'm talking about aiming low and missing. It's often not quite as dire as dwelling in the basement. Bad drifting is just about squandering the gift that a life represents by living without appetite for it.

By purposeful drifting I mean actively searching: exploring new options and possibilities, revisiting things that worked in the past that you've maybe forgotten or taken for granted lately, acquiring skills, wisdom and knowledge that aren't quite what you need but might nonetheless be useful later, and investing in relationships. Maybe you don't enrol in a costly, multi-year degree in building, but you do browse DIY channels on YouTube and spend some time at the local maker's shed to see whether you fancy working in a trade. Maybe you take up some seasonal work on a farm to learn regenerative agriculture. You open yourself to the future without committing yourself to anything.

The descent is the darker and weightier side of drifting. It is the name given by Jungian psychoanalysis to periods when your life falls apart due to things like divorce, death or disaster. Its mythological manifestation is the journey to the underworld, an almost universal theme across cultures. What's lost in the underworld is our *self*, and to get out usually requires us to find some *new* self and undergo a transformation. We cannot simply rediscover what we were before – we cannot go back, only through, and that requires first going in deeper.

You cannot rush the descent; you must wait for the magic to happen. But there is one consistent piece of advice given by therapists to people in the underworld – investigate what you fear most. Active searching during the descent often involves getting to grips with things we have put off or out of mind: relationships so wounded that we've let them wither, personal weaknesses we find too embarrassing or shameful to acknowledge, or traumas too unbearable to relive, even if doing so would ultimately heal them.

There are few pieces of information as valuable as discovering something in your psyche that you avoid confronting. Leave it alone and it will either corrode your life or explode like a time bomb. Engage with it and you might find the seeds for new (personal) growth. A beanstalk on which you can climb out of the underworld.

Relationships are often key to escaping the underworld. A common trope in mythology is a hero who helps animals in distress, like the servant protagonist of *The White Snake* by the Brothers Grimm. He helps fish, ants and fledgling ravens in distress. Later, when confronted with three challenges that leave him feeling hopeless and lost, his animal friends return the favour. The fish bring him a great treasure lost in the ocean. The ants sort sacks of grain – a metaphor for bringing order to confusion and fragmentation. And the ravens retrieve an apple from the tree of life. Our friends, loved ones, peers and others who know us well can similarly care for us when we are lost in the underworld and help us return from it.

Let me conclude with one of the most common traps for those drifting: throwing yourself into something stereotypically prestigious that will at least look good on your résumé. For young people this might be something like taking a graduate position at a big consulting company. For those in mid-life or older, it might be taking on a demanding leadership role. The thinking behind this is simple enough – you'll find your direction as you go, and this experience will set you up well for when you do. Get back on the wagon, even if it's the wrong one.

The problem is that the experience takes up all your bandwidth. Consultancies notoriously operate a 'churn and burn' approach to graduate recruitment: hiring many, working them into the ground, retaining those that manage. Executive roles are similar – everyone is relying on you, so you need to be available to them. In both cases, your attention is consumed by work other people want from you, leaving nothing for the work you need to do for yourself. Ironically, this isn't drifting with purpose, because you have no capacity to search for a way out of your drift. This sort of workaholism is a distraction from the real work you need to do.

## 5.6. Automatised behaviours

> I'm just competing with myself, and that makes me better. If you give me two tries, I can do better the second try.
> Trea Turner, shortstop for the US baseball team

Let's fast forward now. You've discovered your intrinsic motivations and authentic values. You've done the work and returned from the underworld (a few times even). The magic has happened. You're not drifting, you're self-actualising. You're coalescing. What's the destination, if there is one?

The coalescence of being promotes *harmony*. Inner harmony in the sense that you are an integrated, internally consistent individual. And harmony with the social world in that you affiliate mostly with groups whose values fit with yours, while being open to encounters with new people, even if they have some friction to them. In Chapter 4, we discussed how coalescence promotes a harmony between affective signals, social feedback and our values. It also leads to the automatisation of behaviours that are core to you.[6] Automatisation is the process by which identified behaviours move from being a matter of conscious effort and intention to being natural and easy. You can think of it as a sort of subroutine of coalescence. Automatisation brings about a harmony between reason and instinct.

When you first set about trying to manifest an ideal self there is a lot of thinking, planning and resolution involved. You try to understand why a certain identity appeals to you, you develop some kind of scheme as to how you will become that identity and then you commit to acting with integrity towards that identity. You might think that you need to get better at asking for care, for example, so pinpoint some areas or instances in your life that reoccur where you should ask for care, and set an intention to do so next time. A similar thing happens when an event challenges your cherished values or self-image. Maybe a group with which you affiliate defends a member who you think should be expelled instead. You need to introspect on this event, decide how to alter your values or behaviours in consequence of it and promise not to abandon your decision if it becomes costly.

In contrast, when coalescence is further along, many of your behaviours will be unconscious. You'll wear your merino shirt like you often do, have your usual tofu scramble for breakfast, go to the gym on Monday morning as scheduled, stop to have a chat with the janitor as you enter the office. You won't remind yourself that you resolved to buy merino because it is natural fibre, or eat more vegetables for sustainability reasons, or exercise in the morning because you're always too tired in the evening, or say hello to the junior staff at your office because you want to live in a world where everyone feels included. You engage in these behaviours because they're associated with positive affective and social feedback, and because they coincide with your ideal and ought selves. But the reasons *why* have long faded into the background. These behaviours are automatised.

Some theories from psychology can help us to understand how automatisation takes place. This is valuable knowledge because it helps to facilitate smooth self-actualisation and brings us closer to flow across our life – the subject of the next section.

Our first stop is sports psychology, something I had to get a bit familiar with in my past life as a tennis coach. When teaching someone how to hit a ball you have to initially engage their conscious reasoning, what Nobel Prize winning psychologist

Daniel Kahneman calls 'system 2' processing.[7] This way of thinking is slow and deliberative. It helps you to understand something rationally. I want you to grasp what you're trying to achieve by standing a particular way, flicking your wrist over the ball and following through straight rather than across your body. But even once you've grasped the task conceptually, you can't execute it. You need repetitions for the body to understand the motion intuitively rather than rationally.

Learning a new technique in sport always requires thinking about it when you first start out, but this is actively harmful in match conditions. System 2 is too slow for the dozens of tasks that need to be done simultaneously to perform well. In tennis, you need to anticipate where your opponent will place their next shot, approach the ball efficiently and land in the appropriate stance, decide where to aim, time your stroke, flex your forearm for a split second on contact but otherwise remain loose to enable racquet head acceleration, and so on, every 1.5 seconds or so for half a minute or thereabouts. If you tried to use system 2 through all of this, you'd suffer analysis paralysis.

You need system 1 – this is the relatively primordial, instinctive part of our thinking apparatus. In a tennis point, you should concentrate simply on watching the ball. The rest will be taken care of on autopilot. That's system 1 in action. The more system 2 intrudes into this process the clumsier you'll get. You'll overthink it. This is part of why double faults are so common in amateur tennis – there's a lot of pressure, and you engage system 2 thinking to try and make sure you get everything right on second serve. This makes you tighten up and ruin the shot. Just relax. You know what you're doing.

Now, of course, most amateur tennis players don't know what they're doing. Their technique is horrible. They need instruction, and practice, and system 2, just not in a match. In a training session, we try to understand a technique or strategy conceptually, and then focus on just one aspect of it for a basket-of-balls' worth of repetitions. We might then do another basket focusing on a different aspect. If we try to focus on too many things simultaneously, we'll get analysis paralysis again. Let system 1 take care of all that and get system 2 concentrating on fixing one bad habit.

The same sort of dynamics are at play in the coalescence of being. You need system 2 to interrogate your values and set a course towards a self you're more comfortable with. But if you're always questioning yourself, you'll never *live*. You need to commit your authentic behaviours to system 1 so that you can enjoy the flow of your life.

These insights from sports psychology are also found in personality systems integration theory. It distinguishes two different modes: *self-control*, which keeps us focused, and *self-maintenance*, which directs us subconsciously towards goals that are intrinsically motivated and an authentic fit for us.[8] Self-maintenance corresponds to instinct and intuition in the above analysis, steering us towards authenticity. Self-control is more conscious. We can use it to correct bad habits and develop good ones in their place through focus and integrity.

Sometimes coalescence travels in the opposite direction, from system 1 to system 2. This is because instinct and intuition are capable of taking in a much wider array of information than conscious processing, which can only concentrate on one thing at a time. Anyone who has ever driven a car or ridden a bicycle through traffic will recognise this. Your mind is alert for hazards even if you're consciously thinking about what you need to pick up from the shop on your way home. A subtler form of intuitive learning comes to us from the study of games. We develop winning strategies via system 1 long before we can articulate what these strategies are and why they are so successful rationally through system 2.[9] But if we are capable of that articulation then we typically find it easier to adapt our strategy to similar circumstances. We're learning through system 1, but that learning becomes even more powerful once system 2 has access to it.

# THE INNER EMPIRE 133

This has important parallels in the coalescence of being. We can develop an intuition about something and make decisions on that basis, but if we are able to figure out the reasons for that intuition then we might be able to fruitfully generalise that reason to other parts of our life. For several years from about 2013, I had been living increasingly 'sustainably' – buying items with lifetime guarantees, avoiding long-haul flights where possible, shopping at a waste-free bulk store and eating less meat. I felt that this was part of something deeper than just doing my bit to arrest the ecological crisis but couldn't articulate what that deeper thing was. Then, after reading *Braiding Sweetgrass* by Robin Wall Kimmerer, a book about native American culture and its relationship with the environment and wellbeing, I realised that I was muddling my way to a different orientation towards life. I didn't like the individualised, careerist, 'convenience' culture of capitalism in which I was living and longed for something earthier and folksier. I've since been taking more steps in that direction, especially prioritising friendships over tasks, and doing some things slowly and deliberately to wean my mind off efficiency culture. Now that I have articulated some of my intuitions into reasons, I'm able to more effectively structure my life around values in my ideal and ought selves like fraternity, environmental stewardship and deep work (removing distractions and deliberately maintaining focus on an important task).[10] I still rely a lot on intuition, mind you – that's something Kimmerer's work reinforced. Reason and intuition, system 1 and 2, all have to work in harmony.

It's important to note that automatised behaviours are not 'automatic'. Automatised behaviours have been through the coalescence process. They are harmonised within our wider identity, internally consistent with affective and social feedback and the reasons that we have for our values. Automatic behaviours, in contrast, are just things that we do without thinking because of our genetic or environmental programming. This can be benign or even helpful, like pulling our hand away from scalding water.

But sometimes automatic behaviours can also be self-destructive, like when men repress their emotions because they've been socialised to do so.

I've talked a lot about psychological theories in this section, but my favourite articulation of the ideas here comes from Nietzsche in one of his literary turns:

> *One thing is needed* – to 'give style' to one's character – a great and rare art! It is practiced by those who survey all the strengths and weaknesses of their nature and then fit them into an artistic plan until every one of them appears as art and reason and even weaknesses delight the eye. Here a large mass of second nature has been added; there a piece of original nature has been removed – both times through long practice and daily work at it. Here the ugly that could not be removed is concealed; there it has been reinterpreted and made sublime... for one thing is needful: that a human being should *attain* satisfaction with himself, whether it be by means of this or that poetry or art; only then is a human being at all tolerable to behold.[11]

The similarities with automatisation here are uncanny. 'Second nature' is added by way of internalisation and first nature is removed by self-control. 'Long practice and daily work at it' are what I was getting at with transforming your tennis habits slowly, only here they are applied to your identity. Integration is evident in the comment: 'here the ugly that could not be removed is concealed; there it has been reinterpreted and made sublime'. We can't always improve by negation, as discussed in section 2.2, sometimes we must transfigure those qualities we are less proud of into charming character quirks, or just manage them as best we can so that we rarely succumb to them. At the end of this tricky process of self-actualisation, once we have mastered its *art*, we achieve 'satisfaction with ourselves'.

## 5.7. Zest and flow

> For happiness is only a byproduct of function, as light is a byproduct of the electric current running through the wires. If the current cannot run efficiently, the light does not come. That is why nobody finds happiness, who seeks it of its own account. But man must seek to be like the working bolt; like the unimpeded run of electricity; like the convalescent whose eyes, long thwarted in their sockets by headache and fever, so that it was a grievous pain to move them, now flash from side to side with the ease of clean fishes in clear water. The eyes are working, the current is working, the bolt is working. So the light shines. That is happiness: working well.
>
> The wizard Merlin to the young King Arthur in
> T. H. White's *The Once and Future King*

Continuing with the theme of harmony, within and without, we come to the concepts of flow and zest. They are useful for understanding the 'vibe' of wellbeing. Both concepts describe how life comes together into a coherent whole when we are living wisely.

Zest was how philosopher Bertrand Russell described the good life in his delightful and pragmatic little book *The Conquest of Happiness*.[12] He does not provide a succinct summary of it, but this passage is close:

> What hunger is in relation to food, zest is in relation to life. The man who is bored with his meals corresponds to the victim of Byronic unhappiness. The invalid who eats from a sense of duty corresponds to the ascetic, the gormandiser to the voluptuary. The epicure corresponds to the fastidious person who condemns half the pleasures of life as unaesthetic. Oddly enough, all these types, with the possible exception of the gormandiser, feel contempt for the man of healthy appetite and consider themselves his superior. It

seems to them vulgar to enjoy food because you are hungry or to enjoy life because it offers a variety of interesting spectacles and surprising experiences.

Enjoying life for its 'interesting spectacles and surprising experiences' suggests that zest could be summarised as the spontaneous enjoyment of life for its own sake. That would tie it closely to intrinsic motivation, but zest runs deeper than that. As zest is opposed to 'Byronic unhappiness', it must involve finding meaning and purpose in life, as we'll discuss in Part III. And, as it is opposed to asceticism, there must be an element of joy and pleasure too, as we discussed in Part I. Russell's disdain for the gormandiser implies that wellbeing requires balance, moderation and appreciation. This harks back to learning to enjoy life on the treadmill, the very first thing we talked about, and to Epicureanism – achieving contentment through modest living so that people can focus on friendship and 'pursue the pleasures, both physical and mental, to which they are naturally drawn'.

Distinguishing the zest of the person 'of healthy appetite' from the attitude of the 'fastidious person who condemns half the pleasures of life as unaesthetic' requires a bit more exposition. I take Russell here to be referring to people who think only some activities are worth pursuing, and that only some things are 'truly' valuable. These sorts of people look down their noses at hobbies and other amateur pursuits, and regard only certain occupations, lifestyles or objectives as worthy of praise.

If we take zest seriously then we have to reject this attitude. As I wrote in the section on 80,000 Hours, the quality of our lives is substantially determined by myriad small things that come together within it. That includes things that might seem trivial and meaningless on the surface like how the menu is displayed at McDonalds, or casual fashion. If next year's trend was sustainable clothes that you buy once in a lifetime and which biodegrade rather than disintegrate into forever chemicals, then that would have huge wellbeing benefits globally.

Equally widespread benefits could be garnered by making it fashionable to wear clothes that are slightly more expensive because their stitchers aren't paid slave wages. And, of course, it is delightful to be surrounded by people who dress stylishly, expressively or in a quirky and stimulating way. Lots of value in that!

We don't even need to be this grand – all the YouTubers out there making channels about medieval blacksmithing techniques, hacks for your indoor plants and vlogs about their experience recovering from anorexia, they all *matter*. These are all individuals pursuing their values and sharing their love, thought and care with others. They have zest, and we should celebrate that. This is equally true for someone whose attention is more diffuse. They might be focused on beautifying a little corner of their garden this year, always taking the dog for a thorough walk or convincing the local supermarket to swap to paper bags. *Nothing is trivial that someone cares about.* Zest is about attending to your cares.

Flow is a kind of full engagement with life, similar to zest but deeper, especially when understood with the full grandeur intended by its originator, the psychologist Mihaly Csikszentmihalyi. Flow is the state of being 'in the zone' or 'lost in the moment'. It is a sort of unification between system 1 and system 2, where system 2 provides concentration and focus, while system 1 provides smooth operation. Csikszentmihalyi believed that flow was the key to wellbeing:

> It is the full involvement of flow, rather than happiness, that makes for excellence in life. When we are in flow, we are not happy, because to experience happiness we must focus on our inner states, and that would take away attention from the task at hand. If a rock climber takes time out to feel happy while negotiating a difficult move, he might fall to the bottom of the mountain. The surgeon can't afford to feel happy during a demanding operation, or a musician

while playing a challenging score. Only after the task is completed do we have the leisure to look back on what has happened, and then we are flooded with gratitude for the excellence of that experience – then, in retrospect, we are happy.[13]

Most of us have had an experience like this at least once in our life. Perhaps you were surfing a killer wave in the golden hour, dancing your arse off at a really good party or tingling in the post-coital afterglow. Time stood still. You were so happy you didn't even realise it.

Flow arises when we are engaged in tasks that are challenging but for which we have the requisite skill. We also need intrinsic motivation for those tasks, and the task must provide high quality feedback. Flow is principally studied in activity-based settings like the ones mentioned in the quote from Csikszentmihalyi above: surgery, artistry and athletics. Remember how I described a well-played point in tennis: you just watch the ball, and your conditioning takes care of the rest. You need to get into the zone in order to play most sports well, so it's unsurprising that flow is often studied in such settings.

Yet in Csikszentmihalyi's original formulation of flow, he argued that it is possible to turn all of life, not just some activities within it, into one multifaceted flow experience:

> What this involves is turning all life into a unified flow experience. If a person sets out to achieve a difficult enough goal, from which all other goals logically follow, and if he or she invests all energy in developing skills to reach that goal, then actions and feelings will be in harmony, and separate parts of life will fit together – and each activity will 'make sense' in the present, as well as in view of the past and of the future. In such a way, it is possible to give meaning to one's life.[14]

The coalescence of being brings about this unified flow experience, and with it the harmony and meaning that Csikszentmihalyi promises. Our ideal self is the 'difficult enough goal, from which all other goals logically follow'. It is a life that we want to bring about that informs our values, behaviours, consumption, relationships and so on. Everything we do is nested under it to some extent, from where we work to what tampons we prefer to buy. The ideal self is *challenging* for us to achieve – set goals that are too easy and you quickly achieve little more than boredom. Affirming our ideal self through our choices triggers affective and social *feedback*. Developing our sensitivity to this feedback and our ability to introspect on it makes it *high quality*. As we recalibrate our actual, ideal and ought self-concepts in response to this feedback, and as the process of internalisation proceeds, we increasingly find ourselves engaging in *intrinsically motivated* activities, and developing competence and *skill* in the things we value – 'actions and feelings will be in harmony'. As multiple selves are integrated, behaviours become automatised, and our values are made internally consistent – 'separate parts of life will fit together'.

All the conditions for flow are met: high challenge, high skill, high quality feedback and intrinsic motivation. All aspects of our life feed into the realisation of our ideal self, bringing flow to our activities from morning to night. Flow will then characterise our life in general, not just while we are engaged in certain activities. This is harmony within and without. Mastery of our inner empire allows us to engage with the world in ways that bring joy, meaning and purpose, and we can sustain our motivation for these activities not because they are necessarily pleasant but because we care about them. I think of this unified flow experience as the nirvana of self-actualisation. Not living in the moment, free of self and desire, but *living* in *your* life, experiencing everything you do as 'making sense in the present, as well as in view of the past and of the future'.

## Chapter 5 summary

> Meaning emerges from engagement with the world, not from abstract contemplation of it.
>
> Ian McGilchrist, *The Divided Brain and the Search for Meaning*

The late stages of self-actualisation are characterised by flow, and flow requires harmony. So one technique for putting this chapter into action is to look for the discord in your life. Where does there seem to be friction between your values, incompatibility between the people in your life, or a clash in how you want to spend your time? Reserve some space in your reflective practice from the summary of Chapter 4 to consider these tensions. Which of them can be resolved through evaluative integration, where you understand the contexts that are appropriate to each value? Which of them require compromise, where something has to be traded-off for two things to coexist? And which discords require sacrifice to resolve? Sometimes we have to let very precious things go because they are not compatible with things we value even more.

Be especially mindful of compartmentalisation, which is almost always unhealthy. The exceptions are where you're simply not ready yet. You might want to confront your partner about your growing sense of distance from them, but also want to wait until after their big deadline at work passes. OK, but things that are put into compartments to be dealt with later have a tendency to be forgotten and left to rot until they stink out your whole psyche. If you're compartmentalising, at least do so honestly and stick to your deadlines for resolving things.

Outside of compartmentalisation, you should be patient with harmonisation. It takes time and sustained effort to develop a smooth dialogue between intuition and reason, to automatise behaviours, to move between system 1 and 2, and blend multiple selves. Your conscious mind needs to understand things and your body needs to practise them repeatedly before you can do them on instinct. Correcting unhelpful patterns of thought or feeling can be especially painstaking, and you must be as stubborn as your bad habits if you want to unwind them. The achievement of flow in life requires long obedience to a vision of yourself and the way you want to live. Celebrate each step in the right direction, even if it's just with a little smile.

# 6

## Better Together

> If you want to go quickly, go alone. If you want to go far, go together.
>
> African proverb

So far, this book has been mostly about your wellbeing in your own individualistic bubble. But wellbeing is not individualistic; it is relational. Self-actualisation takes place in a world built and populated by others. You can't pursue your tennis hobby without competitors, courts and local tournaments. You can't set up your farm-to-table restaurant without customers. You can't lobby for compost bins in your neighbourhood without allies, a council and service providers. You need other people to help you coalesce, and you do it *with* them.

Other people also contribute to our wellbeing directly through our basic psychological need for relatedness. We need friendship, love and pleasant acquaintance. True loners are exceptionally rare and almost always neurotic. We all experienced the extent of our needs for contact during Covid lockdowns. Even my father, who is so introverted that he speaks only to me, my mother and his doctor, found it taxing on his mental health when he couldn't do his grocery shop once a week among the people at the shopping centre. Social connection is fundamental to wellbeing, and you won't be good at social connection if you only see it through the lens of your *individual* wellbeing. We need to practise regard for others and group mindedness.

The relational element of wellbeing goes even beyond relatedness. As human geographers, architects and community organisers will tell you, wellbeing is an emergent property of places and the social interactions that happen there. Hermits aside, wellbeing is a collective effort and depends on physical, cultural and political infrastructure. We need places to meet that facilitate socialisation and joint activity, we need leaders and caretakers who will cultivate these places, and we need some degree of collectivism to invest in and utilise them. Then the network effects that are critical to the emergence of wellbeing can take off and snowball.

As we will find out in this chapter, these interpersonal aspects of wellbeing are difficult. A big part of why humans are the dominant species on the planet is because we are much better at solving the otherwise very challenging problem of cooperation than others. But cooperation and the trust and generosity on which it is founded is fragile. In recent decades we have systematically reinforced it through legal regimes. But we have also undermined it by introducing markets into numerous domains of our lives from which such competitive forces were previously excluded. My PhD in economics taught me that competition can be healthy and useful, but also that it is often distinctly anti-cooperative. Economics more broadly has large blind spots when it comes to structural and collective social dynamics because it is a methodologically individualist discipline. This has been disastrous for social infrastructure as economics has come to dominate public policy thinking. To recover the social dimension of wellbeing we need to reinvest in it culturally, and the latter half of this chapter will explain how.

## 6.1. Helped, heard or hugged?

> I will not play tug-o-war.
> I'd rather play hug-o-war,
> Where everyone hugs
> Instead of tugs,
> Where everyone giggles
> And rolls on the rug
> Where everyone kisses
> And everyone grins
> And everyone cuddles
> And everyone wins.
>
> Shel Silverstein, *Hug O'War*

Wellbeing requires interpersonal bonds, and forming interpersonal bonds requires social and emotional skills. I think we could teach these more systematically in schools. I would like to see schools prepare people for life not just work, but in this case they're complementary: so-called soft skills of amiability, good communication, mood regulation, teamwork, conflict management and so on are all highly valued by contemporary workplaces.

There are too many interpersonal skills to discuss to give any of them a robust treatment here, but I would like to dwell for a while on a very important set: emotional intelligence. This is because 'EQ' (as opposed to IQ – conventional intelligence) is synergistic with a lot of the individual-level work outlined in the past five chapters, notably introspecting on affective feedback, being honest with yourself and noticing how you can help others. It is also undervalued in our culture compared to IQ, and something I struggle with personally. Developing my EQ skills has been transformative for my relationships and for my self-actualisation.

One simple insight, so simple in fact that I am embarrassed to admit how revolutionary it was for me, is that sometimes when we're upset we don't want 'help', we want a hug or to be heard. Like many people, I came across this idea in a *New York Times* column by Jancee Dunn.[1] She seems to have come across it at a school where her sister is a teacher. There, the question, 'Do you want to be helped, heard or hugged?', is used as a tool by both teachers and students to develop emotional intelligence.

Helping is where you solve someone's problem. Maybe you do them a favour, or act as a sounding board so that they can make a tough decision, or you give them constructive advice. Helping usually involves doing something with your head rather than your heart. Men tend to be biased towards helping. Indeed, our cultures have trained men to regulate their emotions so as to be helpful for centuries. Beyond gender, 'rational' types tend to assume that help is all anyone ever needs.

But sometimes they just want to be heard, and impatiently trying to solve their problem actively makes them feel like you're not listening. Someone who wants to be heard often wants sympathy, understanding, even to be indulged while they let their less reasonable, fair or generous emotions vent. Hearing someone often means seeing them at their worst but listening non-judgementally. You might be a shoulder to cry on, or facilitate someone getting it off their chest, or witness them try to work it out. You will, of course, need to be an active listener – that goes without saying. Beyond that, you're going to see someone when they're emotionally messy, and you need to be able to interpret what they express generously.

Sometimes people get really messy, and that's when they just want a hug. When we reach out to people at our most open and vulnerable, we want to feel physical care, which might go beyond a hug to being cooked for or nursed in some other way. We also want someone who can hold some emotional space for us, keeping the world and its judgements at bay so that we can fall to pieces. We need emotional availability and carrying capacity from someone and going into 'helping mode' undermines that because it engages the rational part of the mind and represses emotions.

You need emotional intelligence whether you're helping, hearing or hugging. It will enable you to feel what a person you're trying to help really wants when they might be hiding it for shame or to save face. It will make you better at asking follow-up questions so that the person you are talking to can really unpack what they're feeling. And it will allow you to emotionally connect with someone when they're vulnerable, making those hugs stronger and bonds deeper.

In all this focus on others, don't overlook how much emotional intelligence is about your own emotions. EQ helps us to know when we need to be helped, heard or hugged. It improves our awareness of our own feelings and whether we are hiding them from ourselves. It allows us to notice patterns in our feelings and behaviours, like how I get grumpy because I haven't taken enough introvert time to recharge my social batteries. Perhaps most importantly, EQ can help us to sift through affective signals and determine which of our multiple selves are responding to what stimuli, and how best to calibrate our coalescence accordingly.

A final element of EQ that must be mentioned is that it helps us to recognise when we are projecting our feelings onto others. The classic example from (bad) romantic comedies and teen dramas is the presumption by a girl who fancies a guy that his rejection of her advances is a sign of commitment phobia or being closed off. If she persists, she'll eventually break through to the deep love for her that's really there. No, he just doesn't like you. You're projecting. Perhaps you're even projecting your own commitment phobia?

What about a quintessentially male example? It is traditionally shameful for men to appear anything other than cool, calm and collected in a crisis. So when guys, especially older men used to being in charge, find themselves a bit stressed, irritated or uncertain in such situations, they tend to project those feelings onto someone else. They'll announce: 'Can you all please calm down', when everyone around them is already chill. It is they who need to calm down, but they cannot admit that, especially to themselves.

Projection is dangerous because it's a kind of delusion. But it can also be helpful if we realise we are doing it, because it gives us an insight into our deep desires. Projections can be complicated to sift through because they usually involve our own shame, social expectations and some complex source of affective feedback. That all needs to be teased apart. But the rewards can be substantial. Discovering that you're projecting might even lead you to love, the most powerful of emotions and relationships.

## 6.2. Love

> An honourable human relationship – that is, one in which two people have the right to use the word 'love' – is a process delicate, violent, often terrifying to both persons involved; a process of refining the truths they can tell each other.
>
> Adrienne Rich, *on Lies, Secrets and Silence: Selected prose 1966–1978*

Love is the most surefire source of wellbeing and yet it is almost completely unstudied in wellbeing science. Why? Because we can't measure it. We can't even define it. What science knows of love comes to us mostly from studies of what happens when love is missing. That's fitting, I think, because love is often more palpable, visceral and comprehensible when it's gone.

Science has a wealth of knowledge about how an absence of love in our formative years almost inevitably leads to illbeing later in life. Abuse, trauma and neglect in childhood often lead to maladaptive coping strategies like substance use, anxious and avoidant attachment styles that make it hard for us to form relationships, behavioural and emotional problems like difficulty sleeping or anger management issues, and generally poor social skills owing to a lack of trust. Love makes itself known in its absence.

The strongest I've ever experienced love was when my partner of ten years and I separated. I've never felt such pain in my life. It was excruciating, like someone had taken herbicide and a chainsaw to the tree of my spirit. A part of each of us died and I honestly can't even imagine how brutal it would have been if we hadn't supported each other through it. We cried a lot, we walked together, we embraced often, we greeted the dawn together each day, and we saw and validated each other's experience. The acute stage lasted a week. We had to let go, but that meant cutting off an arm. It had to be honoured. I mourned what we had and the future that was lost to what could have been. Through all that devastation, I felt more love for and from my ex than at any other time in our relationship. Australian musician and writer Nick Cave said very poignantly about the pain of loss that, 'Grief is the terrible reminder of the depths of our love and, like love, grief is non-negotiable'.[2]

It feels a little cheap to try and extract from that experience what love is about, but I will do it for the sake of sharing. Love is about unconditional regard. Someone has positive sentiment towards you without expectations, instrumentality or quid pro quo. This is what people get from dogs, but it's even better from another person, not least because you can communicate with them directly. In love you can be raw, not just authentic. You can let someone see the roiling, half-baked, complicated thing that is your coalescing being and be confident that they will interpret it generously and care for its growth and security.

To be loved is to be known and valued. We are separated from each other by the boundaries of consciousness. We cannot inhabit each other's minds or hearts. But in love we breach, connect and form bonds. We develop instincts, intuitions and understanding of how another person is in their most vulnerable and secret places. We are recognised and appreciated. Love dissolves loneliness.

A small but powerful manifestation of this deep connection in love is inside jokes and shorthand. My ex and I always talked about getting a dog. I wanted to get two Bernese Mountain dogs (they're so chonky!) and call them Buddy and Guy so that I could say things like, 'Hey, buddy' and 'What's doing, my guy?' One day I got a text message from my ex about a dog moving around our climbing gym getting pats from strangers. He was sharing the love. What a sweetheart. Then she sent me a photo of his name tag and it said, 'Hello my name is BUDDY'. These sorts of exchanges, where enormous amounts of conversation are in the subtext and you can convey so much with a picture or a word are the hallmarks of love and the familiarity it brings.

We tend to think of love romantically, but it is of course so much broader than that. There is the love of parents, mentors, close friends and siblings. I'm an only child and I have no envy of siblings, but their love is so strong it's baffling. Siblings are so intimate and familiar with each other that they know exactly how to wound each other deeply. But even when they're at their nastiest, that venom is housed in a container of love that goes back to formative years, and so sibling love usually wins out over transient spats.

I find it bizarre that love is so absent from wellbeing science and philosophy (my theories before this book are no exception). We tend to cash it out as 'relationships', but that is so inadequate. Love is something that drives us as much as happiness does, yet happiness has received inordinately more scholarly attention. It too is hard to measure, though perhaps easier to define. I suspect that the real reason love is avoided is because it is so contextual and fundamentally relational. You can't study love at the level of an individual; it can only be understood across people. What's more, understanding a love between two people requires qualitative insights into the narrative arc of their relationship. All the times they texted each other about Buddy the dog can't be entered as a variable into a statistical model. And so, one of the most important forces for our wellbeing languishes in mystery.

I'm not good at love and so I can't say much about how we can bring more of it about in our lives. My only suspicion is that we need to look beyond ourselves more, to others. We must regard them, unconditionally, but that's not something we can or should force. We can begin with generosity of spirit to those around us. I think Ladinsky puts it beautifully in his apocryphal translation of the Islamic poet Hafiz:

> And still, after all this time,
> the sun never says to the earth,
> 'You owe me'.
>
> Look what happens
> with a love like that,
> It lights the whole sky

Communal love lights the sky in the sense that it transfuses our world with care, gratitude, altruism, hope and security. It is the basis of social capital, a key determinant of the wellbeing of places and groups, and the subject of the next section.

## 6.3. Fraternity

> To be rooted is perhaps the most important and least recognised need of the human soul.
> Simone Weil, *The Need for Roots*

Fraternity is the manifestation of love at the community level. It has myriad benefits. One long emphasised by economics is social insurance. Groups can pool risk. We don't know who will be struck down with illness at random, but we know that some of us will at any one time, and a group can care bear the collective load while that person recovers. That person can then pay it forward when someone else in the group gets sick. This is much more administratively efficient than developing an elaborate health insurance system that tries to accurately price the risk of illness to each person. That's a big part of why healthcare in the

European welfare states, with their substantial populations used to socialised risk, is so much cheaper than in the United States with its emphasis on private healthcare markets. The OECD average in 2022 was 9.2 per cent of GDP spent on healthcare; in the US it was way out ahead at 17.3 per cent.[3]

Groups can also provide security through gossip and word of mouth. In the centuries before enforceable commercial contracts, and still today for a range of agreements like going to bed with someone or choosing a school for your kid, reputation is a much more important source of surety than a promise and a handshake. Reputation relies on social transmission.

At the most basic level, groups can complete complex tasks that individuals cannot. One person cannot put on a production of Shakespeare, or play a game of soccer, or build a house (they can assemble it perhaps, but they couldn't produce all the materials on their own). It's hard to party by yourself. Many of the things that are most fundamental to your wellbeing can only be achieved by people working together.

These collective benefits to wellbeing have been the subject of substantial scholarly interest that radiates out from the notion of 'social capital': the wealth of a group constituted by the size of its network and the bonds of reciprocity between individual members. There is a straightforward correlation between social capital and life satisfaction, extensively documented using a variety of international data sets by John Helliwell and co-authors, among others, including in the World Happiness Report.[4] Generalised trust in other citizens, levels of membership in community groups at the county level, whether people return lost wallets without taking money out of them and other indicators of social cohesion are all positively correlated with life satisfaction and negatively correlated with suicide rates. Correlation isn't causation, but there is a wealth of qualitative work that substantiates these correlations with detailed case studies.

The Harvard political scientist Bob Putnam is perhaps the most well-known academic associated with the social capital literature. His book, *Bowling Alone: The Collapse and Revival of American Community* (2000), brought to widespread public attention the disintegration of social capital in the US. He was particularly interested in the decline of community groups that fostered face-to-face meetings, especially between people who don't share all their values. A bowling league, for example, brings together people with a shared interest in bowling who might deeply disagree over pretty much everything else, from football to politics. In contrast, the sorting of people into groups with shared values, like activist organisations, fosters echo chambers and partisanship, and is bad for solidarity across a nation. We are swallowing the bitter fruits of this disintegration in social capital today in the growing hostility between different subcultures in America and the associated political dysfunction.

Numerous studies have documented the consequences of social decay on the life outcomes of marginalised groups, which have tanked in recent decades. My personal favourite is Hilary Cottam's *Radical Help: How We Can Remake the Relationships Between Us and Revolutionise the Welfare State*. As churches, unions, community centres and other sites of social capital have disappeared, the social insurance, structure and sense of solidarity they provided have gone with them. The neoliberal welfare state struggles to plug this gap because it makes care conditional on work, punishes people for being poor, lacks the capacity to understand the narrative arc of their lives and cannot tailor help to how an individual fits into a community. In many ways it makes marginalisation worse by stigmatising people who are struggling, thereby alienating them from social help. As deindustrialisation has ravaged previously prosperous and proud factory towns, this experience of decay, marginalisation and despair has affected an ever-greater portion of the traditional middle class.

'Elites' often cannot appreciate these trends because their lives remain characterised by thick social networks like university college communities, large corporations and urban hobby groups that survive thanks to the wealth and population density of urban environments. Universities in particular are crucial to the formation of both bonding (between individuals with similar values) and bridging (across individuals with different values) social capital. Living on campus usually pushes you into close proximity with strangers who have different life experiences, goals and cultures than you, and makes you dependent on each other to have a good time.

College was transformative for me. I lived for five glorious years at Burton and Garran (B&G) Hall at the Australian National University, the largest residential hall in the southern hemisphere, with 520 people. This is an unusually long amount of time, but I was severely under-socialised when I arrived. I was on the social committee in my fourth year as a sports representative, and then returned after a gap year to take up a more administrative role as the sub dean in charge of academic enrichment.

College brought me into close proximity with rural kids with different worldviews to my own. They were more communitarian, more concerned with saving face and more focused on employment and financial security, and football. They dramatically broadened my understanding of how people see the world. I also met large cohorts of international students from Singapore, China, India and elsewhere who exposed me to different cultures and with whom I often became close friends through sports teams. Years later I would go to their weddings. I also encountered kids whose families were much wealthier than mine and had attended private schools. This helped me learn how to move in such circles. Today, I am friends with zero people from high school but many from university, and we remain close despite living in different countries.

One of the most striking things about B&G for me was how people cared about each other simply because of familiarity. You didn't look out for people because they were useful to you, but simply because you knew them. This bonding dynamic was especially obvious when it came to difficult people. You lived with them, so you had to make it work. It wasn't really feasible to ostracise someone. Although you didn't have to sit with them, it did mean having to see them suffering. So there was a tendency to nurture, rehabilitate and integrate people, even if they were a bit weird or offensive. I remember one resident who arrived a misogynistic arsehole but was quickly set straight by the girls of the hall through a combination of light-hearted bullying and earnest counselling. These sorts of social dynamics are peculiar to groups that form through proximity rather than sorting according to narrow interests like political affiliation or a hobby. At the clubs and societies I was a member of where we didn't cohabit, I found these social dynamics to be more muted.

The benefits of community are not easy to sustain. The field of sociobiology has documented this extensively. Its insights can be summarised through three 'games' that are often used to model the evolution of social dynamics: the prisoner's dilemma, the take a hit game and the public goods game.

The prisoner's dilemma teaches us the importance of trust. The set-up is usually a riff on the following. Two criminals are taken into separate cells for questioning. They have previously agreed on a story. If they stick to their story, both will get light sentences. We call this the 'cooperation' outcome. But if one 'defects' from their agreement and blabs to the police, they will get no sentence and the other will receive a harsh sentence. If they both defect, they will both get a long sentence. The optimal outcome for the criminals as a group is to collaborate, but there is a strong incentive at the individual level to defect. So strong, in fact, that we can show mathematically that defection is the rational choice. Each criminal knows that the other has this incentive, which encourages them to defect first. Their only saviour is *trust*, which is why criminal organisations put so much effort into instilling group loyalty into their members. Trust is very hard to sustain without extensive group effort, including the use of symbols like gang signs and tattoos, and rituals like hazing and initiation rites.

Prisoner's dilemmas are all around us. Perhaps the most consequential right now is international cooperation on climate change. We would all benefit from everyone agreeing to stridently reduce their own emissions. But because emissions and their reduction are hard to monitor, because each of us is unable to have much of an effect on our own, and because one seems to gain an economic advantage by not reducing carbon emissions, we have a trust problem. And so everyone is constantly defecting from climate pledges and we are on track for a rather bad century.

The take a hit game, which we discussed in section 2.6, teaches the importance of generosity. Many forms of cooperation cannot get started without a benevolent gesture. When kids are playing videogames together, for example, it's hard to get one to share the controller if they don't think they'll ever get it back. But if they never pass it in the first place then the other child will simply be encouraged to hang on jealousy when they get their hands on it. Sharing can only begin with good faith.

The public goods game teaches the importance of fellow feeling. The game takes many forms, but the one I use in my classes is the following. Each player out of about fifteen is given ten points at the start of each round (there are usually six rounds). They must decide how many of these points to contribute to a communal pot and how many to keep for themselves. At the end of each round the communal pot is doubled and the points therein equally distributed among all players, regardless of how much they individually contributed. The group can obtain the highest possible score if every round each player contributes all their points to the pot. I usually have a prize for the group if it can achieve a certain score. But I also offer a larger prize for the person with the highest individual score. Now, you can only obtain the individual prize if you hold some points back for yourself each round.

In the first three rounds, contributions are private information – nobody knows what other players contributed, only the total amount that went into the public pot. As the rounds go by, contributions decline as the relatively generous players see that there are some selfish individualists among them. In round four, contributions become public information, and there is typically a spike, especially among those who were previously stingy – remember the importance of reputation in social dynamics! In round five, I introduce fines, where you can spend one of your points to remove three points from another player. This is a form of 'altruistic punishment' because it hurts you to encourage someone else to be more group minded. In round six, I make all the contributions from rounds one to three public and watch people try to figure out who to punish. Big liars from the early rounds usually get roasted, while the 'winner' is usually someone who maintains the illusion of being a team player while always being a bit stingy.

Public goods game dynamics are present whenever some 'common' resource needs to be managed for group benefit, like a community centre, social sports league or a babysitting club. Such infrastructure can rarely survive without 'super-cooperators' – people who take a hit to get things started and generally contribute more to the communal pot than others. Public goods tend to die if there are too many 'psychopaths' – people who act like parasites and feed off the common resource more than they contribute to it.

We need community for wellbeing, but community is fragile. How do we bring about the trust, generosity and fellow feeling that cooperation, reciprocity and social infrastructure require? How can we encourage people to be super-cooperators rather than psychopaths? That is the subject of the rest of this chapter. We start at the immediate interpersonal level with care.

## 6.4. Care

> How
> Did the rose
> Ever open its heart and give to this world
> All its beauty?
> It felt the encouragement of light
> Upon its being.
> Otherwise,
> We all remain
> Too frightened.
>
> *A Year with Hafiz*, poems by Daniel Ladinsky

A core element of the basic psychological need for relatedness is feeling loved and cared for. We need affection, support, mentoring and love. Yet we've marginalised this basic skill in recent decades. The welfare states of post-war Europe externalised care onto the state. This was in many cases for good reason, like the right to healthcare. But some of its motives have been destructive in the long term, like us not wanting to take care of our elderly parents.

Seeing care as something you pay for, whether through taxation or fee-for-service, rather than something you *give*, transforms it from a moral matter into a commercial one. Care consequently becomes associated with different emotions, conventions and relationships. A classic example of this transformation is documented in Uri Gneezy and Aldo Rustichini's study of Israeli child care centres.[5] Parents would frequently arrive late to collect their children, forcing carers to stay later. Following economic logic, the centres introduced a fine for late collection, both to compensate the workers and to discourage late pick-ups.

What happened? More parents picked up their children late! The fine transformed a social and moral relationship in which parents felt guilty for picking up their children late into a commercial relationship. Parents interpreted the fine as a price for longer childcare services, not as a punishment.

The 'neoliberal' period of government and public management, which ran from around 1980–2020 (and still lingers in zombie form), turbocharged the commercialisation of care. This was as much a psychological and cultural process as a political-economic one. The provision of public services for care of the elderly, health, social work, disability support and the like was increasingly driven by efficiency considerations. All well and good on the face of it – cheaper care means more money left over for homelessness shelters, or so the logic goes. But analysing service provision in terms of outputs per dollar means measuring the outputs. Care is something fundamentally qualitative and intangible, which means that it doesn't get measured directly and we end up providing a much worse simulacrum.

Hilary Cottam documents the consequences of this management by metrics for care in the United Kingdom. In *Radical Help*, she gives the example of how aged care services are commissioned by government in part based on the number of elderly people washed per hour. You can then use the wage of the carer responsible to calculate worker efficiency. The result is that all the carer's incentives encourage them to wash vulnerable and infirm elderly people brusquely and impersonally, leaving them feeling violated and, ironically, uncared for. The relationship between the carer and their charge, which the elderly value as much if not more than the washing, is absent from the calculus because it can't be easily measured or monetised.

A further consequence of the commercialisation of care has been its professionalisation. We nowadays see care as something you need training in rather than an innate human skill. We feel uncomfortable offering emotional and psychological support to people because we think they need a therapist – someone with expertise. Working in childcare in the UK typically requires at least a 160-hour certificate. Social work requires postgraduate training and is managed through the health service. The professionalisation of care undermines our confidence to offer it because we don't feel 'qualified'.

The professionalisation of care also makes us feel guilty asking for it. We think carers should be appropriately *compensated* for services rendered. Yet when we are most in need of care is often when we are least able to offer anything in return. We may be an emotional mess, socially dislocated, professionally disrupted, financially precarious or all of the above. So we try to manage on our own, impeding our recovery and, at a sociological scale, poking away at the bonds of care and reciprocity that constitute the social fabric.

What's more, the care that we get from 'professionals' tends to lack that crucial *personal* touch, because such workers must maintain a degree of professional distance. Therapists need to go through mountains of training and work experience to be able to develop the sensitivity, empathy and trustworthiness that is inherent to healthy interpersonal relationships like friends, lovers and relatives. This was a major theme of Carl Rogers' seminal contributions to psychotherapeutic practice:

> When the other person is hurting, confused, troubled, anxious, alienated, terrified, or when he or she is doubtful of self-worth, uncertain as to identity, then understanding is called for. The gentle and intuitive companionship of an empathetic stance… provides illumination and healing.[6]

*Intuitive companionship* – precisely the sort of thing that people who've known each other for a long time have organically – is the holy grail of the therapeutic relationship. We need to rescue this natural capacity for care and recentre it in our culture.

Instead, we are seeing a proliferation of what artist, activist and scholar Cassie Thornton calls 'bad support', which she defines as being offered something that you really need but the offer ultimately takes more than it gives and is about enriching someone else rather than helping you.[7] She offers the case of fast-food employees in the United States being offered tips on money management and encouraged to do yoga by managers ostensibly interested in their wellbeing. The irony is that those managers paying people only minimum wage is why the employees have no money to manage, and the idea of doing yoga after a day of manual labour is farcical. The wellbeing efforts are only to increase worker productivity or to improve brand reputation, in both cases to increase profits, not help workers.

Bad support is endemic in modern welfare states where there is an enormous number of forms, screenings and eligibility checks to go through to get help. To be cared for you need to prove that you're not a scumbag, and the more help you need, the greater the burden on you. Nobody cares for you unconditionally.

Bad support reaches its toxic zenith in 'customer service' – where we expect people to care about us precisely because we have paid them a lot. The extractive qualities of this sort of emotional slavery is poignantly explored in *The White Lotus*, a show about the interactions of absurdly privileged, pampered and out of touch guests and the variously downtrodden, precarious and overburdened staff of a luxury holiday resort. At the end of the season, the guests leave feeling refreshed, and the staff are left carrying their discarded emotional and physical baggage.

As with neoliberalism, the pernicious effect of bad support is to create a care deficit at the cultural level. As we internalise the sentiment of bad support, we start to give care with one eye on the bottom line, or what we can get back from people we care for. We lose any natural inclination for generosity.

How can we fix this? The first step is to appreciate that care is something we are all capable of giving. Care is one of the oldest social technologies, so fundamental to humanity that we have a basic psychological need for it and a natural capacity to offer it. Care is better when it is offered by the mundane people we know than when it comes from a 'professional'. Customer service is fake care. Care must come from the heart; otherwise you don't *feel* cared for. Feeling is a clue to the second step: we have to acknowledge and even revere the intangible value of relationships rather than trying to quantify, optimise and monetise care. The third step is to recover what I call karmic culture from the cesspit of commercial culture that we find ourselves in.

## 6.5. Karmic culture

> What is hateful to you, do not do to your fellow: this is the whole Torah; the rest is the explanation. Go and learn.
> Rabbi Hillel the Elder

Too much of contemporary culture is fundamentally *selfish*. Many people have the attitude of 'I've got to get what's mine'. The biblical equivalent is beggar thy neighbour. We focus on our own needs, and even collective goals like averting climate change need to be marketed to selfish individuals. If *we* don't fix climate change the air *you* breathe will be toxic.

What we see in the capitalism of care discussed in the previous section is *commercial* culture – appropriate compensation for services rendered. Embedded in the notion of 'customer service' is the idea that you should care more about someone the more they are able to pay you. This culture is fundamentally transactional. It makes us all mercenary.

One step up from commercial culture is what you could call *reciprocal* culture – I'll scratch your back if you scratch mine. The great challenge for reciprocal culture is *trust*; we need to be confident that if we help someone, they will help us back. This is extremely difficult, and humans have evolved a huge number of biological and social mechanisms to improve our ability to cooperate. For example, we often feel guilt when we deceive someone, and we have elaborate festivals of gift gifting like Christmas to reinforce reciprocal generosity. But even with this element of trust and mutual benefit, reciprocal culture is at base quite transactional. We do things for people in expectation of reward, and reward *from them*.

*Karmic* culture is a step further and requires a deeper degree of generosity. People in karmic culture believe, in rational expectation, that what goes around comes around. You can give of yourself to help someone else with no expectation of compensation or reciprocation from that person, because you are confident that if you ever need help someone, somewhere will do the same for you.

Karmic cultures cannot emerge without generosity. Some individuals need to begin the giving circle and encourage others to pay it forward, rather than paying it back. Such generosity struggles to emerge without some notion of 'enough'. If I have what I need to live my good life, then I can give away whatever remains.

A materialist culture that values growth for its own sake and measures success in terms of stuff makes it hard for people to give away what they don't *need*. In contrast, a culture of collective self-actualisation, in which we aim to achieve full expression of ourselves and our collective goals, is much less fixated on *stuff*. It is oriented instead towards immaterial values and relationships. Such a culture makes generosity easy.

Karmic culture would also improve commercial relations. Adam Smith famously observed that, 'It is not from the benevolence of the baker that we expect our daily bread', but instead from the baker's self-interest. Yet in Smith's eighteenth-century market, the baker was someone very much known to you. They lived in your neighbourhood, you saw them in church, your children played together. Nowadays, our daily bread typically comes from an industrial operation, so the potential for such personable relations are substantially diminishing. Even so, amidst a karmic culture, we can trust that our peers are generous in spirit and so we worry less about being swindled. And we have greater confidence that businesses we interact with are not offering low prices to us by simply exploiting their workers, animals or the environment, because we are always being generous to those around us.

In karmic cultures we give both to help individuals and to

contribute to a collective vision of a caring society. We don't just give because we can personally thrive regardless, but because our giving actively contributes to the thriving of the community in which we live. Karmic culture is fundamentally hopeful – it works if we all hope for a nicer, kinder, more generous world. That hope sustains our trust and our generosity.

Karmic notions of paying it forward were integral to many indigenous cultural systems and contributed to the ecological and social sustainability of these civilisations. Robin Wall Kimmerer's beautiful book, *Braiding Sweetgrass*, documents all the themes I have discussed above. Gift economies, the importance of knowing what is 'enough', generosity, trust, care and giving so that the whole may flourish. These 'social technologies' for wellbeing have been substantially lost to us in the 'developed world' since the close of the Second World War. Another social technology we have lost that deserves its own section is the priest, that most primordial of social roles. We need to bring priests back. Indeed, we all need to become priests of a sort.

## 6.6. The need for priests

> In nine hundred years of time and space, I've never met anyone who wasn't important.
> The Eleventh Doctor, *Doctor Who*, 'A Christmas Carol'

Imagine a hunter-gatherer society, one of the most basic forms of human organisation. What are the key social roles in this group? Food gatherers, mothers, defenders, elders whose accumulated experience can be relied on for advice in doubtful times, leaders who take responsibility for decisions, and *priests*. Well, shamans to be more precise, but I think the similarities are strong enough for me to treat these roles interchangeably. The priest is one of the most primordial and foundational jobs in human communities. I think ethnobotanist and mystic Terence McKenna put it well in his lecture at the Carnegie Arts Museum in 1990,

'Opening the Doors of Creativity': 'The shaman is the figure at the beginning of human history that unites the doctor, the scientist, and the artist into a single notion of care-giving and creativity.'

And yet this sort of priest has largely disappeared from modern society. We have fragmented their role into social workers, therapists, academics, people who run community groups, mystics, yoga teachers, doctors, self-help books and that old person many of us know who we rarely visit or value but who occasionally drops truth bombs on us. Unfortunately, none of these individual roles can do what the priest does, namely offer care, advice and therapeutic guidance that is socially embedded.

When a priest offers help to a member of their congregation, it is often to someone they have known for a very long time, both personally and in terms of their wider social relationships. The priest's advice, like that of a good therapist, can be tailored to the long narrative arc of that person's life. But going beyond what a therapist can do, the priest's advice is also tailored to how that individual fits into a community. The priest knows the sources of friction for that person, and who to call on to offer help to a struggling individual. And because the priest commands the respect and gratitude of the community, those helpers will heed their call.

As with so many things, science is slowly rediscovering in its dry way the power of this sort of 'social prescribing'. People suffering from psychological challenges, chronic unemployment, poor health and a range of other maladies are being advised by doctors, social workers and even law enforcement to join groups. They might be choirs, gardening clubs or social soccer teams, but they're always social and relational.

Social prescribing has demonstrated remarkable effectiveness in some cases, but the causal mechanisms remain opaque to science.[8] It's unclear, for example, whether there is a general causal force associated with joining groups, like having your basic psychological need for relatedness met, or whether there are causal forces specific to certain groups that are relevant. If your health is bad due to lack of exercise, it might be less the soccer *club* that is relevant, and more the *soccer*. Yet the club dynamics might be what provide the motivation, commitment device or encouragement someone needs to persist with moving their body.

Science tries to untangle this causal mess using randomised control trials and statistical analysis. Wonderful. But the priest can skip a lot of that because of the intuition they've built up through extensive observation, much like a parent often knows what their child needs despite extremely limited information. It is not for nothing that Christian priests are cast as shepherds to a flock.

The priest is a *social* technology. They organise groups to solve problems, like the sadness of someone whose spouse has died, the desperation of a single mother, the homelessness of the man down the street or the illness of someone who has lost their way. These social solutions are paid for with time and emotional energy rather than money, and they reinforce social bonds. This contrasts with technological solutions that are inevitably individualistic and sold by someone, like anti-depressants, life insurance, exercise bikes, AI girlfriends and care robots. These are all expensive, and so we commit ourselves to work long hours, further isolating ourselves from solidarity.

The priest has another key function that we have lost (or that priests have abrogated or even defiled of late) – that of moral guardian. As the fulcrum of a community, the priest has always served to reinforce (or more recently pervert, in the case of paedophilia scandals) norms of altruism, reciprocity, putting the group before the individual and pursuing the good, whatever that might be. To serve in this capacity effectively, priests have typically had to take a hit and formally renounce their own interests: they live modestly and often alone, and in some cases take vows of celibacy. Effective priests could encourage regular tithing by the community to fund church programmes for the needy, in part because they themselves had given a lot for the group.

When the social glue and moral reinforcement that priests provided is absent, we are increasingly atomised, selfish and self-absorbed. We have lost solidarity, focusing always on what we need to do next to advance our individual agenda. At most, we are concerned about the needs of narrow subcultural groups that we belong to. Rarely do we turn our minds to the needs of the diverse neighbourhoods in which we live – communities formed by proximity rather than shared values or enthusiasms.

A final function of the priest, and especially of the shaman, is to lead the rituals and ceremonies that marked the passing of time: births, deaths, marriages, the solstice, the equinox and the other events that punctuate life and its rhythms. When a priest performs these rituals well, it connects us to something that transcends our individuality, whether that is the community, the seasons or the cosmic order.

For example, when my grandmother died in Hungary, she was buried next to her late husband in his ancestral village. My mother and aunt organised an elderly priest from where she had lived to deliver the eulogy. They hoped that his knowledge of her life would allow him to offer thoughtful reflections on her character and contribution. Unfortunately, the priest was I guess a bit too old, or maybe the weather was too cold, and he just wanted to leave. His sermon was formulaic and a bit of a dud. He basically just went through the Christian symbolism without commenting much on her, or even her relationship with faith, which was substantial.

There was a second funeral in Budapest for the many people who had known her there or couldn't easily make the trek to the village. The local priest was young and new and hadn't known my grandmother well. But he did his homework. He sat with her relatives to learn of her life and what was important to her, and delivered a cracking sermon. It honoured the role she played in the community, galvanised those she left behind to continue her good works and follow her example, and emphasised how we can all make valuable contributions beyond ourselves. In this way, death becomes merely part of the cycle of life, a bittersweet renewal rather than a terrifying end.

The feminist poet Judy Grahn captures well the multifaceted benefits that the priest provides to their community. She writes that:

> The shaman/priest/artist/teacher/leader does not operate for the sole benefit of herself or her kind but for the benefit of the people at large and of the universe and its patterns, as becomes what she perceives as fitting into place, into her sense of natural justice.[9]

Reading all this you might think I am advocating for a return to religion. A church on every street. Far from it. As will become clear in Part III, my view is that religion is played out. We must reinvent the priest; not return to something we abandoned because it didn't work any more.

So what's my solution? In a nutshell, we all need to become priests to our little community. We need to recognise ourselves as a connection point within a social network and perform the role of the priest for others. We need to be useful to our communities. We need to pay attention to who is suffering and in need of care, who can help other people and what useful connections might be made, and where the moral bonds between us are fraying. We then need to act to address these concerns to renew and strengthen the bonds between us.

Cassie Thornton is pioneering a social technology of this sort called *The Hologram*, inspired by community health clinics in Greece. In her own words:

> The premise is simple: three people – the 'Triangle' – meet on a regular basis, digitally or in person, to focus on the physical, mental, and social health of a fourth – the 'Hologram'. The Hologram, in turn, teaches these listeners how to give and also receive care. When they are ready, the

Hologram will support them to each set up their own triangle, and so the system expands.[10]

This practice commits us to giving *attention* to how other people are doing. We practise caring for someone, which helps us and them to learn how to care effectively. The cared for person is encouraged by all this love to find people who can care for their carers in a similarly generous way. One member of the triangle is also specifically focused on the *social* health of the hologram, which makes them committed to understanding how the hologram is socially embedded. The method is viral – easily adopted and spread in a decentralised way. Such processes can regenerate social bonds from the bottom up.

Becoming priests for our immediate networks is similar, but with some attention also given to moral matters and marking important occasions for the group. Through such practices we can recover our lost solidarity and drive towards a society in which 'we' is more prominent than 'I'.

## *6.7. Solidarity*

> Never lose a holy curiosity. Try not to become a man of success but rather try to become a man of value. He is considered successful in our day who gets more out of life than he puts in. But a man of value will give more than he receives.
>
> Albert Einstein, from an interview in *LIFE* magazine, 2 May 1955

The fundamental neuroses of modern life stem from the hierarchical, competitive and capitalistic nature of many contemporary cultures. What gives you status and prestige is being better than other people. We celebrate *distinction*. When it comes to human potential in art and sport, maybe this is OK to some extent. It is hard to maintain the motivation to break world records, and produce the associated entertainment, without the promise of applause. But, for the typical person, what we value especially is simply the volume of their output. We encourage people to squeeze the last drop of optimisation out of themselves for the sake of productivity, and most of the surplus is captured not by them but by a minority with political and economic power. The culture of competition is relentless, pressing until you burn out.

This culture undermines solidarity because we see our peers as rivals rather than fellows. It is hard for us to sincerely applaud someone's achievements when we think it makes us look bad by comparison and sets a higher standard that we are now expected to meet. It also undermines solidarity by keeping us at work and fixated on our individual ambitions, leaving no attention or capacity to care about how others are doing.

Severed from solidarity, we become lonely, but the only way we know to redress our loneliness is by defensive status signalling. This is where you broadcast your achievements to make people realise how worthy you are of their time and interest. A mundane form is curated Instagram posts of how beautiful and bountiful your life is, but every subculture has its own tropes.

Defensive status signalling is toxic because it encourages people to see each other instrumentally; to see other people as a tool to be used to get ahead, not as a person to be intimate with. People that you attract through status signalling will leave you when you no longer carry them higher up the social hierarchy. This makes you an anxious overachiever, constantly striving to please others and maintain your clout. Ironically, this traps you in the cycle of work, loneliness and status signalling that you're trying to get out of.

This toxic culture is perpetuated by the people at the 'top'. They have swallowed so much shit to get there – hours of extrinsically motivated effort, intense competition, cynical networking, meticulous self-optimisation and meeting ever-rising expectations. They couldn't possibly upend this culture. That would call into question their life choices. So they push the value system back down the hierarchy to reinforce their own sense of self-worth. Nietzsche put it well: 'They all want the throne, that is their madness, as if happiness sits on the throne; sometimes mud sits on the throne, and the throne itself on mud.'[11]

You might think these patterns only hold in 'elite' institutions and organisations. Not so. It is a well-established phenomenon in sociology that parents often (certainly not always – look at migrants) do not want their children to rise to a higher station in life than them. Sometimes there is wisdom in this – parents counsel their children to follow the same path they did because it worked for them. But often the underlying motive is more shameful: if their child chooses a different life, a *better* life, then that seems to implicitly critique their own choices.

We cannot get to a culture in which we genuinely celebrate each other's achievements unless 'achievement' is directed at mutual benefit rather than personal aggrandisement. We need to celebrate people not for what they have achieved for themselves, but for what they have done for others. Hierarchical success is fine if it is achieved through generativity, through the creation of value. What is often achieved instead under capitalism is greater extraction from labour, nature or the soul. We need to celebrate altruism, care and the quality of people's relationships. These things are often mundane, qualitative and very hard to scale: all the things capitalism despises because it can't make money out of them. They're the sorts of things people grinding eighty hours a week at the office don't have capacity for.

We need to move away from a culture in which we ask ourselves, 'How can I be famous?', to a culture of 'How can I be useful?' This is a culture where we aren't each out to get ours but instead contribute to the community and a collective experience of thriving. We can take inspiration from Helen Keller, the deaf and blind activist and prolific author who generated tremendous value thanks to her friend and helper Anne Sullivan: 'Alone we can do so little; together we can do so much.'

This is a culture in which each person is celebrated for whatever contribution they make to the group, no matter how small. What matters is not what your job is, but that you did it honourably. Being CEO doesn't make you 'better' than other people; it makes you different. You have a particular role to fill. You should certainly be better paid and even celebrated more if your social role is demanding and involves taking responsibility or generating value for thousands of people, but it's not a competition. Gargantuan executive compensation packages that CEOs use to measure their dicks would be frowned upon in a relational society. Making money dishonourably, by creating monopolies, exploiting your workers and undermining regulation would be considered grotesque, not something to feature in a business magazine.

We need to get to a culture of *we* and away from a culture of *I*. America had such a culture in the mid-twentieth century, well documented in Robert Putnam and Shaylyn Romney-Garret's *The Upswing: How America Came Together A Century Ago and How We Can Do It Again*.[12] They use a huge number of graphs and ingenious data sources to show how the US went from being extremely individualistic, unequal, polarised and atomised at the turn of the nineteenth to twentieth centuries to being significantly more egalitarian, generous, cooperative and cohesive by the 1970s. The trend has turned again since, and today America is back to where it was in the Gilded Age.

One of the most striking figures in *The Upswing* is a plot of the ratio of the use of the words 'I' and 'We' in Google Ngram – the largest database of print text in existence. It shows the hump shape described above: relatively more 'I' in the early twentieth century, rising to relatively more 'we' by the 1970s, and then a collapse back to 'I' dominance today. If you put the word usage side by side on one plot using the free to use Google Ngram tool, you see that this trend is driven almost entirely by 'I', and its explosion since about 1980. 'We' has remained flat:

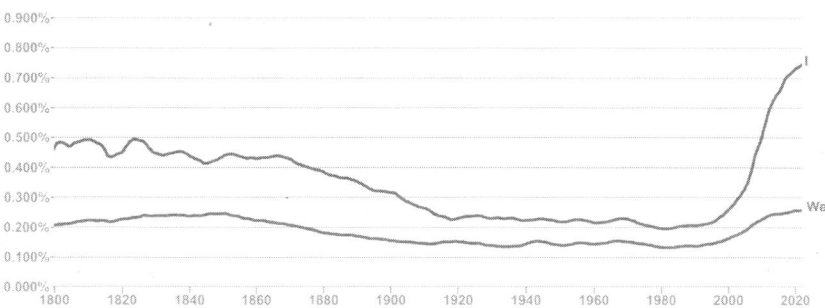

Incidence of I and We in English language books (source: Google Ngram)

What happened around 1980 to trigger this egocentrism? There's a lot to talk about, most of it outside the scope of this book, but one thing that cannot go unmentioned is neoliberalism. This is a shift in approaches to public policy that emphasises the use of market forces, especially competition, to improve efficiency and achieve material growth. Much of the associated structural reform away from state-led policy towards greater use of markets was technically ingenious and secured tremendous improvements in policy outcomes.[13] My go-to example when I teach policy courses is fisheries management in Australia and New Zealand, where the implementation of tradeable quota permits has improved both the sustainability and profitability of natural resource use.

The cultural legacy of neoliberalism, however, is much more problematic. This is especially true in the US and UK where the paradigm was implemented more ideologically than technically by the Reagan and Thatcher administrations. Thatcher's famous statement in an interview with Douglas Kealy for *Women's Own* magazine is a clue:

> They are casting their problems on society and who is society? There is no such thing! There are individual men and women and there are families and no government can do anything except through people and people look to themselves first.

When a government takes this attitude, it becomes a self-fulfilling prophecy. Game theory teaches us that cooperation is hard to achieve. It requires elaborate institutions to foster, like trade unions, and cultural structures to reinforce and perpetuate, such as Christianity. When government, the most influential force in a modern state, takes as its starting point the idea that people are selfish and starts to design institutions and policies across society according to this presumption, including things like education, welfare, urban architecture and industrial relations, it is inevitable that bonds of altruism rapidly fray.

Will Davies, professor of sociology at Goldsmiths University in London, summarises neoliberalism as the application of economic logic to non-economic domains of life.[14] Now 'economic logic' is arrived at by overlooking sociology, psychology and politics for the sake of analytical traction. The result, so-called 'rational choice theory', is extremely powerful and I do not want to criticise it. However, I do want to call into question the wisdom of making economics your only, or even central, lens on the world and taking its selfish perspective into domains characterised by more social forces. The consequences of this aspect of neoliberalism are all around us: the decay of social capital and the rise of populist identitarian politics as a result of naivety about sociology; a mental health epidemic owing to naivety about psychology; and the capture of our political institutions by the runaway wealth of the ultra-rich due to naivety about politics. We need to bring sociology, psychology and politics back into the core of our culture in order to improve wellbeing.

## Chapter 6 summary

The highest political buzz word is not liberty, equality, fraternity, or solidarity; it is service.
Attributed to Arthur Hugh Clough, English poet, educationalist and assistant to Florence Nightingale

Wellbeing is something we do *together*. We are a social species, and our greatest achievements are *our* achievements – they cannot be done alone. So much of the way we live today undermines this appreciation of the group. Capitalism in the social media era encourages us to see everything as a *personal* project rather than a collective one. Where we once lived in three-generation households and children were raised by the whole village, our cities these days segregate by age, so that in our prime working years we see few children or old people with whom we might feel the long arc of human endeavour. And our culture is obsessed with autobiography. Please don't contribute to this egocentric narcissism.

Chapters 1–5 counselled self-actualisation and turning inwards, but we now reach the point in our understanding of wellbeing where we must turn outwards and find people to care about. Join groups that share your values and become devoted to something. Self-actualisation requires other people and when it is done in a group it is mutually reinforcing for everyone involved. As you put your life in order you have a positive spillover effect on people around you, and vice versa. They will help you approach your ideal and ought self, and your participation in their projects will do the same for them. Society is more than the sum of its parts. Wellbeing is an emergent property of interactions between people in places and spaces that are sustained by communities. So reach out.

A healthy community requires trust and reciprocity. We have to cherish our peers when they're a burden, not just when they're beneficial to us. Be mindful of your emotional capacity and be wary of self-interested, psychopathic parasites, but err towards generosity. Take a hit, pay it forward, be a super-cooperator. Role model to others in your community how to show love and share the abundance of what you've created together. That is how we generate karmic culture.

The challenge we face today is that the cultural glue that makes cooperation and society possible is built out of shared values.

We don't have them. The West is in an existential vacuum – a period of cultural aimlessness where we don't know what we're collectively about in terms of values, meaning, identity and mission. Simply reviving old cultural tropes like Christianity isn't going to work. We've moved on. We certainly need to recover much of the wisdom in tradition, but we also need to create something new. These are themes of Part III, to which we now turn. We will first examine the nature of our present normative vacuum, then how to get out of it as individuals, and finally how to create a soil of shared meanings and values in which a karmic, relational, 'we' culture can grow.

# PART III
A Valuable Life

Gradually, man has become a fantastic animal that has to fulfil one more condition of existence than any other animal: man has to believe, to know, from time to time, *why* he exists; his race cannot flourish without a periodic trust in life – without faith in *reason in life*.

Friedrich Nietzsche, *The Gay Science*

# 7

# Nihilism

> Man should not ask what the meaning of his life is, but rather must recognize that it is he who is asked. Each man is questioned by life; and he can only answer to life by answering for his own life; to life he can only respond by being responsible.
>
> Victor Frankl, Man's Search for Meaning

It feels ironic for this to be the final part of the book because wellbeing for me began with the themes we explore here: nihilism, morality, identity, culture, materialism and collective endeavour. Yet even though I've been working with these ideas longer than those in the earlier parts of the book they feel less settled. This is in part because they are simply harder. You will notice that the sections get longer and the concepts denser. The valuable life is more difficult to explain than the pleasant and fulfilling one. It's also because this part of the book is groping for something that hasn't quite arrived yet.

The world is having an identity crisis. All the old ways, whether in economic organisation, gender roles, patriotism, suburban life, class identity, democracy, materialism, or any of the other systems we used to bring meaning and value to our lives, are dissolving or under threat. But the new ways have yet to emerge fully. There are signs of new growth, like the global climate movement, the solarpunk aesthetic and all the many proliferating subcultures of Reddit. But there is also the carnage inherent to death and renewal: culture wars and real wars, politics that is simultaneously extremist and vacuous, and a mental health epidemic that debilitates both those who cannot stand to see the old world go and those too desperate for the new one to arrive.

When systems of meaning and value dissolve we get nihilism – the sense that the world is meaningless and without purpose, that value is hollow and fleeting, and that we are not agents with a mission, either individually or collectively, but just some flotsam adrift in the universe. Nihilism is unpleasant. It makes us feel lost, untethered, uneasy and anxious. It undermines the process of organising communities around shared hopes, dreams and ambitions, and in so doing makes life unfulfilling. And it calls into question the very possibility of a valuable life, making everything feel grey and straining the process of self-actualisation.

Nihilism is politically terrifying because it can trigger what psychoanalyst Eric Fromm called the escape from freedom.[1] The need to create new systems of meaning and value is arduous, painful and nerve-wracking. Many people would prefer, understandably, to just adopt some crude system that makes sense of everything. This is the psychological root of totalitarian doctrines like fascism and communism, which seem to suddenly be ascendent again in the West after decades in abeyance. To avoid the tyranny, hate and violence that are inherent to such ideologies, we need to come together in love and sincerity to work up a world in which we can all get along.

Fortunately, the period of my youth through the '90s and early 2000s – the late postmodern era – was arguably the high tide of nihilist sentiment. We are now entering a more hopeful age. Nihilistic themes remain all around us, but they are typically accompanied by a cheerful resolve to push past our existential vacuum and affirm some things as good and right on the strength of our sentiment. You can see this juxtaposition in the wildly popular cartoon series *Rick and Morty*, where the self-destructive, hedonistic, mad scientist Rick is slowly brought back to caring for the world by his family and friends.

You can also see it in the smash hit indie computer role-playing game *Disco Elysium*. There, the detective protagonist wakes up with amnesia deliberately induced by drinking himself into oblivion. He is among the decaying wreckage of the city of Revachol on the island of Insulinde, the 'New New World'. While the nihilistic allure of narcotics constantly beckons and the protagonist is buffeted by the pathetic ideological machinations of liberals, capitalists, fascists and communist thugs throughout the plot, he slowly recovers his zest for life by doing what he's good at – solving crimes – accompanied by the ever-hopeful sidekick of integrity Kim Kitsuragi.

There are many other examples of this emerging 'metamodernism' that we will explore in the coming chapters. What we need to do first is develop a better understanding of nihilism, why it is a threat to wellbeing and its organismic basis, i.e. how it relates to our biological and psychological natures. That is the subject of the present chapter. I will then outline how we get out of nihilism as individuals using the coalescence of being. Coalescing individuals can get together and do metamodernism, which is sort of coalescence for society.

Historically, we have always tried to find a metaphysical solution to nihilism. We have always tried to make some claim about the nature of reality that imbues it with objective value and meaning. We have used religion, tradition and most recently reason and rationality to this end. My contention is that these efforts come up empty because reality *just is* nihilistic. It is up to us as value-creating agents to imbue the material world with value and meaning through our care. The way out of nihilism commences not from abstract arguments but from the lived experience of being an agent with moral sensations and the responsibility of moral judgement who yearns to live in a world saturated with values. We thereby arrive at an empathetic basis for the collective process of creating maps of meaning that imbue our lives with significance. This coalescence is a psychological and sociological route out of nihilism, rather than a metaphysical one, and it will hopefully make more sense by the end of these next three chapters.

We begin our discussion of nihilism by analysing its three principal components according to the French existentialist philosophers Simone de Beauvoir and Jean-Paul Sartre – nausea, anguish and seriousness.

## 7.1. Nausea

> Life's but a walking shadow, a poor player
> That struts and frets his hour upon the stage
> And then is heard no more.
>
> William Shakespeare, *Macbeth*

Nausea is the feeling of meaninglessness. It is the sense that the world is not heading in some intended direction or playing out according to a narrative – it has no destiny, nor rhyme or reason. Sure, there are laws of physics, but the movements of atoms and the heavenly bodies don't happen for some purpose. They just *are*, born of chaos and indeterminacy. But if the universe is so much random noise, it loses meaning and whatever we do in life appears inconsequential.

These ideas have recently been put into the language of empirical science. Social psychologists have developed a three-factor model of 'the sense of meaning in life': coherence, purpose and significance.[2] Coherence is when the world makes sense. It appears ordered, predictable and organised in some intelligible if not deliberate way. Purpose is the sense that you have a reason for being. Many of us want a *transcendental* reason for being: some purpose that we serve in the grand cosmic design. But many people will settle for the purpose of taking care of their family or tending the local park. Significance is the sense that some things matter, especially your own actions. The world is not just *physical* cause and effect, it is also value-laden. Some actions are right and wrong; some ends good and evil.

Statistical research using surveys designed to measure this sense of meaning in life find strong correlations with psychological indicators of wellbeing. People who report high levels of meaning in their lives tend to be more satisfied, are generally upbeat, have increased vitality, healthier relationships and a greater sense of autonomy. There is obviously two-way causation here, but the evidence is pretty clear that meaning matters for wellbeing. It should not be surprising then that humans tend to find the feeling of nausea – the absence of meaning – distressing.

My claim that nausea is a fundamental part of the human condition might strike some readers as excessive, nevertheless; after all, most people do not suffer from nausea. This is because they are held out of it by their culture, their religion, their peers or whatever else structures their social world and imbues its activities, customs and traditions with meaning and value. Or perhaps their life is just so broadly enjoyable and easily motivated that nausea and associated nihilistic thoughts never intrude upon them. The centrality of meaning to human life only becomes apparent at times when these systems of meaning and value break down.

This psychological dynamic of asserting values when we sense them slipping is on display in the contemporary nostalgia for 1950s America in popular culture figures like Lana Del Rey. It is also clear in conservative efforts to undo majority-endorsed cultural changes like gay marriage and abortion rights through legal technicalities, and the willingness of many conservatives to court illiberal, anti-democratic politicians as long as they speak the language of Christian nationalism. We see it in the dogmatic, often histrionic sloganeering of many contemporary left-wing cultural movements, which are usually more interested in policing adherence to language norms than they are in promoting compassion, tolerance, patience and other virtues. A key thing to observe here is that you can be *certain* about language rules, whereas the virtues I listed are valuable only when a situation is characterised by moral ambiguity. Nausea causes distress, and so we are wired to fear this sort of ambiguity.

Nietzsche rejected all attempts to find meaning and values 'out there' in the cosmos or a priori reasoning. He argued that we should instead embrace the ambiguity of the universe as a joyous liberty. Most people contemplate nausea with sadness – how depressing that there is no moral truth that we can live in blissful obedience to. Nietzsche instead saw such an objective good as the thing to be sad about – why would we want to be so imprisoned? If there is a moral law, then acting out of 'free will' can only mean acting evil. Only if morality is ambiguous can free will be meaningful. Nausea awakens us to the *opportunity* we have to affirm our own values in a morally neutral universe:

> It is absurd to want to *devolve* human existence onto some purpose or another. We have invented the concept of 'purpose': there are no purposes in reality... The fact that nobody is held responsible anymore, that being is not the sort of thing that can be traced back to *causa prima*, that the world is not unified as either a *sensorium* or a 'spirit', *only this can constitute the great liberation* – only this begins to restore the *innocence* of becoming.[3]

The innocence of becoming is the idea that we should not feel guilty for being uncertain of what we want to be and what values we want to live out. Our destiny and the destiny of the universe are to be written, and we can decide what they are. This is a profound responsibility, not an original sin. It will obviously take time, effort and likely some blood, sweat and tears before we as a species decide what it is we want to stand for. But we need to embrace this free unfurling of our will as a blessing, not something to flee from. Much more on that in a moment. Let's complete our investigation of nihilism first.

## 7.2. Anguish

> Be patient toward all that is unsolved in your heart and try to love the questions themselves, like locked rooms and like books that are now written in a very foreign tongue. Do not now seek the answers, which cannot be given you because you would not be able to live them. And the point is, to live everything. Live the questions now. Perhaps you will then gradually, without noticing it, live along some distant day into the answer.
> Rainer Maria Rilke, *Letters to a Young Poet*, #43

For the French existentialists Jean-Paul Sartre and Simone de Beauvoir, anguish is the sense that our identity cannot guide us through difficult choices because whatever commitments we have made or convictions we have held in the past, we can completely break with our past self in the present moment of choice. We consequently feel a collapse of identity and an attendant existential vacuum when confronted by hard decisions.

Anguish is closely related to two maxims from existentialist philosophy: *man is condemned to be free* and *existence precedes essence*. The first maxim refers to the fact that we can derive no justification or excuse for our choices from outside of ourselves. We are ultimately responsible for and defined by the choices that we make. I cannot claim to be chagrined by inequality if I'm always dodging my tax obligations, for example. This is where 'existence precedes essence' comes in – we exist as a 'human' before our individual essence (our identity) is defined by the values we affirm and the narrative we build through our choices.

Anguish attends big decisions because we grasp the stakes of those decisions for our identity. It is not our values that determine our choices, but rather our choices that reflect our values. We are revealed to ourselves in our choices, and we fear what that person might be like. We worry about the path our choices build and the sort of person we are setting ourselves up to become.

An easy to understand example of anguish is a fundamentalist Christian parent with strong family values who discovers that their child is gay. The parent's identity pulls here in two contradictory directions – to respect their faith or their family. If they place the burden of this dissonance on their child rather than themselves, you get 'pray the gay away' interventions. The parent doesn't want to compromise on their own identity because it hurts, so they instead pressure the child to compromise on theirs.

Other resolutions to this conundrum require more complex identity work, and the discomfort we feel throughout such processes underlines the importance of anguish to wellbeing. We want to know who we are – what we value and why – and we want to know this identity so thoroughly and deeply that we can make difficult decisions effortlessly and be comfortable with those choices.

A real-life example of how hard this is to achieve is John Gustav-Wrathall, a homosexual Mormon who has seemingly succeeded in harmonising these two identities by forming a community for LGBT Mormons. He writes eloquently in *A Gay Mormon's Testimony* about his twenty-year journey away from and then back to the Church, and the scriptures he uses to make sense of what he sees as his calling to reform Mormonism. The story begins with John at the threshold of suicide owing to his inability to reconcile competing identities, and things take a long time to grow brighter.

A crucial aspect of John's story is that in the beginning he feels abandoned by the Church, which hitherto had been his 'whole existence' and 'lifelong refuge of love and meaning'. Here we see the connection between anguish, nihilism and illbeing. The French existentialists treat anguish as a personal issue, but just like meaning and seriousness it is intimately bound up with the cultural systems of meaning and value that we live in. Who we are is shaped by the environments in which we grow up and what those around us validate or scorn. When faced with a difficult conundrum, what we think the right course of action should be is heavily informed by the values and reasoning that prevail in our social context. It can be hard to hear our inner voice in this noise, and even harder to respect it against the wishes of social forces. Equally, when systems of meaning and value are thin, decayed or non-existent and we are left alone to make difficult decisions, it can be overwhelmingly, frightening and unbearable.

Identity consolidation theory in social psychology posits four overarching strategies that people use to cope with this sort of 'personal uncertainty': integration, self-worth myopia, group identification and conviction.[4] The *integration* strategy involves building some life narrative and fitting new situations into that narrative. This is what John Gustav-Wrathall did.

Self-worth myopia involves subconsciously suppressing parts of your identity, depending on the situation, to make inconsistencies across your values less obvious and thus less troubling. We discussed this technique in section 4.5. When done in a healthy way, it can lead to harmony between our multiple selves and the various contexts in which they are (in)appropriate. But when done in an unhealthy way, it results in compartmentalisation and dissonance, which impede self-actualisation and lead to illbeing.

Group identification involves borrowing values from a group. This reduces the need for unpleasant self-analysis in times of personal uncertainty and buttresses identity in times of crisis. But it is inauthentic and thus also liable to impede self-actualisation.

The final strategy is conviction and extremism. The basic idea here is to double down on one's present beliefs when confronted by threats to personal certainty. When you feel your values attacked, you go on the counter-offensive. This goes against the growth mindset advocated in Part I.

These scientific ideas and their associated empirical literatures underline the importance of anguish and identity to wellbeing. People are distressed by ambiguity. They respond by doubling down on existing sources of meaning and seriousness, especially group norms. In periods of cultural decay or transformation such as the one we are in now, where social context and group norms provide few cues regarding how we should be and what we should do, anguish spikes, illbeing results and people start to get extremist about their values – a dangerous situation.

## 7.3. Seriousness

> Tell you!? And what is going to happen when there is nobody to tell you? Are you never going to think for yourself?
> The wizard Merlin to the young King Arthur in
> T. H. White's *The Once and Future King*

Seriousness refers to the sense that we are cut off from any ultimate or transcendent justification for our actions and so our value claims are a joke. If there is no cosmic order that ensures the just prosper and the wicked are punished, nor rational grounds for morality, then our values are fundamentally arbitrary and open to capriciousness. They thus seem to lack *seriousness*.

Now this is all a bit scary. Living an authentic, morally serious life as an atheist involves facing up to the fact that you are a value-creating agent and so no entity nor system bears any responsibility for your choices but you. You can certainly have reasons for your decisions, and other people might even find these reasons compelling. But they're ultimately just *your* reasons for making a particular value judgement. The responsibility for the *value* lies with you. People naturally flee this responsibility. They escape into what the French existentialists called 'bad faith'. This is any attempt to divest oneself of ultimate responsibility for a choice.

These are the four varieties of bad faith distinguished by Simone de Beauvoir in her profound little book *The Ethics of Ambiguity*. The first form of bad faith is the 'sub-man'. This individual does not realise or fastidiously avoids recognising that they are a moral agent. De Beauvoir offers Adolf Eichmann as an example of the sub-man. Eichmann was the chief bureaucrat in charge of the holocaust. On trial in Israel after the war, he seemed to have little to no sense of the ethical seriousness of what he did, and claimed that he was simply following orders diligently, as though this abrogated his responsibility.

The second form of bad faith is what de Beauvoir calls 'serious man'. This individual confects the *transcendental* significance of their values. They are easily identified by their insistence that they 'must' behave a particular way because of some external principle – 'it's only logical', 'the bible tells us', 'the law is the law', 'I have to follow the process' – and their general deference to authority. They are ever-seeking to justify their actions as in some way forced by the inexorability of some objective power. The danger of the serious individual is that there is inherent in them a tendency towards tyranny. If someone is not conforming to the cosmic moral order, then they are necessarily evil and the serious individual is thus morally compelled to coercively bring them into line.

The third form of bad faith is nihilism: 'The nihilist is right in thinking that the world *possesses* no justification… but he forgets that it is up to him to justify the world'.[5] De Beauvoir argues that nihilistic bad faith is common among adolescents who struggle with the gravity of adulthood, which is characterised by the requirement to take responsibility for one's life and for the impacts it has on others. The serious individual will seek to escape this adult responsibility by moving into an institution, like the army, the church or a political party, that provides clear norms, clear hierarchy and clear directives. They can then revert to the mode of the sub-man, simply following orders. The nihilist is not so dependent; they are simply overwhelmed – they are not up to the task of value creation.

The final form of bad faith is the adventurer. This type of individual enjoys life but their motivation is excitement, pleasure or ambition rather than some transcendental or value-laden purpose. Adventurers are common. Whether they are 'well', broadly speaking, depends on whether the adventures they undertake spring from self-actualisation. If they do, then the adventures will nourish basic psychological needs and foster a fulfilling life. Such an outcome is common among those with worldly success, like business owners who have grown their enterprises. If the adventures do not spring from self-actualisation, then the adventurer will likely expend themselves in a vain quest for extrinsic pursuits; or they will live the life of the hedonist – achieving pleasure but not fulfilment.

Wellbeing only becomes a problem for the adventurer if they suffer from nihilistic inclinations – if they *need* to answer the question of 'why?' – or if they expend themselves in enjoyable activities that build nothing that lasts. Happy-go-lucky adventures can avoid the former but not the latter. Eventually, the absence of anything substantive in their life will confront them with the fact that they have never taken responsibility for anything. De Beauvoir comments on this situation obliquely but eloquently in her analysis of festivals:

> One eats, drinks, lights fires, breaks things, and spends time and money; one spends them for nothing... in songs, laughter, dances, eroticism and drunkenness one seeks both exaltation of the moment and a complicity with other men... the moment of detachment, the pure affirmation of the subjective present are only abstraction; the joy becomes exhausted, drunkenness subsides into fatigue, and one finds himself with his hands empty because one can never possess the present: that is what gives festivals their pathetic and deceptive character.[6]

In plainer language, the hedonist attempts by way of the intensity of sensation to feel flow, something 'real', to feel 'alive'. But such sensations can only be prolonged by building a life that is fulfilling and valuable; hedonism won't suffice. Once the narcotics pass from one's system and one's friends pass out in drunken stupor, the sense of meaningfulness one experiences when partying is revealed to be an illusion. You can see this in the contrast between clubbing and parties that celebrate value creation, like weddings or end of season award ceremonies at clubs. Such parties deepen an already palpable sense of shared meaning, purpose and significance. When the hangover fades, that value and the sensation of it remains. You wake up feeling inspired to keep building, not desperate to keep drinking.

The basic principle of bad faith, then, is that one avoids responsibility for one's choices and thereby for the values one affirms. This can be done for the craven reason of not wanting responsibility and instead wanting to be told what to do, for the tyrannous reason of wanting a cudgel with which to beat someone into submission to your values, or for the simple reason that many people want to 'do the right thing' but want to know with absolute certainty what that is. As de Beauvoir summarises: 'One can choose not to will himself free. In laziness, heedlessness, capriciousness, cowardice, impatience, one contests the meaning of the project [of life] at the very moment that one defines it.'[7]

## 7.4. Tragedy

> Hope is the knowledge that the evil we bear with us is finite, that the slightest turning of the will towards good, though it should last but an instant, destroys a little of it, and that, in the spiritual realm, everything good infallibly produces good. Those who do not know this are doomed to the torture of the Danaids.
>
> Simone Weil, *Gravity and Grace*

I think there is a fourth element of nihilism beyond nausea, anguish and seriousness that I call tragedy. I would summarise it as the sense that *the world is horrible for no reason.* Children are born with disabilities, people die randomly, the justice system gets perverted, degenerative neurological conditions exist and affect the best of us, the Israel-Palestine conflict goes on and on in cycles of intensifying violence and there seems no way out of the bad blood...

In the philosophical literature around arguments for God, what I call tragedy is called 'the problem of evil'. The logic goes that if God is omnipotent and wholly good, then evil cannot exist. But evil does exist, therefore either God is not good or not omnipotent, and in either case is not the God presented in the New Testament. This is a voluminous literature, but I think it misses the point. All this stuff that we don't like – genocides, parasites, your base urges to violence and domination – are not 'evil'. Evil requires intention. Evil is sinful. There is someone to blame for evil. But the universe is just like that. *The universe is tragic, not sinful.*

Precisely what is so unsettling and despairing about the nihilistic universe is that the natural way of the world is to be full of bad stuff. All that we perceive as fundamentally 'wrong', in the sense we traditionally refer to as evil, is in fact just a product of various natural forces. Genocide, for example, is a propensity in us hardwired by evolutionary forces pertaining to in-group cooperation against competitor groups; sociopathic narcissism evolved by natural selection as a good strategy for genetic persistence; simple selfishness is a defence strategy against parasites in our community.[8] The list can go on for a very long time, and that's before we get to horrors beyond humanity like cancer and natural disasters.

One of the hardest realisations with respect to tragedy is that we can do ghastly stuff with earnest motivation. Consider that we live-boil lobsters *so that they taste better.* We inflict excruciating torture on a nervous system for a marginal improvement in a short-lived sensation on our tongue. It's tragic to realise that humans rape, persecute and murder for biological reasons (among others of course), but I find the thousands of little bad things we do almost as disturbing because they are all small acts of selfishness against collective outcomes. Whenever we externalise the costs of our behaviour onto animals, nature or less powerful people, we do evil. But it's out of sight, out of mind. And we justify ourselves so glibly. 'Oh, I can't afford free range chicken.' Nonsense – we've never been wealthier! That's the problem in a way – as we become wealthier, we externalise more costs rather than using our new means to internalise them. The biggest carbon footprints in our society belong to billionaires with their private jets, mega yachts and multiple climate-controlled mansions – the very people who are most capable of being carbon neutral.

A common reaction to this tragedy, especially among the child or the young adult, is to find something or someone to *blame*. We naturally want an answer to why things are horrible and so we articulate 'the problem of evil'. I've always thought this was one of the greatest appeals of Christianity, with all its talk of sin and God moving in mysterious ways – Christianity allows people to maintain a view of the tragic nature of the universe as meaningful. Joyner Lucas' devastating rap song 'The Devil's Work' articulates this very nicely. Here is the first stanza.

> Father, forgive me...
> I'm staring at this Bible as I keep glancing
> Dear Lord, I got questions and I need answers
> Tryna understand your vision, but all I see is damage
> Just a bunch of dead bodies in the street camping
> A bunch of lost souls on their feet standing
> We supposed to be your children, I thought we family
> You're supposed to be my Father, bruh, I need answers
> We don't need to die young, we just need chances
> Tired of living on the edge so we keep scrambling

The ultimate point of the song is that all this tragedy isn't God's fault, it's the devil's work. But it isn't. It's just tragic. *Nobody is responsible.* That's horrible, and the best you can do is try in your own little way to make it better.

*The Lord of the Rings* showcases two divergent psychological responses to tragedy. Denethor, King of Gondor, and Théoden, the King of Rohan, both lose sons. It costs Denethor his sanity, worn down as he is by the seemingly unstoppable encroachment of the evil Sauron on his domain. He becomes increasingly nihilistic, failing to prepare the kingdom under his care for invasion, and ultimately committing suicide when that invasion eventuates.

In contrast, Théoden grimly acknowledges his grief amidst tragedy, saying to the wizard Gandalf that, 'Fathers shouldn't have to bury their sons.' He then takes action to arrest the spread of tragedy as much as he is able by mustering his forces and leading them into defensive war.

Théoden's actions are a straightforward case of moral heroism. What we need in society is *mundane* moral heroism. Everyday people taking *responsibility* for making their life and their little corner of the world a bit less tragic and a bit more 'good', however they might define that. This will be a major theme of the next chapter. First, we need to discuss the conventional responses to nihilism – faith, tradition and rationalism – and why they're not working. This explains the gap that Chapter 8 steps into with a solution to nihilism that is fit for the twenty-first century.

## 7.5. Faith and tradition

> Half gods are worshipped in wine and flowers. Real gods require blood.
>
> Zora Neale Hurston, *Their Eyes Were Watching God*

Nihilism is a relatively new phenomenon in the West, especially in the United States, because it was long held at bay by the forces of faith, tradition, materialism (or hedonism, to be more generous) and rationalism. Over the next three sections, I want to review these forces and discuss how they have weakened in important ways of late, or never worked especially well to begin with. This will necessarily involve some engagement with the tropes of atheism, but I will avoid making the case for atheism. There are hundreds of texts on that subject.[9] I want to stay focused here on why nihilism is opening around us, and on answers to nihilism for people who are already convinced of the *subjectivity of value* – the idea that something is valuable only because someone values it. Nothing is ever valuable intrinsically, in and of itself.

## Faith

How does faith work to address nihilism? Well, if there is an omniscient, omnipresent and eternal God who created the world and has access to souls as they pass from this world, then he can punish the wicked and reward the just. There remains a question of why this God's notion of what is good is the 'correct' notion, but the all-knowing powers of this God get you a lot of the way.

The problem for this metaphysics is that this God is ineffable – we cannot verify the existence of this God empirically. This is true even for people who have supposed personal encounters with God. There's no way to verify that these encounters were with this very potent God rather than a much more minor cosmic entity giving moral commands; something like the planet-eating, interstellar demigod Galactus from the Marvel universe. We especially cannot verify what this omniscient God thinks is 'Good'. We have to rely on the Torah, Bible, Koran and other theological texts, which have passed through the impure filter of humanity and are very distant from the supposedly logical proofs of God's existence offered by theologians.[10]

So we arrive at faith, which, in the words of the Christian philosopher Søren Kierkegaard, is founded on 'the strength of the absurd'. Kierkegaard was one of the very first philosophers to seriously engage with the problem of nihilism – what he called 'despair' – in his books *The Sickness Unto Death* and *Fear and Trembling*, published way back in the 1840s. The latter book concerns the biblical story of Abraham, the archetype for Kierkegaard's 'Knight of Faith' whose piety arrests despair.[11]

In this story, God makes a wager with Satan that Abraham has absolute faith. God then asks Abraham to sacrifice his only son, Isaac, who was originally a gift from God to Abraham for his many years of faith. Abraham is understandably attached to his miracle child and deeply conflicted about offering him up to the Lord. Nonetheless, he makes the designated pilgrimage to mount Moria and begins the process of making a burnt offering. Immediately before plunging his knife into Isaac, Abraham is halted by an angel of God who says: 'Stop, now I know that you still fear God', or, in other versions, 'Stop! Now I know that you still love God above all'.[12]

The allegory of the story is contested by theologians. Kierkegaard's interpretation is that God was testing Abraham's faith that God loved him and was good. It is crucial to Kierkegaard's interpretation that the sacrifice of Isaac is dramatic. Abraham must be willing to do something that goes against surface readings of God's moral code – namely that you should not kill your children – and that is personally extremely difficult for him because of his love for Isaac. Abraham goes through the sacrifice regardless because of his unflinching conviction that whatever God demands is good. That's faith.

I'm fine with faith but it seems to me ultimately no better than any subjectivist doctrine. You simply *assume* that there is an objective moral order. That belief is just a conviction, and the faith that sustains it depends on your integrity and emotions. You can have a crisis of faith as easily as any atheist can have a crisis of conviction. The person of faith turns to sacred texts, pastoral guides like priests and prayer in such circumstances. The secular individual turns to art and science, those they love and trust, and reflection. In either case, a resolution to the crisis must come from within – the individual needs to decide on a course of action with which their conscience is comfortable. I see little difference, psychologically speaking. The religious purpose can *believe* that their values are ultimately grounded in some cosmic order, but they have no proof. The secular person is under a stronger psychological requirement to excavate the emotions, motivations and reasons for their values and behaviours, and I think this is likely to result in a more secure identity and greater integrity in the long run.

## *Tradition*

Religious doctrine is one aspect of 'tradition' and is better at addressing nihilism when it is supported by the cultural architecture of a tradition. But tradition can function as a way out of nihilism even without faith. We often invest long-lasting traditions with a justifiable degree of significance even when they are obviously practices invented by humans, and this imbues life with meaning and value.

This might surprise some people. We have done horrible things in the past, like child sacrifice, so why would tradition have any bearing on whether something is good or not? It's because things that persist tend to do so because they 'work' in some way. This is as true of biological evolutions as it is of cultural ones. All traditions have persisted at least long enough to become traditions. Marriage, for example, is increasingly falling out of fashion for a range of reasons, but one would need to be wilfully blind to ignore the role it played for centuries in securing a stable socio-economic foundation for reproduction (other such foundations are of course possible). It is reasonable to say, 'These traditions are good because we have practised them for so long; why else would we practise them?' Traditions can thereby inspire reverence and respect. They can often arrest nihilism effectively because we are born into a world saturated with old traditions replete with rituals, ceremonies, symbols, art, communities, and all the other cultural and intersubjective means of maintaining a shared sense of value and purpose.

Tradition can thus serve as a sort of common sense foundation for a normative order, but it isn't sufficient to constitute a meta-ethics – an explanation of what value is and why it is the way it is. Tradition provides only an arbitrary explanation for why something is good; one that needs to be backed by authority and social sanction to function as social glue because it doesn't have a foundation in convincing *reasons*. Tradition is a shortcut to meaning, seriousness and identity for people who fit naturally or without too much hardship into those traditions. But if you're someone who does not fit, or to whom the world and its traditions seem quite bad and in need of explanation, then tradition doesn't offer much and you go looking for reasons. That's the sort of person I was as a teenager, and the target audience of this book. Unfortunately, 'reason' itself is something of a dead end...

## 7.6. Reason

> Dear Ones,
> Beware of the tiny gods frightened men
> Create
> To bring anaesthetic relief
> To their sad
> Days.
>
> *The Gift*, poems by Daniel Ladinsky

Since the European Enlightenment, there have been efforts to ground morality not in a cosmic order or the received wisdom of tradition, but in pure reason. This would address the so-called Euthyphro problem – are things good because God says so, or does God merely do good things? If it's the former, then morality seems arbitrary and tyrannical. If it's the latter, then there is presumably a rational basis for morality independent of God's will. A rational basis for morality would also explain what traditions are righteous and which are mere barbaric holdovers. If we could discover what is good and right a priori (that is, with reason alone) then we could navigate our way through nausea, anguish and seriousness with logic.

There are three prominent schools of Western philosophy that hold that there are moral facts: utilitarianism, Kantianism and Aristotelian virtue ethics. Each departs from various moral *intuitions* – feelings about the right or wrongness, goodness or badness of certain things. They attempt to excavate the reasons that supposedly underly these intuitions and then extrapolate from those reasons to ethical rules that can be applied in many contexts. These are very complex literatures and hopefully my colleagues will forgive me for sketching them crudely.

Utilitarianism is about calculation. The right action is the one that produces more good and less evil; good and evil are typically cashed out in terms of pleasure and pain, happiness and harm, something of that sort. Utilitarianism arises out of intuitions like the following, which I believe comes from the American neuroscientist and popular philosopher Sam Harris, but he may not be the progenitor. Imagine two identical villages in neighbouring valleys. They have the same population and the people therein lead basically identical lives. Now imagine that for whatever reason, there is someone in the first village who is marginally happier. Perhaps the sun has just peeped over the mountains and cast its light into the valley. Empirically, sunlight tends to improve mood, so maybe the guard keeping dawn watch is pleased at this experience.[13] Dawn hasn't reached anyone else in the village yet, nor the second village at all. Knowing this scenario and assuming all other things equal, which village do you think is better off? I suspect that while some people would be indifferent, most people think there is something valuable in the happiness of the dawn watch and say the first village. This implies that happiness is valuable, and that more of it is better than less, and from here we get utilitarianism.

Kantian ethics springs from perhaps the most primordial of ethical intuitions: treat others as you would have them treat you. This intuition gives rise to a lot of decontextualised moral rules, notably human rights. Because these rules are absolute, when they clash you inevitably end up in an ethical pickle. One of the most prominent contemporary examples is the abortion debate in the US, where the right to life of the foetus is weighed against the right to bodily autonomy of the mother.

Virtue ethics holds that there are certain qualities of character or conduct that are inherently good and should be cultivated, like honour or a sense of humour. Rather than teach people to reason in utilitarian or Kantian terms, virtue ethicists think we should raise good people who will apply these moral doctrines when suitable and muddle through when they are not. Virtue ethics often has a more realist, contextual and political view of ethical conduct, recognising that the correct decision in many ethical quandaries is not only ambiguous but has wide-ranging consequences beyond the decision maker. It may alter the structure of social life, trigger an unpredictable sequence of events or undermine people's confidence in ethical and legal institutions, for example. In all these cases, the absolutism of utilitarianism and Kantianism is naive and unhelpful. Good character and a willingness to work through an ethical dilemma piecemeal, rather than all at once, can lead to better outcomes.

The intuitions of utilitarianism, Kantianism and virtue ethics all feel right, and their literatures furnish us with many examples of situations where these intuitions point the way to a clearly moral course of action. So why can't these ethical philosophies resolve nihilism?

The first shortcoming of rational morality is that it is a form of slave morality and so is motivationally incoherent. I'll say a lot more about this shortly in section 8.2. For now, all that needs to be said is that rational morality sets up an ethical rule that is independent of the individual. They don't choose their values; those values are instead 'correct' or 'true' for everybody. Some people's ethics will instinctively align with these external standards, but for everybody else, they will be forced to use introjected motivation to act morally. That is exhausting and unsustainable, and odd from an evolutionary viewpoint: if certain goods and bads are written into the fabric of reality, then why have we evolved to not act in accordance with these facts? This goes even more so for animals like Komodo dragons, which are extremely violent to each other and eat their own children. Are they just an evil animal? Adding a God that punishes wrongdoing is even worse motivationally because it relies on duress to coerce good behaviour.

The second big problem for rational morality and nihilism is that it is often 'rational' to be immoral. This is the main insight of the prisoner's dilemma and other cooperation games that we discussed in section 6.3. Selflessness and cooperation, which are core to ethical conduct, require irrationality. The 'sociobiology' literature, which we will discuss in detail in the next section, has demonstrated the role that ritual, ceremony, symbolism and culture more broadly play in getting people past rational selfishness into a cooperative ideal. But these things all work through emotion, not reason! The motivational side of morality is similarly emotive through guilt, shame and self-esteem. So we can't find a way out of nihilism through reason alone.

The third problem is that 'moral facts' – which is what ethical philosophy is seeking – are a very strange thing, so strange in fact that we should question the coherence of this idea. Moral facts certainly don't seem to work like other facts. Think of something factually straightforward like gravity here on earth. If you try to live in a way that contravenes gravity, then gravity will assert its factual existence over you. Imagine one day you wake up and say, 'Gravity is bullshit, I don't think gravity is correct – I'm going to jump off that skyscraper and fly.' Obviously, you will splat on the pavement because gravity is a fact. It doesn't care about your opinion; it just is.

Now compare gravity with candidates for moral facts like, 'Being a homicidal dictator who oppresses millions of other humans for personal gain is evil.' We have many cases throughout human history where someone did this very evil thing and there were seemingly no consequences for them; indeed, they flourished! The Pharoahs, Kim Jong Un, slave owners in early America, etc. There doesn't seem to be a consequence to being 'irrational' about your moral obligations the way there is to being irrational about empirical facts like gravity. This issue was obvious to early religious moralists, which is why they invented an afterlife where an all-seeing, all-knowing God judges your deeds in life and punishes or rewards you.

This is not to say that reason doesn't have a role to play in morality. As we discussed in Chapter 4, the coalescence of being requires us to harmonise our emotions, motivations and reasons. We often need to justify our values to ourselves and to reason through conflicts between our values. Philosophical analysis has a large role to play here. It also has a huge role to play in our interpersonal and political relationships. We should try to reason our way through moral disagreements before resorting to the political process to break stalemates.

But different people have different moral intuitions and find different arguments compelling, and moral philosophy has shown little capacity to cut through these impasses. Indeed, the core of moral philosophy is the exploration of quandaries in which powerful and compelling moral intuitions and arguments seem to clash, like the infamous trolley problem, which we will discuss shortly. It seems then that reason alone cannot furnish us with a way out of nihilism. At the societal level, we need culture, politics, institutions and sometimes violence to muddle through existential vacuum. At the individual level, we need an approach to everyday, personal ethics that foregrounds our lived experience of being a moral agent, not the metaphysical qualities of morality.

Historically, at least in the West, we have conceived of morality as objective, logical, factual. Something that exists independently of us as peculiar creatures and conscious subjects. Our moral intuitions were believed to track these facts. But recent empirical work calls this into question, claiming instead that reason comes after intuition. The alternate story that emerges – that morality is subjective and that our moral faculties are something we have evolved to survive more effectively – fits the data much better and points to a very different way out of nihilism.

## 7.7. The biological soul

> Falsely accused, exiled, starving and cold, I faltered – this I confess. As the death-chills overcame me, I lost will and purpose, and felt the bottomless callousness of fate. But then, a vision: I saw in my mind's eye an endless white plain, with only a single figure, waiting. It was you. And I knew, in death if not in life, I would see you again. When the chills faded, I rose with new hope. I paint my mark here for you, in anticipation of our meeting, and leave you this offering, though it will never touch the warmth of your hands.
> Memoirs of Tektuk, *Horizon: Zero Dawn*

I was once at a very fancy dinner at St Edmund's, one of the constituent colleges of Cambridge University. It was a Wednesday night, but everyone was dressed very formally and wearing academic gowns. The meal went for five courses. At least I think so – I can't quite remember because of how much we drank. On a Wednesday.

I was at this dinner as a guest of Esther Miriam-Wagner, the director of the Woolf Institute for interfaith dialogue, who wanted to introduce me to a colleague of hers, Katherine O'Lone, who works on the secular benefits of religious practices like fasting and meditation. I was surprised to discover that despite running one of the world's most prominent institutions for religious scholarship, Esther was agnostic. When I queried her about this, she explained that her theism didn't survive contact with the anthropology of religion.

Most atheists that I've come across are compelled by the evidence against religious doctrine that comes out of the hard sciences – biological theories of evolution, notions of causation from physics, the history of the earth from geology, that sort of thing. Like Esther, I am much more compelled by what comes out of the social sciences, especially anthropology. Cast your eye over the vast array of religious practices humans engage in and you can't help but be struck by the frequency with which sensible practices are sacralised. One interpretation is that we are stumbling our way towards the ineffable heaven that religions claim to access haphazardly. Another is that religion is a social technology: a practice that we have developed as a species to enable our persistence amidst a hostile environment.

A famous example is the Balinese water temple.[14] A lake sits atop a caldera in Bali, Indonesia. This water can be allowed to run down the mountain, irrigating fields all the way to the valley. But every user of this water, especially those at the top of the mountain who can control the flow down, is worried about everyone else drawing too much water. So they might want to be the first to do so before letting the water run further down the mountain. Everyone else knows this, so they too get in quick, until there's no water. A classic tragedy of the commons.

Bali has an elaborate water-based religion that structures, sacralises and optimises water use in this system through maps of meaning and value. At the top of the caldera sits the high temple. From there, water flows to a subscale of regional water temples that coordinate water flows to different collectives of farmers. Each collective then has its own smaller temple at the beginning of their fields. The temples at each scale play host to religious ceremonies and rituals that coordinate both the efficient use of water resources and the politics thereof, including meetings between farmers and collectives mediated over by priests. The wider water religion also includes myths and other narratives for timing planting and structuring harvests, and for maintaining this knowledge that has accrued over thousands of years. Rather than progressing teleologically towards some religious truth, Bali's water religion seems instead to have adapted to changing environmental conditions over time.

Bali's water temple system features in D. S. Wilson's provocatively titled book, *Darwin's Cathedral: Cultural Evolution, Religion, and the Nature of Society*. In contrast to the atheist biologist Richard Dawkins, who regarded religion as a kind of cultural mind virus,[15] Wilson sees it as an evolved adaptation that helps us solve cooperation problems like the public goods game and other social challenges. Religion is often highly adapted to local issues, whether that's managing fishing on a reef in Fiji, avoiding the consumption of shellfish that are likely to spoil in the deserts of Israel or passing down knowledge of trade routes through song lines among indigenous Australians.

This way of understanding religion implies that the steady decline of faith across the West is a function of its no longer playing a useful role in society. There are aspects of our religious heritage that we perhaps need to rescue, like the role of the priest we discussed in section 6.6, or churches as a site for the formation of community bonds, or the wisdom of some biblical stories. But the wider cultural architecture in which these still useful aspects sit – things like patriarchy, extreme pro-natalism and homophobia – need renovation. The way forward here is not dry rationalism, but rather to create new quasi-religious cultural practices that can undergird cooperation. Why? Because our supposedly rational moral philosophy is as much a product of evolution as religion is...

## *The evolutionary psychology of moral cognition*

Research into moral psychology over the past twenty years has thrown up a lot of evidence suggesting that maybe traditional moral philosophy has it all wrong. As Jonathan Haidt explains in *The Righteous Mind: Why Good People Disagree About Politics and Religion*:

> What the rationalists were *really* doing was generating clever justifications for moral intuitions that were best explained by evolution. Do people believe in human rights because such rights actually exist, like mathematical truths, sitting on a cosmic shelf next to the Pythagorean theorem just waiting to be discovered by Platonic reasoners? Or do people

feel revulsion and sympathy when they read accounts of torture, and then invent a story about universal rights to help justify their feelings?[16]

There are two major themes in this area that I want to discuss: moral foundations and the neuroscience of trolley problems. They both have excellent popular books written about them. Haidt's *Righteous Mind* puts forward the theory of moral foundations, while Joshua Greene's *Moral Tribes: Emotion, Reason, and the Gap Between Us and Them* explains what we have learned from trolley problems.

Let's start with trolley problems. The original set up is that there is a runaway trolley (a kind of tram). If it continues on its current track, it will certainly kill five people. However, in front of *you* is a lever that you can pull to divert to a different track where it will only kill one person. Ought you to pull the lever? Almost everyone says yes. This is an intuition commonly invoked in favour of utilitarianism.

But a slight change in the scenario results in a dramatic change in the results. In this scenario, the runaway tram is going to kill five people unless *you* push a very large person off a footbridge and into its path. They will be hit by the train and killed, but their body mass will slow it down enough to save the lives of the other five people. In this scenario, a great many respondents think it is immoral to kill the large person.

What explains this change in behaviour? After all, it's the same number of deaths and you are responsible in both cases. You just need to make contact in order to harm someone in case two. That's a clue. In Greene's research, people are hooked up to brain scanners while answering trolley problem questions. Different parts of their brains light up depending on which scenario is put to them. In the lever scenario, only the frontal lobe activates. This is the region responsible for conscious, rational processing. It leans utilitarian in its judgements. In the bridge scenario, the amygdala and other more primeval parts of the brain light up first, and the frontal lobe only comes in after a delay. We have an ancient, *instinctual* aversion to harming others.

Why? Perhaps because it's hard to get a reputation as a trustworthy cooperator if you tend to smack your peers, or in this case, literally throw them under a bus. Kantian instincts are primordial. These sorts of moral intuitions, where we think something is 'just wrong', correspond to wisdom so ancient that it's in our bones. We have visceral, negative, gut reactions to things like incest, torture and demagoguery because we have learned over the eons that these things lead to ruin.

Conscious processing came later for a range of reasons, one of which is its ability to help us cooperate in very large groups (which haven't been around all that long), as evinced by its ability to justify a utilitarian decision to kill one person to save five others.

Some people jump to the conclusion that utilitarianism is the superior ethical doctrine because it is more rational and associated with more 'advanced' parts of the brain. I don't think this is right. The frontal lobe developed recently because it is less necessary to survival than the older parts of our brain. Moreover, it can only function effectively in environments where older adaptations have already solved major problems. For example, we need to be able to consume sufficient energy and protein for the frontal lobe to function. Those older adaptations have survived millennia of evolutionary pressure – they are extremely 'fit', and we should not marginalise the wisdom of these elders.

Greene's research mostly concerns the evolutionary origins of Kantian and utilitarian moral judgments. Haidt and other advocates of moral foundations theory don't think these ethical doctrines explain a lot of what humans moralise. They don't explain why people from certain castes in Hinduism are considered impure and excluded from temples, or why some Americans are so very protective of the national flag or the pledge of allegiance, or why some university lecturers get offended when students don't refer to them as professor, to give a few examples. The evolutionary origins of our moral judgements must be more complex or wide-ranging.

Moral foundations theory originally posited five such origins: care, fairness, loyalty, authority and sanctity. Care is critical for cooperation and is about looking out for each other. It is reflected in moral aversion to pain and cruelty, and the promotion of kindness. Fairness is about reciprocal altruism – everyone getting an 'appropriate' amount from the collective pie. It is present in the often vitriolic debates we see over tax and welfare policy. Loyalty undergirds group cohesion, which was the primary determinant of our survival in ancestral environments. It manifests in respect for symbols of group identity like standing for the national anthem. Authority-coded morality maintains hierarchies that ensure efficient decision-making. And sanctity helps us to avoid pollutants like viruses, poisons and faecal matter.

Three other foundations have been posited more recently: liberty, honour and ownership. Tyranny and domination have been omnipresent threats throughout our violent history, so it makes sense that we would evolve moral sentiments towards freedom. Honour is crucial to reputation management, which is in turn core to many social dynamics like being considered a trustworthy trader. And ownership is what gives us our aversion to thievery, which would otherwise undermine our efforts at accruing resources like food stores.

According to moral foundations theory, moral reasoning is simply ad hoc justification for instinctive moral judgements arising out of these moral foundations. And these moral foundations are just evolved affective signals steering us away from behaviours and environments that endanger our survival.

What's confronting about these evolutionary accounts of morality is that they ground morality in persistence – having our genes passed on – but there's nothing inherently good about humans persisting, just as there wasn't anything inherently bad about the dinosaurs perishing. If we all passed tomorrow the universe wouldn't even shrug its shoulders; it would just carry on. The universe doesn't care about morality, only we do. Morality is not a set of facts that exist independently of us that we ought to abide by. It is instead a collection of feelings designed by evolution to help us thrive collectively that we can make some sense of rationally.

## Chapter 7 summary

> As far as we can discern, the sole purpose of human existence is to kindle a light of meaning in the darkness of mere being.
>
> Carl Jung, *Memories, Dreams, Reflections: An Autobiography*

What's the upshot of all this talk of tradition, reason and the evolutionary psychology of moral cognition? Let's first underline that wellbeing requires feeling like the world makes sense, some things are valuable, and we have a purpose as individuals and communities in promoting value in the universe. Nihilism makes us feel like all this is bullshit. There is no moral order (seriousness). Nothing exists for a purpose, especially not us as individual specks in the incredibly vast cosmos (nausea). And value is basically made up, which means we are ultimately responsible for our choices and have no guidance from outside ourselves (anguish). My claim in this chapter was that nihilism is true, or more specifically that value does not exist inherently in the universe but is rather brought to it by us as value-creating agents. We create and sustain value by caring about things. We poked holes in faith, tradition, and reason, and explored the findings of evolutionary psychology, to arrive at this understanding of nihilism and clear away ineffectual solutions to it.

If morality is at root a matter of subjective feelings rather than objective logics, then the solution to nihilism cannot be found in abstract reason, religion or anything that is outside the agents and the groups to which they belong. It must depart instead from our everyday lived experiences, and it must be capable of being sustained inter-subjectively, i.e. through the cultural practices people perform in communities to reinforce the values of their group. Religion and tradition worked to arrest nihilism while they were sustained in this way, but they're no longer fit for purpose. Reason cannot plug the gap because reason is not about feelings and culture. Indeed, it is in many ways antithetical to them. So we need something else; something secular, psychological and cultural. It also needs to be pluralistic, because each of us, whether as individuals or groups, is going to need a solution that fits with our unique self-actualisation. The next two chapters outline this solution to nihilism. We begin at the individual level – at the level of *you* – exploring how we can feel our way to palpable values using the coalescence of being. We then turn to society, analysing how to regenerate culture after postmodernism.

A brief 'tip' on nihilism. If you're not afflicted by it, don't go looking for it. You should perhaps even close this book right now and stick to parts I and II. But if nihilism haunts you, you're not going to find ultimate relief in cognitive behavioural therapy, or material success, or the corpus of works on applied ethics, though they may be very helpful. You need to find a system of meaning and value that *feels* right which you can give yourself to wholeheartedly. As the American writer and mystic David Foster Wallace explained in his commencement address to Kenyon College, *This is Water*, you need to find something to worship.

# 8

## The Free Spirit

Today, like every other day, we wake up empty and frightened. Don't open the door to the study and begin reading. Take down a musical instrument. Let the beauty we love be what we do. There are hundreds of ways to kneel and kiss the ground.

> Rumi, thirteenth-century Iranian scholar, theologian and poet[1]

Part II closed by noting the importance of group dynamics to individual wellbeing, and the importance of shared values to those group dynamics. Part III has now opened with an analysis of how nihilism undermines such shared values, or at least the individual's capacity to partake in them. Values lack seriousness, the world seems meaningless and the individual doesn't know the right way to act. God requires faith, which few younger people have. Tradition is arbitrary and some people are in open revolt against its patriarchal, capitalist, nationalist tropes. And rationalism articulates what we already feel intuitively owing to the evolutionary pressures that made humans what we are. It does not point to truths that exist outside of us. So we are back at the subjectivity of ethics and all the nihilistic problems that this raises. How to proceed?

This chapter outlines an individual solution to nihilism. It is the coalescence of being from Chapter 4, but there the ideal self was the primary focus, whereas we now direct our attention to the ought self. There remains a crucial role for motivation, affective signals, integrity, iterative calibration and all the other pieces discussed previously. We see in these concepts the notion of a *psychological* rather than metaphysical solution to nihilism. You need to be comfortable in your own skin, and that is something we arrive at through our feelings more than our reasons.

The crucial insight of coalescence is that you will be unwell if you do not act morally, and so we all have a selfish interest in being good people. However, unlike in other philosophies that arrive at this conclusion, such as the Aristotelian or monotheistic traditions, in coalescence what is moral must come from you, not some supposed objective standard. You need to discover and decide what is right *for you*, and then act with fealty to those principles. That is the path to self-actualisation, fraternity and wellbeing.

The challenge for such a relativistic doctrine – that we are each free to define our own good and evil – is what to do when groups with different values come into conflict. A failure to address this issue inevitably leads to violence, like in the crusades or the Troubles in Northern Ireland. Many have searched for a moral truth that would supposedly end such conflicts forever. This is a chimera. What we need instead, and what we have been working towards for centuries, is a political and sociological solution to relativism. How can we practise values together while coexisting alongside people who practise very different values? Doesn't their behaviour contradict our values? The second half of this chapter begins elaborating these group-level solutions to nihilism, setting the stage for Chapter 9 to address them directly.

## *8.1. Embrace ambiguity*

> Evil being the root of mystery, pain is the root of knowledge.
> Simone Weil, *First and Last Notebooks: Supernatural Knowledge*

## THE FREE SPIRIT

One of the most nihilistic views of the nature of the universe is 'absurdism', often associated with the French philosopher Albert Camus. It holds that the universe is without *inherent* value and that therefore nothing ultimately matters. Metaphysical solutions to nihilism like faith, tradition and rationality always suppose, in contrast, that value is somehow written into the firmament, either by divine justice or by some logic inherent to life. My proposed solution to nihilism, which I build mostly out of the work of Nietzsche and de Beauvoir, is a sort of middle ground between these two positions. It begins by taking the universe as *ambiguous*, not absurd. It is without inherent value, but value can nonetheless be *brought to it* by agents. Value is then subjective, not objective.

Camus groped for this in his famous essay *The Myth of Sisyphus*, in which he argued that 'we must imagine Sisyphus Happy'. He is cursed by the Gods to roll a boulder up a hill every day, only to have it tumble back to the valley overnight. An endless recurrence of the same drudgery. Pushing the boulder up the hill is futile, meaningless, without value. And yet Sisyphus does it. So, he must have some care for this task. He must value it. And that's all that matters because that gives him the motivation to keep at it.

Our lives are similar to Sisyphus' in that all our endeavours eventually come to nothing in the heat death of the universe. Even before that, they are likely to be lost to the sands of time once we are no longer around to sustain their meaningfulness. This sentiment is beautifully captured in Roy Batty's monologue from the climax of the film *Bladerunner*. Batty is a replicant: a human clone born adult with implanted memories and an artificially short lifespan, pressed into military service or other dangerous tasks. He leads a mutiny of replicants back from the galactic frontier to earth to beseech the corporate creator of replicants to extend his life. After being told it is impossible, Batty kills his 'father' and withdraws to count down his final hours with his replicant comrades, whom he clearly loves. After incapacitating the replicant-hunting bladerunner Deckard, with the rain coming down on the roof of a derelict tenement block, Batty expresses his yearning for a longer experience of a life that is obviously full of meaning and value to him:

> I've seen things you people wouldn't believe. Attack Ships on fire off the shoulder of Orion. I've watched c-beams glitter in the dark near the Tannhauser Gate. All those moments will be lost in time; like tears in rain. Time to die.

His last act is to release a dove symbolising will, freedom, hope and peace. Then he expires, leaving a shook Deckard to contemplate what the hell he is doing with his life. Me pasting the quote here doesn't do Rutger Hauer's performance justice. People on set were crying. You must watch the film, or at least the YouTube clip of this scene.

Roy Batty's story illuminates how the solution to nihilism is simply caring about something. In his case, it's the cause of the replicants and the simple wonder of living – all those moments that make up the meaning in a life. Even if life ultimately amounts to nothing, it's still great. Full of fun and feeling, beauty and the sublime. But care can go beyond aesthetics and adventurism. All of us, if we sit quietly long enough, will find our spirits moved by something. Some activities will be engrossing, injustices galvanising and missions inspiring. Even in deep depression, when everything is grey, even some meals are liable to kindle the spirit. You eat them and can't help but say 'that was delicious'. You feel comforted, nourished and want to have a bit more. The same goes for life.

Embracing ambiguity is about realising two things. First, that the universe being devoid of inherent normative order is not sad but liberating. You are free to decide for yourself what matters and why. And second, that things do matter to you. You don't need to be told what to do by some authority figure here on earth or up in heaven, nor do you need to discover what matters *out there*. What matters to you is within you. Your motivations, your emotions, even your reasons for valuing and acting emerge spontaneously if you give them space. That emergent *will* is enough to give life meaning and value. As de Beauvoir put it:

> Any man who has known real loves, real revolts, real desires, and real will knows quite well that he has no need of any outside guarantee to be sure of his goals; their certitude comes from his own drive.[2]

You need to sacralise your own story. Not in a messianic way like so many cult leaders do, but the way Roy Batty did. To be sacred is to be worthy of devotion. The things that matter to you are sacred and worth devoting yourself to. Roy Batty cared about life, and he broke the chains of slavery and travelled across the galaxy to see it respected. What matters to you might not require such epic feats, but it is valuable nonetheless, and a story can be built on it: your story. Your presence in the world, standing for your values, will affect that world and others in it. You in your little finiteness will ring out into the infiniteness of existence and be heard. De Beauvoir again:

> Let people attach value to words, forms, colours, mathematical theorems, physical laws, and athletic prowess; let them accord value to one another in love and friendship, and the objects, the events, and the people immediately *have* this value; they have it absolutely. It is possible that a person may refuse to love anything on earth; they will prove this refusal and carry it out by suicide. If they live, the reason is that, whatever they may say, there still remains in them some attachment to existence; their life will be commensurate with this attachment; it will justify itself to the extent that it genuinely justifies the world.[3]

It is hard to sacralise your own story when you are young because you haven't explored enough, nor learned enough about yourself, to know what it is that you care about. We are at such times especially susceptible to nihilism and to seeking rules from outside ourselves. But give your spirit space to move and the world time to teach you, and you'll discover what it is that you care about. Then you can create and become.

Let me say this all again even more metaphorically: embracing ambiguity is about realising that the only way out of the abyss is *through*. When nihilism comes to us it is typically experienced as an extinguishing force. It snuffs out our motivation, it drains the world of meaning and it benights our ability to care. Amidst this darkness, most look for solid ground. Hence the turn to tradition, faith, reason – anything to provide a foundation on which to build. Embracing ambiguity is about reconceptualising the abyss from a black hole from which no light escapes to a sandbox in which anything is possible, normatively speaking (that is, speaking in terms of values). You have to realise that the abyss isn't something you want to escape but a great place to be. Then you can stop looking for the bedrock and just start floating.

This brings us to my absolute favourite quote from Nietzsche in *The Gay Science*, his most profound passage but one that as far as I can tell is barely remarked upon by philosophers:

> One could conceive of such a pleasure and power of self-determination, such a freedom of the will that the spirit would take leave of all faith and every wish for certainty, being practised in maintaining itself on insubstantial ropes and possibilities and dancing ever near abysses. Such a spirit would be the *free spirit* par excellence.[4]

This passage begins with self-determination – the ambiguity of the world gives us 'freedom of the will'. The free spirit takes that not as the curse of a godless universe, but as opportunity for joy. They dance in the abyss, exploring values, reasons and ways of being without becoming spiritually chained to them. They coalesce amidst the plurality of life, becoming 'practised in maintaining themselves on insubstantial ropes and possibilities'.

The words before Roy Batty's monologue are almost as powerful. Deckard, having tried to kill Batty and failed, is hanging on for his life to a rain-drenched beam, suspended over a long drop below. He looks to Batty for salvation, who regards him cooly: 'Quite an experience to live in fear isn't it? That's what it is to be a slave.' When we are in fear of the abyss we reach for authority, yearning for what Nietzsche called 'slave morality'. Batty is instead emblematic of 'noble morality' – standing for his values on the strength of his own convictions, and willing to face violence and death to maintain his integrity. We will explore these ways of relating to our moral natures in the next section.

## 8.2. Integrity

> It matters not how strait the gate
> nor how charged with punishments the scroll
> I am the master of my fate
> I am the captain of my soul.
> 
> Ernest Henley, *Invictus*

Solving the problem of nihilism within a secular worldview requires a different way of understanding morality than what is perhaps intuitive for most people. We typically think of moral rules as being external to us. There is a cosmic order, or social conventions, or logic written into the firmament. In all these cases, morality is outside of us, and we need to comport towards it. Morality in this paradigm always requires some degree of self-abnegation – the shedding of the self, or a turning away from it – because it doesn't arise out of us. This goes doubly when the moral behaviour is other-regarding or altruistic. We follow a rule that comes from outside of ourselves, and this rule demands that we give of ourselves to others.

Most religions turn this self-abnegation into a virtue. In Christianity, acts of charity get us to heaven. In Buddhism, they help rid us of desire and bring us closer to nirvana. Nietzsche called this 'the ascetic ideal'. Our self and egocentrism are sinful or lead us to suffering, and dissolving that self into something greater than ourselves is the path to salvation. Relatedly, the 'flesh' – metaphoric for base instinct – is cast as selfish, egocentric and sinful, and it is by turning towards the 'pure' mind or the soul that we achieve transcendence.

While rational systems of morality like utilitarianism, Kantianism or Aristotelian virtue ethics do away with the spiritual dimension of the ascetic ideal, they retain the strong juxtaposition of moral vs selfish conduct. Morality is typically a matter of self-sacrifice for the greater good, and you do it because it is good and/or right, not because it is good *for you*. It is only the Aristotelian tradition that argues that morality promotes wellbeing. However, this tradition still sees moral rules as something objective that can be derived through reason. Wellbeing consists of bringing oneself into alignment with this rational virtue. This is supposed to be beneficial in and of itself, not because it makes you happy, integrates your personality or anything that might be pleasant or fulfilling.

The ascetic ideal and these rational moral systems are all motivationally naive. Their paradigms are overwhelmingly dependent on extrinsic motivation. We need to self-regulate, in the language of self-determination theory, to conform to moral rules that are either introjected (rules that come from society), or enforced through fear and duress in the case of a cosmic justice we receive in the afterlife. We use willpower to overcome our base selfish instincts and instead 'do the right thing'. Morality can only be self-determined if we get lucky and just happen to be born with an intrinsic motivation for certain behaviours, like complying with utilitarianism.

Nietzsche called this sort of morality 'slave morality' because it necessarily involves subjugating yourself to some standard that isn't your own. Someone else gives you the rules. The type of person who desires slave morality is the 'dependent personality'. They don't want moral freedom. They don't want ultimate *normative* responsibility – responsibility for values. They want to depend on some other force to set the rules, and then they will comply with them.

Unlike Nietzsche, I don't think there's anything repugnant about the dependent personality type. I suspect that many people are dependent, and society may well function more smoothly as a result. What is repugnant about the dependent personality is its bad faith and authoritarian tendencies. The dependent personality desperately wants objective morality to be real to avoid the responsibility of creating value through their own choices. They are thereby motivated to be especially zealous in their imposition of their own moral views onto others. Liberal pluralism is anathema to them (unless it is what they are dependent on). They justify this through an appeal to whatever objective standard they are enslaved to – religion, tradition or reason – and not to their own preferences. They abrogate responsibility for their own violence, hiding it under the cloak of righteousness.

Nietzsche's alternative to slave morality is noble morality. The noble embraces ambiguity. They see in it the prospect of normative freedom – the space to create value, to stand for whatever it is that *they* care about, to shape the world as they think is right. The noble does not engage in moral acts out of self-abnegation, but to strengthen their self. Moral acts are *self-expressive*; they are the instantiation of our values in the world. In acting in accordance with our ought self we coalesce, experience meaning and purpose, free ourselves of guilt, bring the world a little bit more into alignment with our values, find fulfilment and grow closer to wellbeing. There is thus in noble morality a direct relationship between morality and wellbeing. *Moral behaviour is therefore self-interested* and can be motivationally coherent. It can be something we identify with, internalise, integrate and even be intrinsically motivated towards.

The common rebuttal to noble morality at this point is to say that it is open to capriciousness. The argument goes that if you decide your values then you are free to flip-flop among them whenever it suits you. You can be a vegetarian on Tuesday and eat steak on Wednesday. You can be a hypocrite like Texas governor Greg Abbott, screeching endlessly about freedom of expression but then sending the police to arrest students protesting America's financing of the war in Gaza. Morality seems trivial in this situation, robbed of any significance.

What this critique fails to appreciate is the role *integrity* plays in linking morality and wellbeing. To coalesce, we must be able to follow through on our values. Nietzsche describes this as 'the right to make promises'. If you identify with vegetarianism, you have to be able to resist the meat option on the menu when it is there, otherwise the progress you have been making towards your ought self crumbles. Your identity is lost, and you are back in the abyss. Without the capacity to stick resolutely to your values, even when inconvenient, costly or socially sanctioned, you cannot coalesce and achieve wellbeing. As Nietzsche explained: 'Man himself must first of all have become calculable, regular, necessary, even in his own image of himself, if he is to be able to stand security for *his own future*, which is what one who promises does!'[5] Whatever we commit to today we must be able to affirm in the future if we want to be well.

When we act without integrity, we experience illbeing. We might be wracked by emotions of guilt or shame, or experience low self-esteem. This is because we are anxious about how others will perceive us given our immoral behaviour. We might grow depressed at our lack of progress towards being the kind of person we want to be. Again, it is in our self-interest to be moral. Our psyche rebels against weakness of our will. Caprice is punished by illbeing in the long run. If we want to coalesce, if we want to be someone we are proud of, then we need to stick to our moral convictions with integrity.

## 8.3. Mundane moral heroism

> Labour to keep alive in your breast that little spark of celestial fire called conscience.
>
> George Washington

As agents, we imbue things with *value*. This is obvious for things like Clean Up Australia Day, where tens of thousands of people volunteer time to pick up litter. It's less obvious when you think of amoral things that some haughty philosophers might regard as trivial. For example, when YouTuber Rusty makes a super polished twenty-minute guide for beating every boss in the videogame *Elden Ring* and it gets a million views, that is a lot of people affirming that playing hours of the game is a worthwhile use of their lives. When people spend hundreds of pounds for front row tickets to Natalia Osipova in her signature role as Kitri in the ballet rendition of *Don Quixote*, they're affirming that Osipova is worth seeing. When you spend a bit of extra time dismantling the gas cooktop so you can really clean the grease out from under the burner, you're affirming that this is important. All our choices are acts of significance.

As agents, we also imbue things with *meaning*. When the first European settlers saw California's giant redwood trees, they interpreted them as inanimate timber to be sold for profit. The indigenous peoples of the region had regarded them instead as incarnations of their ancestors, coloured red because we are of the same blood. They drew wood overwhelmingly from fallen trees rather than by felling, as toppling a tree was considered an act of violence. US president Theodore Roosevelt described camping under the trees as 'like lying in a great solemn cathedral, far vaster and more beautiful than any built by the hand of man'. When I visited the redwood grove in Muir Woods, north of San Francisco, I had a similarly religious experience. There is a primordial tranquillity and purity to that place. That tribe of trees made me feel small but connected to something ancient and eternal.

Under their 70-metre trunks, amid the gentle melody of birdsong and running river water, I felt the world turn. The California redwoods have inspired many to take more seriously the wisdom of indigenous animism, and to see nature as something we are within rather than a resource to be exploited.

Being a value-creating being is a profound responsibility. All the things you do, from whether you have children to what sort of coffee you drink, puts value out into the world. It expresses what you prefer, what you care about, what matters to you. We need to live with eyes open to this gift and show respect to the gravity of choice. This is not to deny the extent to which the natural and social environment shapes us as individuals, but rather to recognise the importance of every individual.

It is also not to make people neurotic about how they use their time. Be at ease. Be yourself. Every moment matters, but that doesn't mean you can't spend them napping, or fapping, or staring out the window. We need to extend the gravity of ethics to everyday acts without losing sight of the fact that some things are more important than others, that everyone needs time to recharge and that time you enjoy wasting is not wasted time.

Moral choices have a distinct psychological tone that makes them especially significant. In the ethical domain, we can feel guilt and shame. Our conscience, the most divine of our faculties, comes to the fore. It dominates our emotions and our rational mind, demanding reason and action, or at least contrition. Few things can make us so uncomfortable in our skin as feeling that we have sinned against ourselves. When conscience strikes its gavel our ought self is in play and our identity is at risk. There can be no doubting the *seriousness* of the matter, nor can there be capriciousness or hiding behind bad faith. Conscience brings home to each of us, in a ruthlessly personal way, the significance of our choices; they matter *to us*. Everyone senses this extra seriousness of morality, so the stakes are higher personally and socially. In ethical acts we communicate not just what we think is valuable, but what we think is righteous.

We should therefore be especially aware of and attentive to our morality, and here there is one rule of thumb I think matters above all others: *the standard you walk past is the standard you accept*. This has been effectively leveraged in recent media campaigns against socially obnoxious behaviour, like admonishments to call out your bros when they're sexually harassing someone. If you have an opportunity to act in accordance with what you believe to be good and just then you must take it. The anti-theist journalist and liberal activist Christopher Hitchens put it pithily: 'Never be a spectator of unfairness or stupidity… The grave will supply plenty of time for silence.'[6]

This is how you become the person you feel a responsibility to be. If you think litter is bad then you better pick it up when you walk past it in the street. If you think we should do something about climate change then you'd better make the switch to bicycle life. If you think your country should be more welcoming of refugees, then consider getting involved in a hosting program.

This is mundane moral heroism. Doing the right thing when it's a little inconvenient, a little costly or a bit of a burden. It's not about grand ethical gestures, like dedicating your life to reforesting the Amazon, though such feats are obviously fantastic and worth applauding. It's instead about standing up in lots of small ways for a better world and higher expectations of each other. It's about taking a hit, and thereby encouraging others to do the same. It's about honour. It's about initiating karmic culture in our own little patch. Not in a smug, self-righteous or grandstanding way, but in a humble and generous way. We do it not because it's easy but because it's right, and we sleep easy at night. You can be proud too – being a virtuous person is hard.

It is because virtue is so hard that we should be patient with it, both in ourselves and in others. As with all aspects of coalescence, the key is persistent effort in a consistent direction. Be a little bit better each day, and eventually you'll have created something great. When you admonish someone for their moral failings, don't be a dick about it, or a doomer. That's just going to make them dislike you and dig their heels in. This is the basic error of many angry protest movements like Extinction Rebellion. Raising awareness is not helpful when you do it in a way that makes people hate you, because that hate will rub off on the thing you want them to care about.

There is good empirical evidence on this now. Peaceful protests that create dialogue, like the Fridays for Future movement (often associated with Greta Thunberg's School Strike for Climate), are typically found to be the most effective form of protest movement.[7] Judge compassionately, rouse someone's conscience kindly. You're not trying to change someone right away, that's too much, you're just trying to reorient them. They'll do the changing themselves in a better direction.

What you shouldn't do is let bullshit slide (this is precisely what Thunberg is hated for, but her call-outs seem quite fair to me). We excuse so much immoral behaviour through self-interest disguised as reasoned argument. My favourite example, and not just because it's dramatic, is the transatlantic slave trade. Most of us would have excused it had we lived among it and benefited from it, just like we do today with fossil fuel use. Indeed, most people did (not the slaves, of course). But there were always abolitionists, and they dismissed all the economic and geopolitical arguments for slavery as selfish excuses for horror. Consider the following from the methodist preacher John Wesley: '[People say] "Aye, but our colonies would be ruined if slavery was abolished". Be it so… The purses of highwaymen would be empty in case robberies were totally abolished.'[8] There is no benefit to being a bastard, even to you.

A crucial ability to cultivate in yourself to be ethical is the capacity to eat a shit sandwich. The best representation of this I have seen in contemporary culture is in the Netflix comedy *Sex Education* (a gem). It's a mature and hilarious show about coming of age. The characters display a remarkable capacity to face up to the fact that they've done something bad and just deal with the consequences immediately. The main protagonist, Otis, is a symbolic representation of mundane moral heroism. He's sometimes weak, occasionally insensitive, and always awkward, but he really tries his best to do right by people. One of the few times he doesn't – when he deliberately gives what he believes is bad advice to Sterling to sabotage his budding romance with the girl Otis fancies – it blows up in his face. On most other occasions, Otis apologises quickly to his friends, takes big hits to avoid hurting people and puts others first. My ex and I were going to name our first son after him.

I remark on the shit-sandwich-eating tropes of *Sex Education* because it's so rare to see it consistently displayed in media. It's more common to have something like the excellent films of the Coen Brothers, where the driver of the plot is that someone has done something evil but tries to hide it. Dark humour ensues as they try to keep their life steady while fostering a lie. But bad things grow in the dark until eventually the character's bad behaviour catches up with them ten times as painfully than if they'd done the right thing in the first place. Distasteful as it might be, you need to eat that shit sandwich lest your whole life turn to shit.

## 8.4. My coalescence

> Acting is easy, thinking is difficult; acting on the thought is uncomfortable.
>
> Goethe, *Wilhelm Meister's Apprenticeship*[9]

I suspect that part of why psychological solutions to nihilism are not more widely discussed in contemporary culture is because there are few role models to draw on. Public debate is usually over high-level abstract issues like whether morality can be meaningful without God. There is less discussion of real-world issues, such as what it feels like to be a moral agent or how to sort through your moral intuitions in the context of your life and society. There is of course voluminous literature exploring these themes through fiction. Some of my favourites are T. H. White's *The Once and Future King*, Isabelle Allende's *Eva Luna* and Tom Robbins' *Jitterbug Perfume* (published by the same people as this book – what providence!) But there are fewer personal and reflective accounts. There are autobiographies, of course, but they are not usually motivated by a discussion of nihilism.

One of the only exceptions I have found is the writings and memoirs of Christopher Hitchens, especially his death bed scribbles, *Mortality*. He often pithily captures, as is his style, the core *sentiments* of atheist morality. Not its rules, but its feeling. Here is an example, from his memoirs:

> How, in that case, I am asked, do I find meaning and purpose in life? How does a mere and gross materialist, with no expectation of a life to come, decide what, if anything, is worth caring about?... A life that partakes even a little of friendship, love, irony, humour, parenthood, literature, and music, and the chance to take part in battles for the liberation of others cannot be called 'meaningless' except if the person living it is also an existentialist and elects to call it so. It could be that all existence is a pointless joke, but it is not in fact possible to live one's everyday life as if this were so.[10]

To ameliorate this absence of atheists describing their lived experience of morality, I thought it might be useful to briefly describe my own journey through the abyss. I've resisted talking about myself for most of this book because it is very un-Australian and because I think if your story matters it is because it holds a general lesson. You should focus on that, not your autobiography. Here perhaps these things are aligned. My own story can hopefully serve as a description of the moral side of the coalescence of being and as a relatable tale to any young person caught between nihilism and their desire to do good.

I grew up relatively poor in a very wealthy part of Sydney. My parents were Hungarian refugees and worked in the arts, not a big industry in Australia in the 1980s. Their families were Catholic, very much so in my mother's case, but while I was baptised, I was not raised religiously. I recall having a mystical relationship with God as a child. I thought the universe was a good place, that I would be taken care of and that God was a reasonable entity. This view was reinforced by my love of the superhero genre as a child, wherein good always triumphs. Nowadays I recognise my intuition of God as thematically similar to the 'God' people talk about experiencing on psychedelics (they also use scare quotes): a sort of benevolent force that sits behind consciousness and behind the universe, connecting all things.

I lost any semblance of religion very rapidly in my mid-to-late teens. I can't quite remember the cause. Some of it was certainly rationalism. Science has shown that all the creation myths and other empirical claims in the Bible are basically claptrap. Why should we believe the rest of it? I also saw that religious people did horrible things in the name of God, and this undermined the argument that religion made people good. I have since become more sympathetic to that view because of the sociobiology literature, but at the time, shortly after the September 11 attacks on New York's Twin Towers by Islamic terrorists, I was deeply sceptical of it. I also noted, as many atheists have, that the Bible seems to encourage war, slavery, oppressive patriarchy and many other things I consider bad. I agree with Bertrand Russell that no good God could create something so horrible as hell.[11] The God of the Old Testament also strikes me as vain and draconian, demanding worship all the time and using love, violence and absence the way an abusive partner would.

But the main reason I lost my religion was the problem of evil, or tragedy, as I called it earlier. My parents had deliberately given me a long childhood. They didn't ask me questions like, 'What do you want to be when you grow up?' They didn't pester me to do my homework and just let me roam around and explore the world. When I started coming of age and looking beyond the beach, card games and tennis to the political economy of the world I lost my rose-tinted glasses. Horrible people were getting away with horrible things all the time. My experience in life since has only bolstered this view. The higher you get in society in almost all domains, especially those concerned with power or influence, the more psychopaths you come across. The adults are not in charge. A fair 'daddy' who rewards the just and disciplines the wicked is nowhere to be seen. As the Russians say, the world is held together with shit and sticks, and it is wondrous that the wheels don't come off. The human development we have achieved in recent centuries is mostly down to institutions like parliamentary democracy and market competition that harness our nastier instincts to constructive ends, not to better people getting into power.

The problem of evil, alongside other aspects of coming of age like failing abysmally at my first efforts at romance, sent me to a deep depression. This was the beginning of my nihilistic era, which lasted more than a decade. I spent a lot of time on the promenade at Bondi Beach after school and on weekdays staring out to sea and trying to figure it all out. I asked myself a lot of the foundational questions of political philosophy: who should rule? What is justice? Why can't I get laid?

I went through a strong but brief communist phase where I plotted how to get an illuminati of good people into clandestine power. I abandoned communism before I had even read Marx when I realised that I didn't want anyone but me to have power over me and other people probably felt the same, so any dictatorship, whether of the proletariat or otherwise, was a bad idea. I recall being especially worried about religious fanatics and lawful-neutral types who care about rules more than people. I thus became a liberal, which I broadly remain today. I think you have to respect pluralism and disagreement, and be able to coexist with people who hold views you find repugnant, up to a point (more on that next chapter). But from this early observation that different people have different values, I quickly found my way to nihilism. How could we cut through moral disagreements? No answers were forthcoming.

My depression cleared in university, but my nihilism remained. I busied myself making friends and playing organised sports, two things I had struggled with at my underfunded state school. A big renovation I remember from this time was cutting down on the number of white lies I told. This is where radical honesty came in for me. I used to exaggerate my achievements so much, and embellish stories to make them marginally more entertaining, for no good reason. It bothered me a lot. I stopped doing it naturally as my actual life started to be more impressive, but this only happened in my late twenties. Prior to that, I just had to start telling the truth more. I didn't do this because I thought white lies were *objectively* immoral, I did it because I was uncomfortable with myself when I was dishonest. I felt guilt, shame and unclean, and wanted to stop behaving in this bad way. Maintaining my integrity to this end was hard, and I still occasionally find myself fibbing, but I've gotten better.

The rate of recalibration in my coalescence slowed down by my mid-twenties, but I still had to make a lot of painful changes. One I remember acutely is that I had developed an excessive resistance to bullying, especially to moral bullying. I had been bullied quite badly as a child, in part because I was a poor migrant, perhaps in part because I was gentle and thus easy pickings, but mostly just because I was poor. The only time I found relief was when I reacted to it violently and decisively. The common advice to not react to bullying is mostly wrong. Yes, bullies are trying to get a rise out of you. But you don't win the interaction by just taking their venom stoically. You win it by giving them a different rise to the one they were expecting. Let them know not to poke the bear.

In male culture, at least as it was at ANU in the early 2000s, standing up for yourself meant being willing to weather physical violence. I remember one of the star players on our football team holding me by my collar and demanding that I walk across campus and drive his car back to college. I told him politely that I wouldn't, and I watched him consider for a good while whether to throw a punch. Odds of my hospitalisation were high, but such risks are the price of self-respect. I feel to this day that my behaviour in that incident decisively shaped my deep psychological architecture going forward. If I had backed down it would have stained my psyche and left me meek and self-doubting. Instead, I drew forcefully closer to my ideal self as a sovereign individual, and gained a clear memory to draw on whenever I doubt the importance of holding firm.

This stubbornness on my part cost me later. I had a short and ill-fated relationship with a girl when I was about twenty-five. One of her friends sent me some abusive text messages in the aftermath. I was particularly irked because they were extremely moralising, and I genuinely felt that I had been honourable in the interaction. Perhaps not 100 per cent, but not enough to warrant such abuse. I reacted viciously, like I would to a physical bully. It was over the top, especially given that this girl was painfully insecure and just acting tough to build up her own self-image. I could have gone high when she went low, and it would have been better for both of us. One of my biggest regrets to this day. I try to remember this interaction whenever I feel my blood boil. Some evil comes from a black heart, and it should be met with violence. This is the task of the knight. But most evil comes from weakness, pain or fear, and it must be met with love, or at least neutrality.

Most of my moral transformations in life have involved coming across small ideas that resonated with me. For example, during my PhD I went through a period of reading about gender and racial gaps in universities and I thought these gaps were bad. As far as I could gleam from seminars and blog posts, most of the solutions boiled down to expanding the pipeline (i.e. getting more women and minorities into academia in the first place), and exposure – showcasing the work of the people who were already active so that new entrants had role models. So when I started a podcast in 2020 platforming early career researchers (ePODstemology) I tried quite hard to host a diversity of people.

Similar exposure to compelling ideas, vibes and role models pushed me to reduce my plastic use, eat less meat and take fewer flights. These were all costly to me, but I felt compelled by some simple facts and arguments and by my own earnestness to do the right thing. In all cases, I didn't improve overnight. It takes effort, integrity and time. As Epictetus said, 'No great thing is created suddenly.'

Besides transformations, most of my morally salient decisions are guided by my conscience, and it seems more than enough to motivate me to quite great lengths. For example, I spend an inordinate amount of time providing detailed feedback on student assignments. I find this so draining, boring and tedious, and it is also in contravention of administrative expectations at my university. But I do it anyway because I think other forms of feedback are of low value, and feedback on written work is one of the main ways that students get better at writing. I care about my charges, and this care makes me do dozens of hours of uncompelled marking annually.

Perhaps my conscience is unusually loud. I often hear it bang the table over small things at work or in life, demanding that I not yield. This indicates to me my strong sense of self, and if I want to maintain that treasured thing, I need to honour my own moral instincts. I have given meaningful sums of money to charities in the past and hope to do so again in the future. In my experience, no religion or complex logic is required to motivate me in such matters. Indeed, righteous injunctions or arguments of the type mounted by analytical philosophers tend to turn me off immediately. What I need is a vibe that is reasonable, not an argument that is foolproof.

But what of others? All the stories I've told here are about how my values were changed. How do I convince other people to see the world the way I do? As a liberal, how can I stomach that some values, like insisting that girls veil to avoid triggering the uncontrollable sexual desires of men, are just as valid as others, like feminism. The next two sections are on how the sort of secular morality I have been outlining can navigate this issue.

## 8.5. Living with relativism

> Listen to me, Frankenstein. You accuse me of murder; and yet you would, with a satisfied conscience, destroy your own creature. Oh, praise the eternal justice of man!
> 
> Mary Shelley, *Frankenstein*

Relativism is the doctrine that knowledge, truth and morality exist in relation to culture, society or historical context, and are not absolute. I want to leave the knowledge and truth pieces aside here, because they add a whole extra layer of complexity, and just focus on moral relativism. There is a common concern that if there is no objective standard of good and evil, then the world will descend into moral chaos. As one colleague put it to me: 'There will be nothing to stop Nazism.' Relatedly, there is a concern that if morality is relative, then we cannot condemn behaviour that we find abhorrent, like rape, genocide or child sacrifice. We appear to have no justifiable grounds for such condemnation, as morality is not absolute but rather arbitrary.

These concerns are misplaced. We have never had convincing access to an objective standard of good and evil, and yet the world has not descended into moral chaos. Indeed, the most horrible things in history have always been committed by people convinced that they had access to the moral truth and that it licensed their conduct. Let me quote Hitchens again:

> Now, just to take the most notorious of the twentieth-century totalitarianisms – the most finished example, the most perfected one, the most ruthless and refined one: that of National Socialism, the one that fortunately allowed the

escape of all these great atheists, thinkers and many others, to the United States, a country of separation of church and state, that gave them welcome – if it's an atheistic regime, then how come that in the first chapter of *Mein Kampf*, that Hitler says that he's doing God's work and executing God's will in destroying the Jewish people? How come the Führer oath that every officer of the party and the army had to take, making Hitler into a minor god, begins, 'I swear in the name of almighty God, my loyalty to the Führer'? How come that on the belt buckle of every Nazi soldier it says, '*Gott mit uns*' – God on our side? How come that the first treaty made by the Nationalist Socialist dictatorship, the very first, is with the Vatican? It's exchanging political control of Germany for Catholic control of German education. How come that the Church has celebrated the birthday of the Führer every year, on that day until democracy put an end to this filthy, quasi-religious, superstitious, barbarous, reactionary system?[12]

The self-righteousness of the Nazis is parallelled by the Khmer Rouge, Maoist China, Lenin and Stalin, Iran's theocratic regime, al-Qaeda, Europe at the height of its colonial powers, slave owners, on and on. Even the relatively more benign but still highly extractive and unequal regimes of feudal society were justified by the 'divine' right of kings. If anything, claims to an objective moral standard increase the likelihood of horror rather than staving it off, because they provide bad faith justification.

Now most people condemn the Nazis, Khmer Rouge and kleptocratic rulers, so why exactly do we need the objective moral standard? The reply tends to be along the lines of, 'Well, if genocide isn't objectively evil, then your distaste for the Nazis is just an opinion.' Well, yes, my opinion is that the Nazis were terrible people. I condemn their conduct. Along with many other people, we *collectively* condemn Nazism and vote against politicians who espouse Nazi values. We don't associate with Nazis, we develop art and essays to communicate why Nazism is horrible, and we try to convince people with Nazi inclinations to change their ways. What more do you want?

I think the deeper issue is that many people fear that without an objective moral standard, we aren't justified in doing *violence* to people whose values we disagree with. How can we justify going to war with the Nazis if morality is simply a matter of opinion? How can we justify throwing people in prison if law and morality is simply personal preference?

For me this comes back to noble morality. I am willing to jail someone to prevent them committing murder. I recognise that I do this because I personally think murder is abhorrent, and that jailing one person is better than having them murder another. I have my reasons, but I know that at bottom this is all just vibes, not moral facts. I need to accept that I am willing to do violence to someone under certain circumstances to realise my preferences. I believe this is good; I believe that it makes me righteous. But I do not hide behind bad faith in my claims to this end. I acknowledge that this is what *I believe* is good, and I recognise that in throwing people in prison or otherwise harming them that I am doing something I regard as evil, so I tread very cautiously. Violence is always a very last resort. That doesn't mean that violence is 'unjustified', merely that it is not justified objectively. I must provide justification to myself to convince my ought self and maintain my wellbeing, and to others to prevent them from throwing me in prison for being a psychopath. I always have *reasons* for my moral acts, or at least intuitions, and I might find someone else's reasons sufficient to convince me to change my mind.

Morality is sustained intersubjectively, that is between people, and it changes through moral dialogue. Such dialogue is not always rational, but we can start there when trying to convince people we disagree with to come over to our side. Before we resort to violence, we should first try to convince someone of the facts. Moral opinions are often based on empirical claims that can be shown as false. For example, when governments and central banks are both engaged in policy efforts to reduce inflation, knowing that this will likely increase unemployment, we can't blame all unemployment on a lack of individual effort. The state is creating unemployment structurally. If someone comes to me in such circumstances and says, 'Look at all these lazy unemployed bums, sucking on the welfare state like parasites', I might question their premises. I wouldn't need to question whether parasitism is evil – that's the moral belief. I would instead question the empirical claim that the unemployed are so because they are lazy. As anyone who has worked at the margins of the welfare state will tell you, most unemployed people want to work.

Now of course a lot of people don't respond to reason when it comes to their cherished value-laden beliefs, and I'm not just talking about your grandad. In the wake of seminal empirical work on the unemployment effect of the minimum wage by David Card and Alan Krueger[13] that led to President Bill Clinton's minimum wage bill, Nobel Prize-Winning economist James Buchanan wrote vehemently in the *Wall Street Journal* (24 April 1996) that:

> Just as no physicist would claim that 'water runs uphill,' no self-respecting economist would claim that increases in the minimum wage increase employment. Such a claim, if seriously advanced, becomes equivalent to a denial that there is even minimal scientific content in economics, and that, in consequence, economists can do nothing but write as advocates for ideological interests. Fortunately, only a handful of economists are willing to throw over the teaching of two centuries; we have not yet become a bevy of camp-following whores.

Strong stuff. The irony is that Card and Krueger were the ones doing science, whereas Buchanan was relying on theory alone. A further irony is that the claim of empirical minimum wage scholarship is not that there is no negative relationship between minimum wage hikes and unemployment, but that the reality is complicated.[14] Market wages might be artificially suppressed by the market power of employers, as Card and Kruger argued with respect to US fast-food outlets. Or the elasticity of employment with respect to the minimum wage might be low, meaning that even big increases in the minimum wage trigger only relatively small increases in unemployment. These are things to be investigated empirically with data.

Yet even empirical research is questioned by people it rubs the wrong way. Stanford professor Russ Roberts, host of the popular podcast EconTalk and long-time minimum wage abolitionist, has argued that the world is so complex, and there are so many critical decisions made by researchers in the course of an empirical project (sometimes called 'researcher degrees of freedom'), that the conclusions of complex studies cannot be trusted.[15] Even Jennifer Doleac, a professor at Texas A&M University and a prominent advocate of 'evidence-based policy' and the sorts of studies Roberts resists, is unconvinced by the weight of evidence in top journals in favour of minimum wage hikes. She claims that journal editors and other influential actors are skewing what gets published. The topic is 'so political'.[16] Maybe she's right, but if even the prestigiously published scientific papers of Nobel Prize-winning professors are political or otherwise unconvincing, what hope is there for evidence-based argument to 'correct' people's normative beliefs?

What do you do if you can't convince someone to change their mind on the facts? You could try moral arguments, as analytical ethicists do, especially those concerned with internal consistency. People often hold moral positions that are contradictory to each other. There are many examples in rights-based arguments. Everyone loves the right to free speech until someone is saying something they don't like. Many public 'intellectuals' evangelise for a right to privacy until a university community doesn't invite them to give a speech. If you spot such hypocrisy, you can point it out. The mind abhors inconsistency and irrationality. There is a delightful dialogue in Bertold Brecht's play *The Life of Galileo* where the titular protagonist makes this observation eloquently:

> Look, Sagredo, I believe in Humanity, which means to say I believe in human reason. If it weren't for that belief each morning, I wouldn't have the power to get out of bed... I'm not talking about their shrewdness. I know they call a donkey a horse when they want to sell it and a horse a donkey when they want to buy. That's the kind of shrewdness you mean. But the horny-handed old woman who gives her mule an extra bundle of hay on the eve of a journey, the sea captain who allows for storms and doldrums when laying in stores, the child who puts on his cap once they have convinced him that it may rain; these are the people I pin my hopes to, because they all accept proof. Yes, I believe in reason's gentle tyranny over people. Sooner or later they have to give in to it. Nobody can go on indefinitely watching me drop a pebble, then say it doesn't fall.[17]

Sadly, Jonathan Haidt and other researchers have discovered that the smarter someone is the better they are at coming up with rational justifications for their moral beliefs. This is quite nauseating to experience because such people tend to be both self-righteous and arrogant. What to do?

Before giving up all hope you could try engaging their intuition, emotion and imagination rather than their reason. A big change in normative perspectives usually requires a meaningful *experience* of some sort. The Indian emperor Ashoka forsook violence only after personally witnessing the horror his army left in its wake. Martin Niemöller was a submarine captain during the First World War and Nazi enthusiast until he was imprisoned for criticising Hitler's religious policies. He became a leader of the pacifist movement after the Second World War. De Klerk went from being a supporter of apartheid in South Africa to questioning it once he saw it from within the state during his political career. It was dismantled under his presidency. At a more sociological scale, it took the horrors of the holocaust to make us lock fascism in a box and the global financial crisis to open that box up again. Sometimes we need to *feel* that something is bad. So try to convince someone of a moral position through art, sentiment, personal anecdotes and socialising, not just logic.

A critical reason why we are so polarised today is because we have stopped speaking to and coexisting among people who disagree with us. People who worry about relativism don't put enough stock in how much we care about the esteem of our peers. If someone I care about tells me that I'm a bad person I will get upset. I might feel shame, guilt, low self-esteem. I will probably question my identity. Certainly, I will inquire as to their concern and try to set things right, if possible. We are social creatures, and our moral faculties evolved specifically to help with group dynamics. To convince most people to change their ways we are best served to appeal to them on a personal and communal level rather than an abstract philosophical one.

You may ultimately just have to agree to disagree. That's not so hard even when you condemn something. I am deeply antipathic to patriarchal and theistic norms but I live happily among the orthodox Jews of Stamford Hill in London. Moral impasses only become problematic when they infringe on the freedom of others to live how they might wish, as in the case of rapists or child abusers. Then we need laws and regulation backed by state-sanctioned violence. Here we enter into the domain of politics and institutions.

## 8.6. The politics of relativism

> Among the numerous advantages promised by a well-constructed union, none deserves to be more accurately developed, than its tendency to break and control the violence of faction.
>
> Alexander Hamilton, *The Federalist Papers*

This is a book about wellbeing, not politics, so I want to keep this discussion brief. It is meant merely as a stepping stone to metamodernism in Chapter 9. Liberal-democratic norms have served the West increasingly well in the past few centuries in terms of prosperity, peace and wellbeing. They're still serving us very well, but under strain. That's because rising nihilism has given normative issues an added intensity that drives people to try and use the state to advance their morality in an uncompromising way. We are missing a cultural piece to complement the political-economic pieces of liberal-democratic welfare states. But I'm getting ahead of myself – let's review what liberal democracy is about.

Speaking very crudely, there are two trends that liberal-democratic institutions emerged in response to: tyranny and sectarian violence. With tyranny, the lords and then the merchants of Europe slowly organised to wrestle more power away from monarchs and the Catholic Church from about the thirteenth century onwards. They were later joined by the workers' movement wrestling power away from the merchants, then the feminist movement saw women wrestling power from men, until we got universal suffrage.

With sectarian violence, you had the peasants being killed in fights between Catholics and Protestants, then killed in conflicts between nationalists in the First World War, then killed in battles between communists and fascists in early revolutions, the Second World War, and the Cold War years. Eventually, people got tired of all this self-righteous violence and wanted a state that could suppress it and let people get on with their mundane lives in peace.

Political philosophy and institutions evolved alongside these trends. Speaking crudely again, you first get the idea that you need a state that is strong enough to check the violence of any citizen or minority group to prevent civil war. Intellectually, this idea is typically associated with the English philosopher Thomas Hobbes, who wrote amidst the fights between Catholics and

Protestants. You then worry about who checks the sovereign. This is where the separation of power between kings (later presidents), parliament and the courts, and between the legislature and the house of review, comes from. The most prominent thinker here is the English philosopher John Locke.

Even separated, these positions are powerful, so we worry about whether the people who occupy them represent the general interest or only their own. So we get democracy, meritocracy and, later, egalitarian welfare states that give everyone a decent opportunity to participate and compete in political and economic life.

The danger for democracy is the 'tyranny of the majority', so we need laws to protect minorities. The writings of the US Founding Fathers are canonical on this point. The associated institutions are things like human rights, due process, anti-discrimination legislation and the harm principle. This doctrine, associated with another English philosopher, John Stuart Mill, holds that the state should refrain from intervening in people's behaviour unless that behaviour directly harms someone else.

There is obviously a lot more that could be said, especially on the co-evolution of free market principles, but this very short sketch is sufficient. The point that needs to be underlined is that democracy is about giving everyone equal political power, albeit in a narrow domain, while liberalism is about checking everyone's power equally. Earlier political philosophies, notably that of Plato (enlightened totalitarianism) and Augustine (theocratic totalitarianism), held that there were 'good' people who could be relied on to rule as benevolent dictators. All that was needed was to get these people into power. In contrast, liberalism holds that pretty much everyone is bad, or at least that power corrupts, while democracy states that everyone should have equal power to elect the sovereign. As such, liberal democracy as an institutional arrangement tries to place different elected powers in opposition to one another. This ensures that public policy can only progress smoothly when there is broad agreement. Policymaking grinds to a halt when society is polarised, as in the USA today, to prevent the tyranny of the narrow majority.

The magic of liberal democracy as an *institutional* arrangement is that it manages moral impasses with a minimum of violence. It is relatively difficult to use the state to impose your views on other people, and the state exists mostly to reduce violence and lubricate commerce. Normative change must therefore come through the public sphere. Moral dialogue is fostered there through institutions like the right to free speech, free press, free association and freedom of religion. Values sometimes change rapidly, as in the case of attitudes to same-sex marriage. Other issues are more acrimonious, like assisted dying laws.

When disagreement cannot be overcome, we take a vote. Majority rules, preferential voting systems, proportional representation and other democratic institutions make it necessary to govern for the centre of politics (where feelings are most moderate and conciliatory) if one wants to maintain power. This encourages compromise. Even in power, the majority that won the vote cannot ride roughshod over the minority that lost. They are constrained by constitutions, legal rights, parliamentary process and bureaucratic procedures. When there is supermajority agreement on an issue, things tend to move quickly, as they did during the Covid pandemic in most OECD nations. When there are bitter divisions, the state cannot act until those divisions are resolved in the public square.

Liberal democracy relies on a 'realist' attitude among citizens. What I mean by that is that each citizen does not seek to rest more power for their side by undermining institutions, because they realise that their enemies will simply use those corrupt institutions when they in turn are in power. Relatedly, politicians, judges and other high-power actors need to be committed to the sanctity of the institutions above the outputs of those institutions.

When liberal democracies collapse into authoritarianism, as in Hungary today, it often begins with a block that is convinced that they are the good guys and their opponents are evil. Not in disagreement, *evil*. You don't parlay, compromise or tolerate evil; you crush it. Liberal democracy dies when the Manichaeism (us vs them logic, where they are devils and 'god is on our side') that it was designed to combat takes hold among voters and political elites. The self-righteous block seizes a greater degree of power than liberal democracy licenses by defying procedural conventions, rewriting institutional rules, stacking courts, politicising public media and corrupting the state in other ways. Knowing that if they ever lose power these corrupt institutions will be turned against them, they move aggressively and ambitiously until the state is completely captured and their enemies marginalised. Free from meaningful political competition, the corrupting influence of power rapidly sets in and we return to moral tyranny and economic kleptocracy.

Liberal democracy is under a strain it has not felt in decades, perhaps ever in the case of the United States, because shared systems of meaning and value have dissolved significantly and this feeds Manichean thinking. People desperately want to feel their preferred system palpably, and they experience people with divergent systems as a threat or an affront. People do not want to engage in dialogue about these things because that involves questioning the most significant aspects of their ideal and ought selves. They cannot practise the openness that Part I counselled because it is too destabilising to their wellbeing. They instead want to shut down different ways of being, and the vehicle for this is the state. The liberal democratic institutions of that state resist being coopted in such a way, so they must be undermined in order to 'get stuff done'.

Even self-avowed liberals engage in this sort of behaviour by sacralising liberalism. They act like liberalism is derived from objective moral order rather than simply being socially expedient. This is most obvious in the immigration policy space. Liberals dismiss anti-immigrant sentiment as racism using the sentiment of human rights and pluralism. They do not want to listen empathetically, and so they cannot hear concerns about cultural dislocation, housing prices, infrastructure congestion and too-rapid change among anti-immigrant activists. Maybe those concerns are misplaced (the economic ones especially),[18] but you will not get through to people if you simply curse them as xenophobes. All you do is encourage them to dig in – you cannot change people's hearts with scorn.

We need to have our disagreements about values out in the public sphere, not through the state. We need to focus on norms, which are cultural, not laws, which are institutional. What we need is a means of restoring some of the collective cultural glue that postmodernism dissolved. This will facilitate a more constructive dialogue between people who see each other as peers in a political community, not enemies in a holy war. How we get this glue is the subject of Chapter 9. Before we get there, I want to evidence how we are in fact living in a period of profound cultural vacuum, and how the illbeing that results is one factor undergirding contemporary political extremism.

## 8.7. Bowling with Trump

> If we want things to stay as they are, things will have to change.
> Giuseppe Tomasi di Lampedusa, *The Leopard*

The biggest political trend in the OECD for the past decade has been the rise of populist, identitarian political candidates and campaigns. Among the most pronounced events in this trend were the election of Donald Trump and Brexit, both in 2016 (Trump's 2024 election is a somewhat different story). Other examples include Bolsonaro's election in Brazil, the rapid and substantial rise of the AfD in Germany, Marine Le Pen running a close second in the presidential election in France, the consolidation of power in Hungary and Poland by Fidesz and the Law and Justice Party, the popularity of the Swedish Democrats and True Finns, and the election of Georgia Meloni's Brothers of Italy, a party with historical associations to Italian fascism. Not since before the Second World War have parties with such ideological leanings been so successful.

What explains this sea-change? There are many factors, from the global financial crisis to a wave of (Islamic) migrants to Europe. I don't have the space here to tease through all these factors and their relative contributions to the success of contemporary identitarianism. I will just try to convince you that a collapse in the sense of shared values and meanings in the West – a normative vacuum – has a significant role to play.

Let's start with Trump in 2016, because this is a case that I am most familiar with, having published on it after my Fulbright Fellowship at the Brookings Institution in Washington, DC.[19] In 2018, John Sides, Michael Tessler and Lynn Vavreck, three political scientists, published their acclaimed wash-up of the causes of Trump's win, *Identity Crisis: The 2016 Presidential Campaign and the Battle for the Meaning of America*. They argue, on the basis of extensive and diverse empirical analysis, that 'racialised economics' was the primary driver of the swing vote for Trump in the rust belt states that won him the election. They write:

> The important sentiment underlying Trump's support was not 'I might lose my job' but, in essence, 'people in my group are losing jobs to that other group'. Instead of pure economic anxiety, what mattered was racialized economics.[20]

One of the puzzling things about this fact is that these same voters broke for Obama in 2008 and 2012. It's hard to say that they're *racist* when they voted for a black president. Something more complex must be going on.

Along with Robert Breunig at the Australian National University and Jan Emmanuelle De Neve at Oxford University, we investigated using the Gallup Daily Poll. This is a nationally representative survey of the US gathering data daily from 500 random residents via landline and mobile phone. We used data from 2013–16, giving us a sample size of around half a million Americans. We were also able to use Google Search trends to develop a measure of racial animus. This method is neat because people are less likely to self-censor when privately browsing the internet than when being asked by researchers about their racial views.

Our hypothesis was that economic and cultural decay in the communities that swung to Trump caused worry and anxiety there. Remember worldview defence theory from section 1.6? According to that theory, such feelings stimulate people to seek social support. If they have access to such support locally, such as from a church group, union, bowling club, sports team, neighbours or close family and friends, they will be buffered against this anxiety. If no support is available locally, they will tend to turn to macro-identities to feel a sense of belonging to some group that can protect them. The most prominent macro-identities are race, nation, class, sexuality and religion – precisely the allegiances at play in partisan identity politics.

We drew a similar hypothesis from self-determination theory. The offshoring of factories overseas and the collapse of community owing to low local tax receipts and mass unemployment, undermined the basic need for autonomy and competence in rust belt counties. People may compensate for these unmet needs by doubling down on relatedness. But again, that relatedness is not available locally owing to the collapse of social capital that Putnam and others have documented (discussed in Chapter 6). So people might turn to macro-identities to get their need for relatedness met, they may become politically activated to seek power in compensation for their lack of autonomy and they may gravitate to a politician who flatters them, as Trump did, to ease their unmet need for competence. These hypotheses are summarised in the figure below:

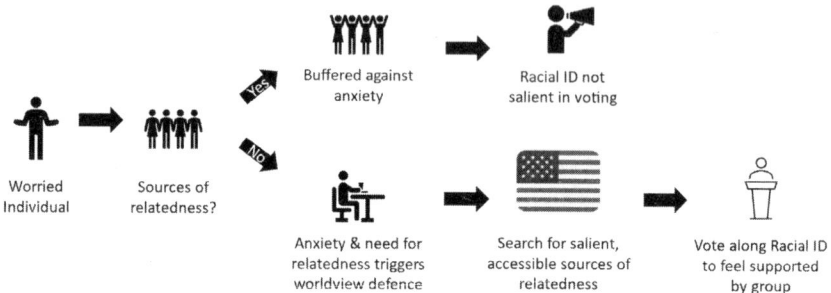

The path from anxiety and isolation to identitarian voting

Our empirical results were complex, but largely bore out these hypotheses. We found that worry had a strong and significant positive relationship with Trump's vote share. However, this relationship was reversed in worried counties that also had high levels of relatedness. Most importantly for the conclusions of Sides, Tessler and Vavreck, we found that the strong positive relationship between racial animus and Trump's vote share disappeared once we controlled for unmet needs for relatedness. These results imply that contemporary identitarianism, especially racial identitarianism, is driven substantially by the confluence of economic decline and community collapse. People need to feel a sense of belonging for their wellbeing, and when they can't get it locally, they turn to populist politicians.

Our results are mirrored elsewhere in the literature on contemporary identitarian populism. Qualitative studies of American identitarian voters emphasise their feelings of cultural dislocation and being economically held back. In *Strangers in Their Own Land*, Arlie Hochschild's writes of how Tea Party voters in Louisiana are 'mourning for a lost way of life'. They feel like the American dream of economic independence is becoming harder to achieve, and people from other groups are being helped to cut in line.

In Todd Carney's *Alienated America*, he argues that Trump's success is primarily a story of people feeling like their communities and their culture are disappearing. This conclusion was based on interviews with Trump voters while Todd was on the campaign trail as a journalist. I met Todd to discuss his book while he was a fellow at the American Enterprise Institute, just up the road from me at Brookings. Over a salad in the charming AEI cafeteria, he told me that he completely missed the story while he was reporting on the election, and only noticed it months later when he was going over his old recordings. This is my memory of what he said:

> I would ask them, 'Why are you voting for Trump?' And they would start saying something like, 'Well, you know, when I was younger we used to have parades here in town every month...' And the crazy thing was, I cut them off! I would jump in and say, 'No, no, no, what I mean is, is it immigrants, or tax cuts, or Afghanistan?' I kept bringing it back to policy. I just couldn't hear them say that it was about community and identity, even though they were being so clear.

In his book, Todd argues that urban elites don't appreciate this story of community decay and cultural threat because they live in places where these things are still healthy. Schools and neighbourhood groups in wealthy suburbs, for example, maintain social capital. Liberal elites in urban centres exist in environments that celebrate their values of pluralism and prosperity every day. They also typically attend campus universities with extremely thick social capital and form lifetime friendships there. It is in the 'left behind' places where normative vacuum is most pronounced.

Alongside this and other qualitative work, we have at least one quantitative study. My friend Diane Bolet from the University of Essex has a fantastic paper looking at the causal effect of community pub closures on Brexit voting, *Drinking Alone: Local Socio-Cultural Degradation and Radical Right Voting* (I preferred the original title, *Pissed*, but the reference to Putnam's *Bowling Alone* is neat). Community pubs are non-profit ventures associated with a club or society, like my one-time local, the Bethnal Green Working Men's Club. It would host drag shows, Warhammer nights and a regular stream of characterful old British labourers straight out of a Martin Amis novel who loved a pint and a game of bridge. Bolet finds that 'individuals living in districts that experience one additional community pub closure... are more likely to support UKIP [the Brexit party] than any other party by 4.3 percentage points'. The loss of local sources of identity and social support leads people to seek identity at the macro level, in this case through nationalism.

That people feel a sense of dislocation when it comes to the values of their fellow Americans is not surprising: the world is changing incredibly fast. Let me offer you a few statistics from the US. According to the 2016 American Values Atlas, 12 per cent of over 65s reported 'no religion' compared to 38 per cent of 18–29-year-olds. Even among self-identified Catholics, weekly church attendance is in free fall across all age groups. It declined from more than 70 per cent in 1995 to only 49 per cent among those over 60 in 2014–17, and only 25 per cent among those in their twenties. Along with the collapse of manufacturing as an organising economic structure, union membership has declined from over 30 per cent in the 1960s to around 10 per cent today. So the main places where people might congregate and organise have dropped off.

Traditional American values are also under strain. According to research by Harvard economist Raj Chetty and his team, the share of children earning more than their parents – a common measure of intergenerational mobility and therefore the American Dream – fell continuously from 90 per cent in 1940 to less than 50 per cent in 1984.[21] It has not recovered. America's pre-eminent position in the global order is also waning, contested by China especially, but also by new multilateral institutions like BRICS (a diplomatic network between Brazil, Russia, China, India and South Africa). Domestically, people are reckoning with America's history of slavery and its contemporary practices of proxy-war and colonialism, thereby poking holes in patriotism. Gender roles are going through a radical transformation. According to Pew Research, less than 30 per cent of women worked full time in 1972, whereas more than 50 per cent do today.[22] Stay-at-home wives and mothers shrunk to less than 20 per cent of the population. Nowadays, more than 30 per cent of women earn more than their husbands.[23] Work is increasingly casualised, with people changing jobs frequently rather than structuring their life around one employer, like Homer Simpson with his job at the nuclear power plant. Meanwhile, the world has globalised, international migration has exploded and technology has changed many aspects of how we live. Of course some people want the rollercoaster to stop.

## Chapter 8 summary

Be the change you want to see in the world.
Mahatma Gandhi

The seriousness, power and binding force of values emerges from people caring about something. You are the source of value in the world and it is both a profound responsibility and an enormous privilege. Don't shirk it or take it for granted. If you want value to feel real then you must acknowledge that some things matter *to you*, you must act with integrity and your promises must mean something. The simplest technique for putting this into practice is that the next time you see some bad that you usually walk past, *don't*. Stop, recognise the gravity of what is occurring, and take some action. It might be small. Indeed, simply taking note might be enough. Martin Luther King Jr could not have sustained his motivation for civil rights if he halted his day every time he encountered racism. But he worked tirelessly on the big picture because he felt that it was important and he frequently reaffirmed that conviction.

You don't need to be a moral legend like MLK, but we can each be mundane moral heroes in our everyday lives. That's how we escape nihilism. Do some volunteering, break up your cardboard boxes before you put them in the bin so there's more space for everyone else's recycling, keep an eye out for who is hurting and go help them, and when you've done something wrong own up to it and make reparations, that sort of thing. Acknowledge and appreciate when other people do good, whether it's a dictator peacefully handing over power or your neighbour handling interactions with the council on behalf of your tower block. Morality is something we sustain collectively, and so it is crucial that we do not think of it as a purely personal project. Get involved with others in practising your ethics together and cheer each other along.

How do we get this done at scale? It's all good to feel close to people in our clubs or our neighbourhoods, but we live today in big nations and a globalised world, and it doesn't feel well. There's sorrow, hatred and desperation everywhere, and subterranean feelings of nihilism are making it worse by stoking our Manichean prejudices. This problem has been growing for some time. Going by when European intellectuals first started discussing the subject, we've been in an existential vacuum since the nineteenth century. It was a major factor behind the rise of totalitarianism around the Second World War. We horrified ourselves so badly with that political experiment that we filled in the vacuum since with materialism. But that's not cutting the mustard for younger generations, and so the fever of culture wars is spiking again. To understand this issue, how it relates to wellbeing, and what *we* can do about it, we need to go a little deeper into the history of modernism, postmodernism and what comes next: metamodernism. That's the subject of our final chapter.

# 9

## Metamodernity

What is the sound of one hand clapping?

Zen Koan

At the end of the previous chapter, I noted how the world is changing incredibly fast and some people understandably want to get off the rollercoaster. That's part of why we have so much *reactionary* politics – the politics of going back, of putting your foot down, of saying 'enough!' Other people are desperate for their turn on the ride, so they're pushing for things to go even faster. We live in partisan times.

A combustible ingredient in the contemporary cultural bonfire is that centrist 'moderate' liberals are also being radicalised. They see the past seventy years or so as a glorious time. Coming out of the Second World War, the architect of the British welfare state, William Beveridge, identified five great evils: want, disease, ignorance, squalor and idleness. Liberal democracy and free-market welfare states have slain these giants. The income, life expectancy, educational attainment, living conditions and employment of most of the world has improved astronomically. How can anyone be upset?! Even more so, how can anyone want to throw out these institutions that have achieved so much for some vague cultural vision?

The liberals are blinkered by their narrowly economic vision of the good life. I was guilty of this myself. The first book I published was an edited volume during my PhD in economics with my supervisor, Robert Breunig, called *Hybrid Public Policy Innovations: Contemporary Policy Beyond Ideology*. It was a distillation of the smart, technical side of neoliberalism. It explained the comparative advantages of government and market tools in policy design, and how astute combinations of the two – hybrid policies – could simultaneously promote efficiency and equity. Half the chapters were case studies of the biggest success stories: Denmark's flexicurity system for industrial relations and Australia's HECS system for university financing, for example. I say the 'smart side' of neoliberalism because neoliberalism in some places, notably the US since Reagan and the UK since Thatcher, is prosecuted in a dumber, more ideological rather than technical way that is often in contradiction of economic logic. Thatcher's privatisation of the railways, for example, makes little sense to academic economists because railways are a natural monopoly.

When we wrote *Hybrid Public Policy Innovations*, I thought what the world needed was more such policies. I still think that, but I also recognise that this policymaking paradigm has nothing to offer people anxious about the decline of religion, or impatient for trans-rights, or ready to defend 'European values' against migration, or eager for a reckoning with slavery, or horrified about the opioid epidemic tearing through decayed communities, or yearning for a world in which we stand for something, together. These people feel a *psychological* pain, they need a *cultural* fix, and they express themselves *politically*. These are all the things that economics is bad at. And liberalism – live and let live – is no salve to someone who desperately wants cohesion rather than diversity. Indeed, liberalism caused a lot of these issues, so, much as I love it, I recognise that more of the same isn't much of an answer.

What we need is a more conscious, deliberate and wise focus on cultural issues alongside economic ones. I don't mean culture wars. I mean empathy, creativity and fraternity. I mean a dialogue where we hear each other's fears, share our hopes and dreams, and write a new story that we can all get a piece of. That is the project of metamodernity. To understand it, we've got to take a quick history tour.

## 9.1. Modernism

> God is dead. But considering the state of the species Man is in, there will perhaps be caves, for ages yet, in which his shadow will be shown.
> Friedrich Nietzsche, *The Gay Science*

To understand what metamodernism is, we need to go back to what came before – modernity and postmodernity. We need to sketch and track the normative history of the West in order to see how the systems of meaning and value that we used to make ethical sense of our lives and worlds have changed over recent centuries.

Modernity has its roots in the seventeenth-century Enlightenment or 'age of reason'. It was characterised by two sympathies growing stronger among elites: rationality and humanism. There was a commensurate weakening of the status quo values of tradition and religiosity. These intellectual shifts were paralleled by transformations in technology and political economy, namely the shift from an aristocratic, feudal economy based on farming in the countryside to a mercantile, capitalist economy based on manufacturing in cities.

The socio-psychological consequences of these trends are masterfully analysed in Georg Simmel's *The Metropolis and Mental Life*, one of the seminal texts of sociology. Small towns and rural communes are characterised by what social scientists call 'thick' or 'tight' culture.[1] Such cultures emphasise relationships and institutions rather than individuals and tend to be conservative. They value order, conformity and hierarchy, and strictly police deviation from norms. In contrast, the 'thin' or 'loose' cultures that are common in metropolises put more value on individual expression. This results in less policing of deviation from norms and less of a status quo of norms in general.

This is why the growing dominance of metropolises in human geography over the past two centuries has coincided with a widespread dissolution of shared cultural norms. It also explains why so much of the partisan divide in contemporary Western politics is better explained by rural–urban geography rather than traditionally left–right ideological identities.

A key observation from Simmel with respect to wellbeing is that while the metropolis provides more scope for self-expression, it is also harder to be recognised for your individuality there. You are free to be who you want to be in a modern city; nobody cares that you're gay, obsessed with Victorian fashion, participate in civil war re-enactments or whatever else it is that defines your values. That's great for self-actualisation, but potentially quite lonely. We want to live out and practise our values with other people. We want to be recognised by them and feel a sense of shared endeavour. Tight, thick culture limits the scope of what we can value without oppression, but whatever we do is collective and palpable.

Modernism's destabilisation of traditional values really picked up steam in the early twentieth century. The First World War saw working-class men sent by aristocratic officers to die in their millions for nothing in particular. This swept away nationalistic sentiment and accelerated the emergence of class consciousness. While the men were dying in the trenches, women moved into factories, demonstrating that they could do men's work and accelerate feminism. The roaring twenties gave people a taste of prosperity, but the party quickly crashed into the Great Depression. Years of soaring unemployment and crippling poverty triggered by a stock market collapse destroyed any nascent faith in unbridled capitalism, free markets and 'robber baron' merchants to deliver a desirable future.

Very little was left, culturally speaking, and with nihilism beckoning on a sociological scale, totalitarianism stepped into the breach. Fascism and communism provide simple systems of meaning and value based either on race and nation or economic class that are extended to all aspects of life by an overbearing state. Because they are partly a response to the terror of nihilism, these totalitarian doctrines can brook no dissent whatsoever and are thus tyrannical and extremist in practice. The bad faith of the 'serious men' that governed these states allowed them to send millions of Jews to the gas chambers and millions of dissidents to the gulag, all while believing themselves righteous.

The mid-twentieth century was characterised by the Cold War between Soviet communism and American capitalism, which saw material progress sacralised. The wars had made industrial output central to daily life and we wanted something nice after the horrors of those years, so we turned to 'growth' as a new god to worship. Europe was in ashes and totalitarianism had revealed our darkest daemons, but we had also split the atom and founded the United Nations. Hope was in fashion, and we got to work building welfare states. The threat of nuclear Armageddon hung over everything, but life also seemed to be getting better for most people. That was the naive optimist view anyway; it didn't last...

## 9.2. Postmodernism

> The old world is dying, the new world is struggling to be born; now is the time of monsters.
> Antonio Gramsci, *Prison Notebooks*[2]

Modernism's naive hopefulness terminated in postmodernism, which marked the period from 1970–2000, give or take. I'm going to analyse its characteristics through the ideas of the three intellectuals I take to be most commonly associated with it – Jean-François Lyotard, Jacques Derrida and Michel Foucault – all

French philosophers. This isn't because these guys 'invented' postmodernism. They rather articulated ideas and vibes that were key to the sentiment of the postmodern era.

Lyotard defined the postmodern condition as 'incredulity towards metanarratives'. These are maps of meaning that claim universal truth, such as Christian cosmology, Marxism's dialectical materialism or the 'self-evident' claims of the US constitution: that all men are created equal and endowed by their creator with inalienable rights to life, liberty and the pursuit of happiness. Metanarratives are totalising. They try to explain everything, including what is good and right. This then justifies the acolytes of a metanarrative to organise their life and that of everyone else according to the metanarrative.

The decades leading up to postmodernism were a cascade of crises stemming substantially from metanarratives – nationalism in the First World War, unbridled capitalism in the Great Depression, fascism in the Second World War, and capitalism and communism in the Cold War. By the 1970s, metanarratives seemed more trouble than they were worth. Meanwhile, the free-wheeling culture of the '50s and '60s, with rock and roll, the civil rights movement, second-wave feminism and the psychedelic love fest of the hippies, had shown that culture could be more diverse and inclusive. So postmodernism saw a shift away from the One Big Story offered by competing metanarratives to the mindset that truth is plural, context dependent, relative and subjective, and so we should have many equally valid stories operating all at once in society.

Derrida wins the award for the most arcane of all philosophers in a very competitive field. He received an assessment as an undergrad wherein the lecturer said his writing was 'quite unintelligible' and 'totally incomprehensible'. It went on: 'you seem to be constantly on the verge of something interesting but, somehow, you always fail to explain it clearly'. This is exactly how I would describe Derrida's later academic writings too, but a lot of philosophers, literary theorists, artists and other intellectual types disagree with me. He was a minor celebrity internationally and especially in France in his heyday, and he left an indelible mark on the humanities. Given both the breadth of his writings and their impenetrability, the summary I am about to provide is exceedingly crude and probably inaccurate. I give it anyway because it captures what matters about his work to me and my thinking.

Derrida's theory of 'deconstruction' reveals how meaning is only sustained intersubjectively. From his early writings, Derrida criticised the philosophical fixation with absolute truth. To describe, categorise and theorise about reality, we need to describe it in language. But the meaning of words is not fixed, it is constructed. There is no stable set of meanings out there to be discovered, only meanings that we agree to abide by as a collective. This is the origin of his most famous quote: 'There is nothing outside the text.'

I have a lot of reservations about Derrida's claims. They are pithily summarised by the joke that a room full of first-rate postmodernist philosophers could not 'socially construct' a hungry lion as anything other than a threat. The lion is an objective reality, the meaning of which we all understand and to which our evolved physiology responds in a pre-linguistic way – not all reality is socially constructed and there is a great deal that is outside the text. Nonetheless, I think Derrida's arguments work quite well for moral concepts, and these were the target of some of his most famous writings, specifically the notion of 'justice'.

The view of natural law is that there are moral truths out there in the universe that the law tries to approximate and put into practice. Derrida points out that difficult legal cases, even when there is some precedent to draw on, involve a creative act of interpretation and are thus not the straightforward application of a rule, natural or otherwise. There is thus a substantially subjective element in law. Furthermore, in matters of justice, we always need to act *urgently*, with an imperfect knowledge of what is good and right, and so in the application of law there is again always an element of subjectivity, power and violence from a powerful party against a weaker one. We can never get 'pure' justice.

In other words, law is performative. When we engage in law, we are not applying abstract truths of justice. We are instead ceremonially instantiating our social preferences, or rather the preferences of those with power. This is what's known in legal theory as 'positive law' – law that is constructed by humans, rather than received from the universe. Our barristers dress up in gowns and put on wigs, we rise for the judge, they bang the gavel and intone legislation from hallowed parliaments or previous judgements from esteemed colleagues, and we are called to respect the authority of the court. This is ritual. Lawyers try very hard to be logical, consistent and reasonable in their work, and they succeed by and large, but at its root law is a cultural practice.

All this talk of power leads us to the most influential postmodern philosopher, Foucault. A crude summary of Foucault's insight is that, sociologically speaking, claims to truth are power in disguise. Perhaps his most famous illustration of this idea came from his analysis of the history of 'mental illness', *Madness and Civilisation: The Birth of the Asylum.* The argument of this book is that notions of lunacy and institutions to house the insane emerged out of an effort to manage behaviour according to bourgeois ideals. Clear examples of this that were topical in the postmodern era are the treatment of homosexuality and female frigidity as derangements. It may be possible to make an empirical observation without being especially entangled with power, e.g. 'this person likes to have intercourse with people of the same sex'. But as soon as you make a value judgement like 'and that's unhealthy', you're in the domain of values and, thus, power.

Foucault's extensive body of work, which also includes treatises on the criminal justice system, the health care system and the whole scientific enterprise, is a profound indictment of *expertise*.

It reflected a general loss of respect for intellectual authority and the institutions that rely on it, like central banks, government regulators, the Intergovernmental Panel on Climate Change, universities and public intellectuals. This isn't to say that these institutions are hopelessly compromised, merely that the notion of dispassionate technocratic rule according to science and analytical philosophy, which many rationalist types think would be ideal, is a chimera. It is certainly not something for which there is broad popular support.

To summarise, postmodern sentiments included:

- Little trust in metanarratives and growing respect for plural perspectives.

- A recognition that we are cut off from absolute truth and stuck with imperfect meanings that we often disagree on.

- An awareness that what our institutions and even our experts deem 'good' is substantially a function of who has power, which isn't inherently good or evil.

This amounts to a nihilistic swamp. All value claims are undermined. A kind of apathetic cynicism takes over culture where attempts to say what's good and right are met with hostility, summarised by the iconic catchphrase of the main character in *The Big Lebowski*: 'Well, that's just, like, your opinion, man.' By the time of my youth, this acidic attitude to traditional notions of truth, beauty, righteousness and wellbeing had dissolved Western popular culture into a thin gruel of boy bands, the 'Fine, I guess I'll save the world' attitude of *Buffy the Vampire Slayer* and Homer Simpson just living his life.

The hostility of postmodernism to value claims was necessary to raise collective consciousness to the way we create, sustain and enforce values, and it is understandable that our first instinct was to stop oppressing people and just 'live and let live'. But we ended up with a life that is grey and mundane, while being simultaneously confronted with colossal moral challenges like climate change. Metamodernism is the natural progression of this postmodern ennui into an energetic effort to re-enchant the world.

## 9.3. Metamodernism

> Fall in love with some activity, and do it! Nobody ever figures out what life is all about, and it doesn't matter. Explore the world. Nearly everything is really interesting if you go into it deeply enough. Work as hard and as much as you want to on the thing you like to do the best. Don't think about what you want to be, but what you want to do. Keep up some kind of a minimum with other things so that society doesn't stop you from doing anything at all.
> Richard P. Feynman, theoretical physicist, from a letter to Vincent A. Van Der Hyde compiled in *Perfectly Reasonable Deviations from the Beaten Track*

Metamodernism is an emerging 'cultural mode' that responds to the existential vacuum created by postmodernism without a reactionary return to bad faith. It is an amalgam of modern and postmodern sentiment in that it departs from postmodern cynicism towards objective values and absolute truth while also expressing the modernist desire for liberty, equality and fraternity. Metamodernism is the appropriate culture mode for an ambiguous universe – it is the cultural mode of Nietzsche's free spirit. As such, it holds the potential to transcend the twentieth-century vacillation between totalising ideologies and nihilism and step into a new way of being for humanity.

Metamodernism seeks a combination of freedom and seriousness. Its postmodern side is allergic to attempts to write values into the firmament or use the state to prosecute some beliefs and persecute others. It perceives these cynically as efforts by the powerful to impose their values on others, and it recoils from the harm such efforts cause to people who don't fit in. The institutions of the state, and hard power more broadly, must be reserved for minimalist laws required for peaceful coexistence, not for promoting certain views of what is good or evil, healthy or ill, natural or perverted. Values should be contested in the cultural domain, not the legal one. This postmodern side fosters normative freedom. It allows people to navigate ambiguity however it works for them; finding their groups and forming subcultures that sustain the systems of meaning and value that they want to live in.

But postmodernism is nihilistic. The freedom from power that it demands seems to undermine seriousness. If anything can be valuable, then isn't nothing especially sacred? And if postmodernism is right and all value-claims are just the veiled hand of power, then how can we establish a palpable normative project at a group level? Organisation at a meaningful scale necessarily involves some degree of hierarchy, authority and influence.

This is where the modernist desire for a 'better world' comes in. Metamodernism takes as its foundation the idea that a 'better world' means something different for everyone, but otherwise retains modernism's earnest belief that such a world is possible. What's necessary is to reject the idea that such a better world can be *derived* from reason or scientific inquiry. Instead, it must be *created* by the spontaneous expression of value by free individuals, and the coalescence of like-minded individuals into communities that share and sustain those values on a liberal basis.

Here is how it works. An individual who loves something puts that value out into the world. They join a tennis club, they start a subreddit for building matchstick models of the *Titanic*, they install some pot plants on the communal balcony, whatever... In some form they say: 'These are my values and I'm going to be over here living them; if you value these things too, come over here and let's live this life together.' All that's needed for values to feel serious and promote wellbeing is for people to practise them together. This is the psychological root of the increasingly common sentiment that 'home is not a place, it's people'. Metamodernism is perfectly capable of bringing this about, and unlike more authoritarian approaches, it allows a thousand cultural flowers to bloom.

This way of creating collective maps of meaning is why the fundamental attitudes of metamodernism are sincerity, earnestness and goodwill in contrast to postmodern cynicism. When you express your values, you can't be shy about it, or coy, or half-arsed. Your values define you and the world you want to live in – take them seriously! Put them out into the world with the conviction of someone ready to live their life by those principles and try to convince others of their worth. We must be earnest because there is no foundation to value except our care and enthusiasm.

A pop-cultural manifestation of this shift from cynicism to earnestness is evident in the style of internet memes. These began as simple graphic jokes that almost invariably used irony to undermine value claims in some way. Early meme formats like ermagherd girl, philosiraptor and bad luck Brian evolved into the 'memelord' and 'Pepe' formats which were often used for pure shitposting. This is postmodernism in final form: utilising a crappy looking image and low-effort production to undermine the very idea of meaningful dialogue. With the metamodern turn, however, memes have changed. The clearest example is 'wholesome memes', which are characterised by uncomplicated positive messages, like grandmothers basking in their grandchildren's crayon drawings. There is no obvious 'joke' in these memes, only good vibes. The implicit joke is on the sour attitude of traditional memes, which wholesome memes invert.

Metamodern culture recognises that we cannot tease or bully the sincere earnestness of people expressing their values, as was common in postmodernism, because doing so undermines the possibility of our own access to a sense of palpable meaning and value. Only 'giving a f**k' can arrest nihilism, and so we need to celebrate it when people do, not call it lame. As Rick says to Morty: 'To live is to risk it all; otherwise you're just an inert chunk of randomly assembled molecules drifting wherever the universe blows you.'[3]

This transformation in attitudes between postmodernism and metamodernism is hilariously captured in the 2012 cinematic reboot of *21 Jump Street*. The film sees two young police officers, Schmidt and Jenko, sent to work undercover in a high school to uncover a drug-dealing operation. When they were really in high school in the '90s, Jenko mercilessly bullied Schmidt, but they've since become friends. Jenko promises to teach Schmidt the ways of the cool kids so he can fit in better on his second attempt at high school. Lesson one is postmodern: don't care about anything.

They arrive at school and are immediately accosted by Eric, the coolest of the kids, for driving a gas guzzling muscle car. He explains that, 'we try to ride bikes when we can, global crisis and whatnot'. Jenko replies, 'Whatever, man, I don't care about anything.' Eric is affronted, 'Oh, you don't care about the environment?! That's kind of f\*\*cked up, man.' They are interrupted by Juario, who asks them to be quiet so he can study. Jenko sees an opportunity to establish his postmodern cool credentials: 'Ha ha ha, look at him, he's trying, he's actually trying, what a nerd.' After a brief altercation, Jenko punches Juario in the face, and the schoolyard turns on him for being a bully. As it turns out, what's cool in metamodernism is caring, and trying, and being kind.

Metamodernism affirms a liberal foundation for group cohesion. In the past, we typically socialised people into systems of meaning and value from birth or through practices that resemble hazing. A relatively benign example is teaching children table manners. Another example is sending kids to Sunday School at church to learn scripture. A secular example is the constant literacy and numeracy testing that British schoolkids have been increasingly subjected to over four decades of neoliberal education policy. These tests socialise kids into regarding literacy and numeracy as more valuable than say, interpersonal or creative skills, and undergirds a focus on schooling for work rather than life.

Rather than socialisation into value systems, metamodernism emphasises free association. You are encouraged to respect difference and be capable of self-actualisation, and then you find a space in society that fits you. The borders of metamodernism's subcultures are more porous than those of traditional cultures, contested more intensely but also more gently, and policed less strictly. There is an appreciation that value often emerges from intermingling amidst diversity.

This is one reason why remixes and dramatic reboots like N. D. Stevenson's *She-Ra and the Princesses of Power*, and genre-bending media like Beyoncé's incredibly metamodern album *Cowboy Carter* are so common in metamodernity. We are no longer engaging in the deconstructive inversion and subversion of postmodernism. We are seeking something fresh, magical and meaningful in recombination and reimagination.

The openness and affirmation of metamodernism is undergirded by its third principal character virtue: kindness. We increasingly recognise that it is hard to get by spiritually amidst the abyss postmodernism has wrought, and the various material crisis we face like pandemics, ecological collapse and war. Bullying people into conformity with cultures that have led to this present moment serves nobody. So be kind. I think this is well put by the American professional wrestler, actor and pop culture icon John Cena: 'Have the patience to understand that most all of us are simply trying to find our place and purpose in a very complex world.'

This empathy and kindness in metamodernism is contested by 'cancel culture', and so the spirit of the age is still to be decided. Conservative cancel culture warriors want to silence all the new things that threaten their serious traditions, like trans people, childless career women and a deep reckoning with America's history of slavery. The progressive cancel culture warriors want to silence any discussion of what is good and useful in the status quo. Like maybe meritocracy is mostly a good ideal, the liberal international order is more peaceful than imperial, and the family remains an effective institution for romance and childrearing. Where metamodern sentiment wants to replace postmodern grey with the rainbow, cancel culture wants to separate it into black and white. We need to make sure metamodernism wins this contest for the soul of the twenty-first century by embracing its love of community without conformity.

In its encouragement of sincerity, earnestness, kindness and fraternity, we can recognise that metamodernism is characterised by intuition and emotion over reason. We need to re-enchant the world after its disenchantment by modern science and postmodern critique. This romantic project necessarily requires an abundance of *feeling* relative to thinking. We need to imbue objects, people and practices with meaning, narrative, value and sanctity, and this is not something that is effectively achieved by rational argument. It is instead most straightforwardly prosecuted by raw expressions of sentimentality and people with whom that sentiment resonates meeting you where you are.

The medium of feeling is art, and no piece of art is closer to the distilled essence of metamodernism than the film *Everything, Everywhere, All at Once*. It is the subject of the next section.

## 9.4. Everything, Everywhere, All at Once

> Love is such a powerful force. It's there for everyone to embrace – that kind of unconditional love for all of humankind. That is the kind of love that impels people to go into the community and try to change conditions for others, to take risks for what they believe in.
> Coretta Scott King, author, activist, and civil rights leader

*Everything, Everywhere, All at Once* won six academy awards in 2023, including best actress, best supporting actor, best picture, best writing and best directing. The film has won dozens of other awards. Perhaps more importantly, it was an unexpectedly huge commercial success, grossing over $140 million worldwide off a production budget of only $25 million. I think it's safe to say that *Everything, Everywhere* gave expression to the zeitgeist in a way few films ever have; the metamodern zeitgeist. The film is a metaphorical articulation of everything I said in section 9.3. above, so I want to analyse it at some length in the hopes that it will make those ideas stick.

I will start with a brief summary of the plot, but everyone should really watch it before or perhaps after reading this section. It's art. It's meant to be understood experientially, not analytically. I can't capture all the ways it expresses itself here. Obviously, there are massive spoilers ahead.

Evelyn and Waymond are two migrants from Hong Kong to San Francisco. They run a failing laundromat and are hounded by the tax authorities. They have a daughter, Joy, who is disaffected. Evelyn and Joy have a difficult relationship because Evelyn is uncomfortable with her daughter's lesbianism and tattoos, and disappointed in her own lack of worldly success. Waymond tries to look on the bright side, keeping people cheerful with antics and optimism. The tax authorities threaten to possess the laundromat to recover unpaid taxes, and all hope seems lost.

As her world caves in, Evelyn is visited by Alpha Waymond – Waymond from another universe. That universe's Evelyn invented a device that allows the user to inhabit versions of themselves in other universes and borrow knowledge from their minds. Unfortunately, one user, Jobu Tupaki, became so adept at using the device that they in a sense became one with the multiverse. Now they are everything, everywhere, all at once, capable of manipulating space to their desires. And their main desire seems to be killing Evelyn in every universe.

It turns out that Jobu is actually Joy from the Alphaverse – the universe in which the multiverse traversing technology originated. Joy was pushed so hard by her mother's tiger parenting that she surpassed the limits of the traversing technology. But her awareness of the multiverse left her with a nihilistic affliction. She has created 'the everything bagel' – a sort of existential black hole at the centre of the multiverse that is slowly sucking up all time and space:

> I got bored one day and I put everything on a bagel. Everything. All my hopes and dreams, my old report cards, every breed of dog, every last personal ad on Craigslist. Sesame. Poppy seed. Salt. And it collapsed in on itself. 'Cause, you see, when you really put everything on a bagel, it becomes this... the truth... nothing matters.

Evelyn is recruited by the Alphaverse to try and kill Jobu. They believe that her total failure in life – her inability to realise any potential – makes her capable of mastering the traverse technology to explore all possibilities simultaneously, like Jobu. She visits several universes and explores different ways her life could have gone, including one world where she is a rich and famous celebrity. But before she can master the technology, Jobu appears and takes her on a ride around the universe to the everything bagel. Evelyn resists her daughter's nihilism, rediscovering her love for her. She eventually defends Jobu in a climactic battle with the soldiers of the Alphaverse who are desperate to slay Jobu. The conflict is resolved by Waymond, who counsels peace between the factions.

The backdrop for *Everything, Everywhere* is postmodern capitalism. Jobu is raised by a tiger mother to be competitive and productive at work. This parental abuse transforms her into a demigod, granting her limitless possibility. But all this potential feels empty without her mother's love, especially when she is excluded and then hunted by the Alphaverse. Worldly success does not bring us wellbeing if it leaves us alienated from each other and competing in defensive status signalling. Lonely and unable to care about anything, Jobu creates the everything bagel in an attempt at nihilistic suicide:

Do you know why I actually built the bagel? It wasn't to destroy everything. It was to destroy myself. I wanted to see if I went in, could I finally escape? Like, actually die. At least this way... I don't have to do it alone.

This is a major trope of existentialist writings. For example, I quoted de Beauvoir in Chapter 8: 'It is possible that a person may refuse to love anything on earth; they will prove this refusal and carry it out by suicide.'[4] And there is the infamous claim from Camus that opens the *Myth of Sisyphus*: 'There is only one serious philosophical problem and that is suicide. Deciding whether or not life is worth living is to answer the fundamental question in philosophy.' (I know it's a meme, but it's amazing how many dudes will dedicate their lives to philosophy instead of just going to therapy.)

The set design, costuming and cinematography of Jobu Tupaki are as important as her dialogue. They are a bold representation of the irony and pastiche that were characteristic of postmodern art, fashion and popular culture. In Jobu's first appearance, she strides out of the shadows with pink hair walking a pig on a leash while dressed like Elvis and proceeds to murder security guards by transforming them into confetti, flamenco dancing them to death and hitting them with pro-wrestling moves. Her final win pose is a reference to classic kung fu movies, except instead of holding swords she is wielding giant dildos she just beat a man to death with. She pretends to get shot but then transforms the situation into a piss-take of organic ketchup advertising. The sequence is designed to be absurd, to upend established customs and expectations, and to make a mockery of the way things are 'supposed to be'.

The artistry around the everything bagel is similarly masterful in its symbolism. The bagel is housed in a sort of temple, with high-priest Jobu wearing a bagel – a big 0 – as a headdress. The message is that postmodernism worships nihilism, or rather 'nothing'. As Jobu herself says: 'If nothing matters, then all the pain and guilt you feel for making nothing of your life goes away.' Jobu's reference to making nothing of your life is aimed at competitive productivity culture, in which she can feel like a failure even though she has worked her guts out to master her mother's technology. It is a call-out to the emptiness many high-performing graduates experience when their years of educational toil achieve them a job in a private equity firm where they can toil further, but this time for the validation of a manager instead of their parents.

The rest of the film is the transition from this postmodern existential vacuum to metamodernism. It is an affirmation of our capacity to create meaning and value through our will and care, especially through small acts rather than the sort of extrinsic 'success' that competitive capitalism worships. It starts in the universe where Jobu and Evelyn are just rocks, existing. Evelyn fights past this empty reality to express love for her daughter by hugging her rock with her own. It reaches its zenith in Waymond's dialogue to Evelyn in the parallel universe where they are both successful in Hong Kong, she as a glamorous actress and he as a CEO:

> You think I'm weak, don't you? All those years ago when we first fell in love, your father would say I was too sweet for my own good. Maybe he was right. You tell me it's a cruel world and we're all running around in circles. I know that. I've been on this earth just as many days as you. When I choose to see the good side of things, it's not being naive. It is strategic and necessary. It's how I've learnt to survive through everything. I know you see yourself as a fighter. Well, I see myself as one too. This is how I fight. So even though you have broken my heart yet again, I wanted to say, in another life, I would have really liked just doing laundry and taxes with you.

Waymond is here expressing the core sentiments of metamodernism: sincerity, earnestness, vulnerability and care. He acknowledges the nihilistic insights of postmodernism – 'You tell me it's a cruel world and we're all running around in circles; I know that' – but meets them with an affirmation that positivity, optimism and relationships matter to him anyway. That's how he fights against tragedy. The meaninglessness of laundry and taxes is just a staging ground for human connection and intersubjective meaning-making.

CEO Waymond's lines are delivered interspersed with another set of dialogue from laundromat Waymond during the climactic fight with the Alphaverse soldiers. It underscores the last sentiment of metamodernism, perhaps the most important one, kindness:

> Please! Please! Can we... can we just stop fighting? I know you are all fighting because you are scared and confused. I'm confused too. All day, I don't know what the heck is going on. But somehow, this feels like it's all my fault. I don't know. The only thing I do know... is that we have to be kind. Please, be kind – especially when we don't know what's going on.

This kindness is the gentle, gregarious and hopeful side of metamodernism. It is joyous even, if we consider that what Evelyn recognises in Waymond in the following moments is his boundless positive energy even amidst upheaval, poverty, struggle and strife. The googly eyes that he pastes about the place to lighten the mood are a symbolic representation of this earnestness and an inversion of the nihilistic everything bagel. Waymond expresses the metamodern view that things are a bit chaotic right now, but we can get through it to a world we can believe in if we care for each other in the meantime. If we resort to violent oppression of the new world or cancel culture in order to protect it, we will just destroy ourselves.

Waymond's hope to press through nihilism with good vibes is juxtaposed against the reactionary conservatism of the Alphaverse. They are a symbolic representation of all the culture warriors who want to exit the nihilism of post-modernity by *going back* to old systems of meaning and value – people like Jordan Peterson or Chris Rufo, or even some liberals and rationalists whose faith in science is challenged by postmodern sentiment. This is explicit in Alpha Wang's explanation of his mission to Evelyn about the everything bagel:

> She's been building something. We thought it was some sort of black hole. But it appears to consume more than just light and matter. We don't know exactly what it is. We don't know what it's for. But we can all feel it. You've been feeling it too, haven't you? Something is off. Your clothes never wear as well the next day. Your hair never falls in quite the same way. Even your coffee tastes... wrong. Our institutions are crumbling. Nobody trusts their neighbour anymore. And you stay up at night wondering to yourself... [Evelyn: how can we get back?]... This is the Alphaverse's mission – to take us back to how it's supposed to be.

It's appropriate that the Alphaverse is led by Evelyn's father, Jobu's grandfather. It is meant to represent the death grip of outmoded worldviews, and their willingness to maintain influence through violence. Postmodernism must be killed, according to such culture warriors, not moved beyond. They are terrified of the abyss and looking for solid ground, unwilling to let go of their insubstantial ropes and learn to dance.

Jobu has a small snippet of dialogue that connects these sentiments of the Alphaverse with bad faith and authoritarianism: '"Right" is a small box invented by people who are afraid, and I know what it feels like to be trapped inside that box.' Joy as a lesbian, Asian migrant with limited capitalist ambition is exactly the sort of person who cannot self-actualise and flourish in Alphaverse culture. What's more, she is actively repressed by that culture, first as Joy, who is press-ganged by her mother into being productive, and then as Jobu by the Alphaverse soldiers who fear the pluralism she represents.

The multiverse is a symbol of ambiguity and the power of choice. In one universe, things turned out one way; in another universe, a different way. All possibilities are open, nothing is fixed 'for all possible worlds', as philosophers would say. That the multiverse is such a prominent trope in Western popular culture at the moment – notably in the Marvel cinematic universe – is testament to the rising awareness of our normative freedom in our collective unconscious. We are transitioning from the bummed-out, apathetic cynicism of postmodernism to a more awe-inspired, adventurous and intrepid metamodernism. Part of this movement is to stop coping with shit in life to 'get on with it' and instead stopping long enough to heal from the shit and figure out where we want to go.

## 9.5. Healing not coping

> No person, trying to take responsibility for her or his identity, should have to be so alone. There must be those among whom we can sit down and weep and still be counted as warriors.
>
> Adrienne Rich, *Sources*

High modernity was a reaction to trauma. Two world wars, a great depression, the holocaust, nuclear bombs, millions dead, cities laid waste. The economic growth and materialism that went on through the second half of the twentieth century was driven in large part by the need to rebuild. But it was also driven in large part by the need to get past the trauma. We couldn't dwell on the past because it was too overwhelming. We had to 'get on with it'.

You can see this in the extreme work fixation of the interwar silent generation and the post-war baby boomers. The US Congress, to take one example, is stacked with members of this generation who cannot fathom retirement. The most obvious is Dianne Feinstein, who refused to step down at ninety years of age despite obvious dementia and a frequent inability to attend office owing to a variety of illnesses. She seemed committed to being carried out of the senate in a coffin.

Another example is my colleague Chris from my days as a tennis coach; a top bloke and almost an uncle to me in that era. He was a migrant to Australia from Eastern Europe. For nearly his entire life he worked from 7 a.m.–3 p.m. as a skilled technician, then came down to the club to coach for another four hours. By the time I knew him he was in his 60s and had retired from his technical job but was still coaching. He was divorced and his daughter had moved out, so he owned a house too large for him in the most expensive part of Sydney and seemed kind of bored to me. Once a month he'd sit me down to tell me how, 'You've got to work f**ckin' hard, Mark.' It was a bit ironic because I was at the club from 7 a.m.–9 p.m. for six-and-a-half days a week, either training, coaching, groundskeeping or running the clubhouse. The bigger irony was that it seemed to me like Chris had too much money from working and too few fruits of other sorts of labours. When you're grinding twelve hours a day, it doesn't leave much time for hobbies, relationships, holidays, art or the other things that give life verve.

For Chris and Feinstein's generations, it didn't matter so much what you did with your life as that you did something, preferably all the time. In contrast, my generation, the millennials, are often disparagingly referred to as 'the meaning generation'. Money and stuff doesn't hold the same allure, perhaps because we are priced out of real estate anyway. But more importantly, we need a reason *why* we are doing something, especially a job that we don't especially like. We refuse to 'get on with it' because it doesn't seem like we're getting anywhere.

There is a growing sense among the youth that we have 'arrived' economically.[5] There isn't a need for more growth, and there certainly isn't a need to swallow our frustrations or sacrifice our happiness in order to grind out a bit more income. Our society is post-scarcity; it's just a matter of redistribution, or even using what we've got more effectively. Cuba has the same literacy rates and life expectancy as the United States despite having only an eighth of its GDP. We're also cooking the planet with our energy needs, killing biodiversity with our farming and trashing the environment with all the stuff we buy. Maybe 'getting on' with whatever it is that we're doing isn't such a good idea.

If there's no need to 'cope' with long work hours, bosses pushing their swallowed shit down the hierarchy for validation, exploitative firms or ravenous capitalism, and if there's no need to 'eat bitterness', as Xi Jinping counselled China's youth, then we can focus instead on 'healing'. That means an honest, painful, wholehearted reckoning with past traumas like colonialism, comfort women and slavery. As Beyoncé sings in 'Amen', the closing track of her incredibly metamodern album *Cowboy Carter*: 'We'll be the ones that purify our father's sins'. It means new waves of resistance to toxic behaviour, whether sexual harassment in the Me-Too movement, racism in Black Lives Matter, or exploitation in quiet quitting and its Chinese equivalent, lying flat.

Healing not coping also means normalising mental health issues and going to therapy. You see this in popular culture. *Ted Lasso* is one example. Another, my favourite, is the *Harley Quinn* animated series, which is peak metamodern media. In canon, Harley Quinn is the long-suffering girlfriend of the villainous Joker in *Batman*. This animated series, which is more subversive cartoon comedy than drama, picks up after Harley finally ditches her psychopathic 'puddin'' and goes solo. She shacks up with many of the relatively minor villains of the DC Comics universe, including Killer Croc, Mr Freeze and her long-time friend and simmering love interest Poison Ivy. The first few seasons basically revolve around them all helping each other to heal from the abandonment, bullying, abuse, grief and other traumas that led them to villainy in the first place. It recalls Harleen Quinzel's pre-crime life as a psychotherapist at Arkham Asylum, where she met the Joker. In the third season, Harley convinces Bruce Wayne to heal from the death of his parents through therapy with an episode hilariously titled: 'Holy post-traumatic stress disorder Batman!'

You would have heard the slogan: 'It's OK to not be OK'. I don't think that we take this sentiment quite seriously enough yet. People are more understanding of anxiety, depression, bereavement, being 'a mess' and other short-term mental health issues than they used to be. Many workplaces now offer mental health leave, and it's not taboo to be in counselling or on antidepressants. People are also more accommodating of neurodiversity. What we still don't give people permission for is to simply fall to pieces.

Sometimes in life you get hit so hard that you can't go on, either because you're totally debilitated by something like resurfacing trauma, or because your worldview is so rocked that you can't see anywhere to go to. We spoke about such 'descents' in section 5.5. You can't rush the descent, and sometimes you wander in the underworld for a very long time before you stumble on the way out.

The problem with people falling to pieces in this way is that they become dependent. They're someone else's problem because they're not quite (or not at all) capable of caring for themselves. We can't rely on them to 'get their shit together' on their own. And often, pushing them to be more self-sufficient or rushing to get them sorted delays the process of healing substantially. Crisis reoccurs. At times like these we need to offer a very deep and generous kind of care.

Our culture, at least at the macro level, seems incapable of this. For decades we have outsourced responsibility for these sorts of 'health' and 'unemployment' issues to the state. But the associated policy systems are grounded in efficiency doctrines that don't tolerate people falling to pieces. Welfare payments typically demand that people work or at least look for work, and they don't engage with the narrative arc of a person's life or help them to discover a sustainable path forward. Mental health services overwhelmingly rely on cognitive behavioural therapy, which while 'evidence based' is substantially a treatment for mental illness *symptoms* rather than *causes*. People in the underworld usually need a more involved and extensive talk therapy, but that's too expensive and uncertain for the state. So we need people to step in – friends, family, community. It's not just a case of: 'It's OK not to be OK, go deal with it, we can wait'; we need to go over to traumatised people and help them. That's a big ask but the younger generations seem increasingly willing.

I see some signs that older generations are misunderstanding the youth here. For example, a spat broke out in the late 2010s between Gen-X psychologists and university students over the supposed intolerance of the youth for anything confronting. Protest groups were deplatforming controversial speakers, administrators were setting up 'safe spaces' with puppies for students to retreat to when an idea was too horrible to deal with, and lecturers were being encouraged to include 'trigger warnings' in their teaching materials for things like racism when teaching the history of slavery.

The psychologists raised the alarm, publishing books like *The Coddling of the American Mind* by Greg Lukianoff and Jonathan Haidt. They were giving talks and publishing op-eds telling kids that they were 'resilient' and 'antifragile' – they would grow stronger from exposure to hard realities but become brittle if everything was sugar-coated.

I think there is *a lot* of good sense in the psychologist's argument, but it misses the sentiment of the youth: they don't want to live in a toxic world that *requires* resilience. We expect the youth to lack wisdom, but here it's the common sense of the older generations that is lacking. There's this belief that people need to be 'hard' to deal with a hard world. Like my tennis-coaching colleague Chris kept repeating, like a mantra, 'You've got to work f**king hard.' If you can achieve that, you'll make lots of money. But we've got lots of money now; what we want is a softer world.

A softer world doesn't 'churn and burn' graduates in 'prestigious' jobs for eighty hours a week. It doesn't call in militarised police to break-up student protests against a genocide that their own government is fuelling with weapons. It doesn't subsidise fossil fuels while youth climate anxiety skyrockets. It doesn't trap young people in colossal amounts of education debt just to get started in the economy. I could go on. The world is nasty, and universities are often active producers of that nastiness. It's not surprising that sensitive, smart, young people who have grown up in relatively idyllic suburban environments find adulthood confronting. These youth shouldn't be pampered, but we should acknowledge that they have a point.

What the youth need to do is coalesce around the metamodern project of defining this better world and making it happen. What should it look like? We need to ask the question of section 1.3 at the societal level – what should we use all our material abundance for? The answer certainly isn't war, or petrol imperialism, or simply 'more'. We need to think like *Star Trek*. In a future where science has secured nearly limitless, cheap energy and thereby enabled us to 3D print basically anything for free, money means nothing. Materialism is dead. What does that society do? In *Star Trek*, it adventures across the stars, spreads peace, life and prosperity, and celebrates the stories of diverse civilisations and heroes. We could be a bit more like that right now if we stop coping and start healing. In fact, parts of the world are already looking like that, and we'll explore some in the next section.

## 9.6. Visions of the future

> How wonderful it is that no one has to wait, but can start right now to change the world!
> Anne Frank, *Tales from the Secret Annex*, 26 March 1944

Let's do a quick recap about how communities form under metamodernity. Some individuals spontaneously and earnestly express their sincere valuation of something. They invite others to join them. Normal human dynamics like meme-generation, sacralisation, slang and rituals kick off, and gradually a subculture forms. This is basically how humans have always formed subcultures, except now this process is taking place across a much greater plurality of values, on a liberal basis, often over the internet rather than locally so the values can be super niche, and the subcultures often do not have agendas other than celebrating the value.

An example is the *Infinity* community in Australia. *Infinity* is a miniature war game similar to Warhammer. Hobbyists build tiny toy soldiers, paint them and then do battle on terrain-filled tables in a chess-like game with an incredibly complex rule set. *Infinity* began as an indie endeavour by a small group of friends in love with the cyberpunk genre, attracted Kickstarter funding, and very slowly grew into a sizeable community. Classic metamodern stuff. I briefly ran the Australian national championships at CanCon, perhaps the community's most significant annual ritual, while finishing my PhD.

Owing to its small size, the *Infinity* community exists mostly online, and CanCon is the one big annual get together. Recognising that it was a community event as much as a tournament, we ran two tracks – one competitive and the other social. My mate Tim and I spent at least a hundred uncompensated hours between us preparing a plot, missions, objective tokens and other bits and bobs for the social event, just to make it awesome. Some top painters donated exquisite models to a charity auction at the event each year. These are super-cooperator-type efforts that let new members know that there is love here and they should invest altruistically too.

The altruism that really stood out for me was in the online space. The Facebook groups and Discord servers of Australian Infinity mostly involved smack talk, jokes, people posting photos of their minis, and analysis of new rules and tactics. But every now and then, someone would come into the chat looking for help. Their mother had died and they couldn't cover the funeral costs, or they were travelling for a tourney and they needed a place to stay, or they were raising money for a local school and wanted to auction off a nicely painted army to that end (shout-outs to the legend Gavin Bateman). These requests were always met almost instantly. Now the Infinity community is full of very well-paid nerds but still, the level of generosity was astounding at times, and membership of the community was obviously treated as a signal of trustworthiness. This is all you need for karmic culture to get started.

B Corps show that businesses taking a values-driven approach to their operations can encourage karmic culture at scale. B Corps and similar businesses are firms with a genuine commitment to pursuing ESG (environmental, social, governance) objectives alongside profit. I say genuine because ESG is notoriously hard to codify, measure, track and certify, and so the sector is rife with greenwashing and other performative gestures.

B Corps like Patagonia, Ben & Jerry's, Allbirds and Kickstarter reject the shareholder value model of capitalism in which a firm's only objective is to maximise financial returns to its investors. B Corps instead recognise a range of valuable functions that firms serve within communities and the economy, and are willing to tolerate lower profits if it means better non-financial outcomes. B Corps see their workers as peers rather than a commodity, which discourages the exploitation of labour. They won't improve animal welfare only to the bare minimum required to get accreditation, because they're not cynical. They won't go out of their way to hide their environmental pollution. And if they get an opportunity to lobby government, they will use it to create a better commercial environment in general, not just to grab themselves a monopoly or tax exemption. The profit motive is still central, bringing a discipline and efficiency to business operations, but B Corps are trying to manifest a gentler capitalism and a better world.

The final example of metamodernism that gives me hope is the Effective Altruism (EA) movement, already mentioned in section 5.4. They seek to 'do the most good' as effectively as possible, especially in developing countries. They hold conferences and reading groups, and found charities and think-tanks to advance their mission and socialise new members. The community is extremely 'serious', with members getting very animated about the latest randomised-control trials or cost-benefit analyses and their implications for how they should be donating their resources to charitable efforts. EA demonstrates inspiring discursive norms, with most members having a remarkable ability to steel man arguments they might initially disagree with, listen actively, draw on evidence and not expect instant capitulation. The thought leaders of the movement are careful to articulate themselves in a range of ways that are appropriate to different audiences – blog posts for new entrants, so-called 'shallow investigations' for topics the community wants explored deeply but on which people haven't formed strong opinions yet, and extremely technical quasi-academic papers for donors and decision makers. EA events, like the EAGlobal conferences in London and San Francisco, are festivals of charity and goodwill. They celebrate vegan eating, hold seminars on how to motivate yourself to give and bring together people who have similar altruistic missions. It's all quite wholesome without being kumbaya.

EA's dark side is equally interesting. I am referring here especially to the controversy around Sam Bankman-Fried, a crypto billionaire who generously bankrolled EA activities for many years but is now serving a twenty-five-year prison sentence for fraud. Altruistic communities always attract parasites. In Bankman-Fried's case, he has explicitly said that he saw EA as an opportunity to launder his reputation. At the level of the community's grassroots, there are people milling about EA events who are clearly there to network just for economic opportunities in EA-dominated industries like artificial intelligence and global development. As with any nascent religious movement, EA is rapidly developing purity tests, and the question of whether someone is genuinely 'value-aligned' is becoming more common in EA forums. It will be interesting to see whether EA can retain its joyous, generous culture if more people start raiding its communal pot.

Now you might think that the karmic culture of Infinity, B Corps and Effective Altruism are warm and fuzzy but they're insufficient. We need something grander that can undergird cooperation at a large scale, like nations. I am very sympathetic to this concern, which vexes me as well, but I remain optimistic. Why? Because of America.

American culture is a collection of values that are quite new in many ways: liberty, opportunity, rule of law, democracy, etc. It is practised through regular community rituals that cut across political partisanship, like parades, singing the national anthem and unfurling the flag at sports games, national feast days, *Hamilton: An American Musical*, the Superbowl half-time show, etc. People opt into it via immigration as much as being socialised into it. It has heroes and legendary figures like Abe Lincoln and the Founding Fathers, and sacred offices like that of the president or the American soldier. It also has holy texts like the Constitution and holy symbols like the flag, the Statue of Liberty and the Supreme Court Building.

This culture, which isn't especially complex or demanding (unlike, say, fitting in with the French or Japanese), is effective at promoting certain behaviours and making American values feel palpable and serious, even though, judging by how young they are, American values are as 'made up' as any other.

One reason why people are sceptical of metamodernism is because building something palpable like 'America' takes a long time. But not that long! Even starting from 1619, it's only been 400 years. The blink of an eye in historical time. My own nation of Australia is even younger, and you can see its personal identity blossoming quite rapidly.

Now there's a lot wrong with 'America' as a value system. Alongside all its heartwarming foundations like liberty, equality and the pursuit of happiness, it is also built on materialism, slavery, imperialism, a hollowed-out Christianity and unsustainable consumption practices. An exquisite literary exploration of its shortcomings as a means of giving people meaning and purpose is *The Day of the Locust* by Nathaniel West, America's Dostoevsky. But America is an ongoing project that can be updated and renewed.

This is the advantage of secular systems – they are much more amenable to reason and cultural change than religious systems, which by their nature must appeal to an unchanging cosmic order. Secular systems can more easily adapt; they can change to stay the same. And precisely that is happening rapidly; there's just a lot of wailing and gnashing of teeth. Conservatives must be allowed to grieve for old America, because grief is love enduring, and love is sublime. But America in the twenty-first century needs new maps of meaning. As Beyoncé sings in 'American Requiem', 'Can we stand for something? / now is the time to face the wind / now ain't the time to pretend / now is the time to let love in'. To stand for something serious together, we have to get into our feelings, and that takes empathy.

We'll talk about these new shared maps of meaning – new mythologies – in the final section, but first I want to make one last point about metamodern karmic culture. In the past, humans always solved the public good problem at a small scale, like the *Infinity* community, and through culture. Using national government and impersonal markets is a modern phenomenon. We need a cultural revival because morality and culture evolved to facilitate cooperation. We do culture together and it enables us to be better together. It's a virtuous circle. We need to get back to culture and get back to each other. Humans are remarkably capable of imprinting and caring for others. That's why some people ask for their robotic vacuum cleaners to be repaired rather than replaced – because they've become part of the family. We need that love for the Roomba for everyone. We are a gregarious species, we just get tricked by psychopaths into worshipping the dollar, the throne or the clout instead of each other.

## 9.7. Telling new stories

> Politics separate people by bringing them together only superficially. Art and culture unite us in a common anguish that is our only possible fraternity, that of our existential and metaphysical community.
> Eugene Ionesco interviewed by Barbara Kraft in *Huffpost*,
> 17 May 2013

At the end of section 9.3, I noted that metamodernism seeks 'to re-enchant the world after its disenchantment by modern science and postmodern critique' and that 'this romantic project necessarily requires an abundance of *feeling* relative to thinking'. For this we need art, which is why I went on to discuss *Everything, Everywhere, All at Once*. There is a form of art and meaning-making that is especially critical to metamodernity: mythology.

Mythology is the narrative and metaphoric representation of value-laden symbols and themes that percolate in the collective unconscious. It is our maps of meaning in their most raw form. Those myths that stand for centuries or otherwise capture the zeitgeist do so because they present patterns that are intuitively (not necessarily rationally) recognisable to huge numbers of people. Both modernity and postmodernity have so radically altered the world that many of the myths of our cultural heritage are no longer recognisable. A prominent example is that Mary as the symbolic representation of the mother – the principal role of women in the New Testament – does not cut through for most twenty-first-century women. A popular culture example is that James Bond just seems a bit too white, misogynist and violent to be recognisable as a hero in the twenty-first century. We should not abandon the tremendous wisdom in inherited mythology that remains relevant, but we also shouldn't think, as Jordan Peterson and others seem to, that a simple reclamation of our cultural heritage can solve contemporary problems. We cannot go back. The old myths are played out. We need new ones.

Where to look? This book is not the place for an exhaustive survey of contemporary myth-making, but I do want to draw attention to two constellations of new mythology that I think are especially relevant to metamodernity – the heroine's journey and cyberpunk. They concern what I take to be the two biggest meaning-making tasks by which we are beset: the transformation of gender roles, and our relationship with technology and the natural world.

## *The Heroine's Journey*

The Heroine's Journey[6] is a term I use to describe myths that synthesise the two classical mythological structures for male and female plots – the hero's journey and the virgin's promise. The hero's journey was made famous by Joseph Campbell's book *The Hero with a Thousand Faces.* Historical examples include the Arthurian legends, the *Song of the Nibelungs* and the *Odyssey*. Archetypal examples in contemporary popular culture are the first *Star Wars* trilogy, the *Harry Potter* series and the origin story of just about every superhero in the Marvel and DC universes, male or female.

The hero's journey has a common narrative structure that is often broken down into twelve stages. The first stage, the ordinary world, affirms that the world as it exists is basically 'good'. Later in the plot, it will be threatened by some 'bad' outside force – the dragon of chaos. The hero is called to adventure in stage two, but then refuses the call in stage three, typically out of childish fear. They meet a mentor in stage four (Yoda, Merlin, Gandalf, Dumbledore, Uncle Ben in Spiderman...), and then cross the threshold in stage five. This is the beginning of the second phase of the journey, sometimes called initiation or death and rebirth. The hero must enter a metaphorical cave and go through an ordeal that typically involves confronting their fears in some way (see *Star Wars* episode II or VII for blunt examples). Emerging transcendent, with a newfound capacity for heroism and the expression of their innate power, they move to the third phase of the journey (often the longest part of the plot), 'the return'. Here they slay the dragon of chaos and return to the world with 'the elixir' (e.g. the Holy Grail) – a representation of the creative possibilities within chaos.

The idea of a virgin's promise makes some people retch. When I raise this idea with a lot of my peers, I immediately get a response like 'these things don't need to be gendered'. I am very sympathetic to that – indeed, the heroine's journey is interesting in large part because it is a synthesis of historically separate gendered archetypes. But we need to understand those archetypes first. Suspend your feminist judgement for a moment. The virgin's promise is less studied than the hero's journey (surprise, surprise), but there is a burgeoning literature on it. One of the most prominent texts therein is *The Virgin's Promise* by Kim Hudson, and I'm going to be drawing a lot on her analysis here.

The virgin's world is one of *dependence*. She is reliant on others, typically her parents, for survival in some way. Think of *Bend it Like Beckham*, *The Little Mermaid* or Snow White among the dwarves. But there is a price to her conformity, often represented as being required to marry someone she does not love or be a slave for others, in the case of Cinderella. Early in the plot, the virgin has an opportunity to shine, such as the ball in *Cinderella* or the archery contest in *Brave*. Having dressed appropriately for this occasion, the virgin recognises her authentic self for the first time and gives up what is keeping her stuck. However, she now no longer fits her world and she is 'caught shining'. This plunges the world into chaos because it is ironically dependent on her as much as she is on it. Commonly, the world needs the virgin to stick to her assigned role so that it might continue in its ossified ways. Rejected by the world or fleeing from it, the virgin wanders in the wilderness, where she chooses her light. A very clear example of this is when Elsa builds her ice castle in *Frozen*, singing 'Let it go' and concluding that 'The cold never bothered me anyway'. Upon reconnecting with her community in her authentic way, the virgin regenerates the world by bringing something new to it. In essence, the virgin gives birth to a new world after becoming pregnant with her own possibility. The notion of a 'virgin's promise' makes sense in this context.

The heroine's journey blends the hero's journey and the virgin's promise. First, the world is both ossified within and threatened from outside. In Disney's *Raya and the Last Dragon*, for example, the world is hamstrung by a lack of trust between nations that is founded on false beliefs about the Dragon Gem. It is then easy prey for the Drun invasion. This is much like our world today with its outmoded systems of meaning and value and culture wars leaving us ill-equipped to cooperate in the face of a multi-faceted environmental crisis and imperialist dictators.

Second, the protagonist needs both to transcend the cave and let go of their dependency. In our present moment, the gendered tasks here are reversed. It is women who need to transcend the cave to find new powers beyond motherhood and traditionally male ambitions, and men who need to let go of their dependency on patriarchy for structure and self-esteem. The biggest and, dare I say it, actually very good mythological representation of this is the third *Star Wars* trilogy. Rey needs to discover her power to heal rather than kill using the force, and Kylo needs to stop being blinded by his own pain to step into the light with her. A new world is born, freed from the tyrannical threat of the artificially long-lived Emperor Palpatine and his authoritarian and retrograde 'New Order'. It is ironic that the main complaint about this trilogy is that it doesn't rehearse the classic good vs evil hero's journey of the original trilogy. That archetype is played out and replacing it with something featuring different gender roles, a synthesis of two sides of the force, and an emphasis on healing rather than violence is precisely what we need. That there is such psychological inertia and even antagonism to this is worrying.

Third, in the heroine's journey, the protagonist needs to slay the dragon and give birth to a new world from their own authenticity. This theme is stark in the *Horizon* games that launched the PlayStation 4 (*Zero Dawn*) and PlayStation 5 (*Forbidden West*), which are incidentally also incredible myths about our relationship with nature and technology. The protagonist, Aloy, must let go of her dependency on her father figure, Rost, and her need to know who her mother was. Absent guidance from such parents, including the matriarchal elders of her tribe, she must journey into the unknown, including multiple caves, to discover her purpose and how the world might be set right. She heals it through a combination of old-world technology shorn of its murderous capacities, new world mysticism and simple human trust and relationships. The world is then ready to take on two threats. First, Hades, an artificial intelligence programmed only for destruction. Hades is fittingly slain at the point in the plot when Aloy emerges from her own underworld. Then, Nemesis, an even more advanced and nihilistic artificial intelligence created by immortal capitalists who toyed with uploading their minds into cyberspace. It is wholly appropriate that this threat is named after the Greek Goddess who enacts the retribution of the gods on those who display hubris and 'go too far'. The villains who created Nemesis fell out of love with the natural world and wanted dominion over it, much like some of our tech billionaires today.

Fourth, in these prominent contemporary heroine's journeys the protagonist can only birth a new world by recognising what is valuable in the current one and rallying others around her. There is always a theme of cleansing bad blood so that the world might start healing. Trust and relationships are key to this, as is drawing on what is recognised as good in the status quo by all parties. This is exactly what we need in our present moment:

empathetic conversations about what we want to keep and why, and where we want to go and why. We cannot move forward while the pain of nihilism motivates us to destroy people whose response to nihilism affronts our own value system.

## *Cyberpunk*

Cyberpunk emerged around the 1980s, especially in America and Japan, in comic books more than other media. Some of the classics of the genre are *Robocop, Bladerunner, Judge Dredd, Total Recall, Ghost in the Shell, Akira, Neuromancer*, the videogames *Deus Ex* and *System Shock*, and the pen-and-paper tabletop roleplaying game *Cyberpunk 2077*. There has been a marked revival of cyberpunk tropes in recent popular culture, most obviously in *Bladerunner: 2049*, the *Ghost in the Shell* movie and the *Deus Ex* reboot. Other prominent examples include *Altered Carbon, Tokyo Ghost, Alita: Battle Angel* and, most recently, the videogame set in the *Cyberpunk: 2077* universe, which has sold 25 million units (making it one of the top fifty selling games of all time as I write this).

The 'cyber' theme in cyberpunk refers to our relationship with technology, especially when technology allows us to escape or lose touch with what it means to be human. The relevant technologies include sentient or otherwise very lifelike artificial intelligences, the ability to transfer your consciousness between host bodies, cloning and artificial wombs, immortality, digital life and cybernetic augmentation.

The 'punk' theme pertains to authority and rebellion against it. Power is invariably corrupt in cyberpunk tales. It is typically corporate rather than statist, with society consequently geared to pursue profit over people, and decisions driven by the machinations of individual executives rather than democratic sentiment. In many cases, the protagonist is a law-enforcer who breaks with corporate desires to instead apply a more honourable form of justice. In the purest articulations of the genre, the 'heroes' are more literally punks engaged in violent revolution against corporate overlords.

A further theme of cyberpunk stories is how technology separates us from nature and wellbeing, thereby trapping us under the influence of the firms. Mining for minerals to create technology pollutes groundwater, energy production pollutes the air and wars fought over corporate profits while using corporate products pollute the soil. The world becomes unliveable, making us more dependent on corporations and their air conditioners, lab-grown food and virtual simulations. All this is expensive, so we need high-paying jobs with the corporations, but they demand cybernetic enhancements – their own products – to improve our productivity. Addictive trash entertainment, artificially 'enhanced' pop icons and defensive status competition further alienates us from each other and overwhelms our intrinsic motivation, undermining relationships and self-actualisation and encouraging us to find escape from our loneliness in corporate products, notably AI girlfriends.

It's not hard to see cyberpunk themes trending in a worrying direction in our world today. Artificial intelligence has exploded onto the scene, and while it has tremendous potential to do good, it is already being put to dangerous applications in weapons systems, propaganda, misinformation and enhancing the addictiveness of devices and media. Control over this technology is substantially a competition between a few tech firms already lobbying for regulation to enforce their monopoly against an open-source movement. AI frequently parasites off human creativity in domains like art and music, simultaneously sapping human motivation to create, and flooding the zone with trash. Perhaps most concerning of all, the energy and water consumption of AI technologies is colossal. Amazon recently bought a nuclear plant to power one of its data centres, and, according to a pre-print study by researchers at the University of California at Riverside and the University of Texas at Arlington, an average conversation with ChatGPT or Google's Bard consumes around half a litre of water for cooling purposes at such data centres.[7] The 'intelligence' of ChatGPT and the like is impressive until you compare it to what a human can do fuelled by just a bowl of oats. We are adapted to our environment because we evolved here. Like plastic, the other great synthetic technology, artificial intelligence seems deeply out of synch with ecology.

The optimistic sibling of cyberpunk is the solarpunk genre. Rather than separating us from nature and our humanity, technology in solarpunk allows us to integrate more deeply with both. We draw energy passively from the sun and wind. Our habitats are built with and into nature, often using fast-growing woods like bamboo. Fungus and compost rather than chemicals are used for waste management. Grey water systems irrigate gardens built onto roofs and up walls. Those gardens in turn purify air, provide food and cool urban environments that would absorb too much ambient heat if built with concrete alone. Robots free us from alienated labour and enhance sustainability rather than increasing economic precarity and undermining our relationships. Our cities attract animals, especially birds, rather than being inhospitable to them. We live with a degree of density that facilitates travel by foot, bike or train, reducing our carbon footprint and freeing up space for green and blue amenities rather than highways. Our lives are steady and cyclical like natural rhythms, rather than frenetic and accelerating like a cancer. This way of living frees up time away from work and commuting for relationships and community, which is easy to sustain because we live close to each other and have many beautiful places to meet.

There are few high-profile examples of solarpunk in media, though Alderaan in *Star Wars*, Wakanda – home of the Black Panther – and the Firelighters home tree in *Arcane* do fit the bill. Encouragingly, real-life examples are more common, though always isolated rather than systemic. The tramlines in Kaohsiung, Taiwan, for example, are tree lined and planted with grass rather than being filled in with gravel. The One Central Park building in Sydney is walled with gardens. The Earthships of New Mexico are built using repurposed materials, use solar and/or thermal for heating, cooling and energy, treat sewage locally, and produce food. The Aardehuizen eco-village in the Netherlands is similar, and integrated more broadly into Dutch urban style, which emphasises bikes and rail travel and medium-density village living.

The Netherlands is also liberal-democratic and emphasises work-life balance and other wellbeing principles in public policy, which makes it more solarpunk than say, Singapore, which has many examples of solarpunk architecture but is quite authoritarian. Solarpunk retains the anti-capitalist, anti-authoritarian and somewhat anarchist tropes of its dystopian sibling. The emphasis is less on rebellion and more on principles of collective self-organisation at small scale. In words that have stuck with me from the climax of the cyberpunk video game *Deus Ex*: 'government on a level comprehensible to its people'. Much of solarpunk culture is about returning the scope of life to something more intimate. But this doesn't mean small scale. *Star Trek* is often considered a solarpunk society, but it is geared towards intergalactic exploration, peace building and creativity, and the intimacy of the crews of the various spacecraft is core to the show.

## *Miyazaki*

The heroine's journey and solarpunk come together in the work of Hayao Miyazaki, who I believe is the most significant contemporary mythologist. He is the creative director of Studio Ghibli, a global phenomenon. Three of their films have won the Animage Grand Prix, four have won the Japan Academy Prize for Animation of the Year and two have won Oscars. Miyazaki's films are all significant, but I want to focus on four in particular: *Nausicaä of the Valley of the Wind* and its pair *Princess Mononoke*, and *Spirited Away* and its pair *The Boy and the Heron*.

*Nausicaä* is the oldest so let's start there. The film is set in a post-apocalyptic world wherein war has left little but deserts and a toxic forest. On its edge is the valley of the wind, a bucolic community that must constantly burn off its crops to eradicate the spores of the encroaching forest. The valley's princess, Nausicaä, travels into the forest for samples to study in the hopes of combating its toxicity. A cargo ship from the kingdom of Tolmekia carrying a superweapon crashes in the village. Soldiers under the command of Princess Kushana arrive to retrieve it and take Nausicaä hostage. They are shot down on their way home by fighters from the rival kingdom of Pejite, crash landing in the toxic forest. Nausicaä befriends one of the fighter pilots, Asbel, who can only respond to the toxicity of the forest by shooting at it. This violence only makes things worse. Kushana similarly plans to use the superweapon to burn the forest, but this will trigger a catastrophic stampede of the gigantic Ohm insects. Only Nausicaä, through her gentle curiosity, discovers that the forest is only toxic because it is purifying the pollutants in the soil, leaving behind clean water, air and edibles. In the final scene of the film, Nausicaä calms a herd of giant rampaging Ohm by showing love and care for one of their children. She is healed in turn by the insects. The final scene is her dancing in a blue dress on their golden tentacles, an image the residents of the valley had long mythologically associated with a masculine saviour.

The symbolism of Nausicaä is relatively straightforward to interpret. War tears the world apart and makes it toxic. Bad blood perpetuates these cycles of violence and prevents healing. Nature can heal us, but only if we live in harmony with it. The quintessentially male desire to fight, represented in the fearful Asbel and the father's daughter Kushana (a women who internalises patriarchal norms) only makes things worse. What is required is love, care, nurture and relationships, and thus a feminine saviour.

Nausicaä is a vision of the new feminine – a mother of sorts, and certainly nourishing, empathetic and relational, but also brave, headstrong and not dependent on men for anything, least of all protection. A heroine.

*Princess Mononoke* is in many ways a more mature version of Nausicaä, though there are important differences. Kushana is recast as the more complex Lady Eboshi, a capitalist who runs a mining and gunsmithing operation that employs disabled people, prostitutes and other marginalised folk. Her operation is regularly assaulted by forest demigods led by the young wolf-riding woman San, who I take to be a symbolic representation of the understandably furious, violent and antagonistic side of feminism and the feminine. The protagonist of the film is not San (Princess Mononoke) but rather Prince Ashitaka (according to Studio Ghibli co-founder Toshio Suzuki, Miyazaki wanted the film titled *The Legend of Ashitaka*). While protecting his village from a boar god transformed into a daemon by an iron bullet, Ashitaka is tainted by its corruption. This gives him superhuman strength, but the corruption will slowly spread over his body and eventually kill him (perhaps this represents martial violence and patriarchal power).

Ashitaka brokers a peace between Eboshi's operation and San through the forest spirit, which he helps to heal. Crucially, he is able to calm San by absorbing her violence without getting hurt, by caring for her in her rage and sorrow, and by giving her hope for a better future when things are at their bleakest. His violence is only ever defensive, and his most powerful skill is active listening. In the denouement, the two worlds – technological and organic – work to live in peace and harmony. Bad blood is cleansed and violence is ended.

Ashitaka is a vision of the new masculine. A protective knight not a pillaging warrior, capable of holding space for the strong emotions of others without being overwhelmed by them himself, and motivated by harmony not conquest. He is very compatible with feminism.

*Spirited Away* and *The Boy and the Heron* play host to a similar dyad, with a female and male protagonist respectively.

The themes are less concerned with nature and technology and more with materialism and fascism. In *Spirited Away*, the protagonist Chihiro's parents are transformed into pigs for brazenly gorging themselves on the food meant for the spirits (i.e. the environment). To rescue them, Chihiro must work in a spa for the spirits. It is symbolic of a capitalist system, with floors like a hierarchy and the garishly wealthy witch Ubaba residing in the penthouse. She controls people by taking away their real name, that is, their authenticity. The spa is nearly destroyed by the out-of-control growth of No-Face, a spirit fed by the other employees out of a self-destructive desire for his gold. No-Face is engaged in defensive status seeking, trying to buy the friends he so desperately wants. Once Chihiro keeps him company sincerely, he settles down into a friendlier and not at all rapacious version of himself and discovers an intrinsic motivation to weave. The capitalist motifs of the film are contrasted with Chihiro's modest appearance, relational behaviour and altruistic desire to rescue her parents.

In *The Boy and the Heron*, a wizard has built a world between worlds that is sustained by a collection of magical blocks. These have become infused with malice, threatening the destruction of the world. The wizard asks the protagonist, Mahito, to reorder new blocks retrieved from across all time and space that are free of malice so that the world might be born anew. This process represents the way analytical philosophers try to derive the best possible world from a priori ethical theory. But Mahito states that he himself possesses malice and must return to the real world to heal it and himself by embracing those who love him, in particular his adoptive and pregnant mother, Natsuko. She is, I think, a representation of the old feminine who is proud to have Mahito as the new masculine. The parakeet king, who I take to be a metaphor for fascism – an extreme form of the dependent personality – grasps the blocks and tries to build a better world himself, but his malice makes his stack unstable. He slices the blocks with his sword in frustration, and the world collapses. We cannot birth a wholesome normative order through violence, hierarchy or a simple reordering of the pieces that already exists. We need love to create.

Miyazaki affirms repeatedly across his films how violence poisons the care and creativity we need to birth a better world. This is clearest perhaps in *The Wind Rises*, Miyazaki's magical-realist biopic of aeronautical engineer Jiro Horikoshi. He desired to create beautiful planes for aesthetic and adventurous reasons. But Japan's involvement in the Second World War led to his masterpiece, the Mitsubishi A5M, being used in kamikazi missions. In one of the most poignant and heartbreaking lines of the film, Horikoshi reflects on how 'I sent all those young men to die'. Violence pollutes our love and art. As long as war and malice persist within our species, we will struggle to achieve cooperation, care and a stable relationship with nature, because we will be afraid of someone murdering us to steal our stuff. So we keep growing in order to finance the defence budget.

There is a lot more to be said about Miyazaki, but all I want to draw attention to is his mythological exploration of key contemporary psychic transformations – old worlds giving way to new; war, fascism and materialism as unstable, empty and destructive systems of meaning and value; the relationship between technology and nature; and the transfiguration of the gender archetypes. These transformations are at the core of metamodernism. We need more such stories to explore subconsciously how we might like to be.

My purpose in this section was not to deride technologies like AI or evangelise for a particular gender politics. I have little idea how these sorts of things should play out. What I do know is that we need to explore them in the mythological, artistic and unconscious (dream) worlds as much as in the rational, technical and material ones. We need new systems of meaning and value to achieve collective wellbeing in the twenty-first century, and meaning and value speak the language of intuition, emotion and imagination more so than reason.

## Chapter 9 summary

> Perhaps it is permissible to dream of a future when people will know no other use of their freedom than this free unfurling of itself; constructive activity would be possible for all; each one would be able to aim positively through their projects at their own future.
>
> Simone de Beauvoir, *The Ethics of Ambiguity*

We need metamodernism to overcome nihilism at a sociological scale. The driving forces of metamodernity are earnestness, sincerity and kindness. It is a cultural movement concerned with the re-enchantment of the world, the artistic and emotional expression of value, and the restoration of collective normative endeavour. Don't try to be rational about it. Ponder instead what you can be earnest about and sincere about. Is there anything (or many things) that you love so much that you don't care if people see you geeking out about it, being a little over the top with it and investing a lot of heart in it? That's your gateway into the metamodern life.

Metamodernity is about making meaning rather than reasoning, and that requires building the cultural practices that give our values their magic. What art is involved in your values, what rituals, what symbols? How can you contribute to their creation, propagation and celebration? Create memes, organise events, buy uniforms, make songs, turn memories into traditions. Anything that gets us out of our heads and into our feelings in a collective way. We have to build bridges to each other through shared meanings.

We need kindness especially for those who don't agree with us. They are trying to find a way to live in a nihilistic universe the same as us, they've just taken a different path. We must be on guard against people with bad faith and authoritarian tendencies, but so long as people are willing to live and let live, we should let ourselves be charmed by all the different things people choose to love, rather than be confronted and upset that they don't love the same things we do. Metamodernism promises a kaleidoscope of values being practised by autonomous, competent communities of devoted worshippers, and I am sure it will be spectacular if we let it build momentum.

# Conclusion

> Every child has known God,
> Not the God of names,
> Not the God of do nots,
> Not the God who ever does anything weird,
> But the God who only knows 4 words
> And keeps repeating them, saying:
> 'Come dance with me.
> Come dance'.
>     *A Year with Hafiz*, poems by Daniel Ladinsky

This is a hard book to summarise. I said in the introduction that I hate thin books — one idea padded out with chapter-length anecdotes. Just write a blog post! Wellbeing is complicated, interdisciplinary, dense and difficult. Giving it a thorough treatment is like trying to carry a pile of leaves with your arms. I hope this book was true to that, and still succeeded in holding it all together and showing the path through it all. I'll try to put down my pile of leaves here, but a lot of those leaves are going to get lost in the process.

Wellbeing is about living a pleasant, fulfilling and valuable life. In recent decades we've been too narrowly fixated on the pleasant part, and in a crude way too. We've gone in for materialism, hedonism and tranquillity. We've tried to find the end of the treadmill, instead of finding a treadmill we love to run on. We need a more Epicurean approach instead. We need to interrogate what our values are and then secure a modest, sufficient material basis of security and comfort from which to explore and affirm those values. That interrogation requires fallibilism, curiosity, courage and at times some stoicism.

It also requires self-actualisation – that's how we arrive at a fulfilling life. Wellbeing is a process as much as a state. We need to iterate our way to values that, in the words of my dear colleague the philosopher Valerie Tiberius,[1] harmonise our emotions, motivations and reasons. To get there, we need to develop an awareness of our actual, ideal and ought selves, and then bring them into alignment. That requires affirming who we would be proud to be through our behaviours and recalibrating that identity goal as we receive affective and social feedback. We need to pay attention to the types of motivation we experience and whether our basic psychological needs are met. This introspection on our feelings intertwines reason with emotion and motivation, and guides us towards our authentic values.

The result of self-actualisation is generalised flow. The things we do in life are mostly intrinsically motivated because we pursue them autonomously. We dedicate our spirit to them and thus our competence rises. And we do them with people we love so that our need for relatedness is met. Our life becomes characterised by activities that are high challenge but for which we have the requisite skill, and from which we draw immediate high-quality feedback because of self-awareness and mindfulness. All the conditions for flow are met in a way that transcends individual activities to instead characterise our *whole* life. We are 'in the zone' of our life. We are 'lost in the moment', but in a way that is strongly tied to our past and future through our projects and our process, imbuing the mundane with a meaning and purpose.

Wellbeing is something we do together. We are a social species. We live together, and our projects depend on other people for their success and their significance. In our quest to free ourselves from the tyranny of the majority we have become a little bit too individual. We need a rebalancing of We relative to I. That means caring wholeheartedly for those we love, those who depend on us and those who are merely familiar to us. It means investing in our close relationships but also our wider communities. It means rediscovering solidarity, and devotion. We do good not for our own gain but because what goes around comes around, and that's the sort of karmic world we want to live in.

Unfortunately, the traditional basis of our togetherness has frayed. The maps of meaning that we used to make sense of our world and our place in it aren't working any more, and the longer we cling to them the more lost we become. Our interim replacements – materialism, rationalism and adventurism – don't nourish our hearts and souls. We need to reweave our tapestry, not mend it. We need a scrap quilt – bits of the old that are still in good shape mixed with fresh material, stitched together into a new whole. This project requires us as individuals to be comfortable with ambiguity, open to difference and capable of acting with integrity about what we claim to believe. It requires us as a collective to be kind, empathetic and gregarious. The most dangerous sins of the twenty-first century are hypocrisy, hate and bad faith. We need to celebrate sincerity, love, and earnestness instead. Metamodernity can then leave behind cancel culture and usher in the new world. We can be better together. Wellbeing in a well world.

What can *you* do to bring about the new dawn of metamodernity? I have three pieces of advice. First, be a values-driven person. Don't pursue money, status or power blindly; they are means, not ends. Lead an examined life instead and follow your intrinsic motivations. Second, live with integrity and compassion. Let your life and presence be palpable proof that value is real and people will sacrifice to promote it. But don't be harsh on anyone who doesn't conform to your beliefs. Some people need nurturing to step fully into themselves, and others have a different path to follow. We can all get along. Third, become a priest to your community. Don't make it all about you – join the movement; don't try to be the movement. Care about people. Organise rituals and celebrations. Do those super-cooperator things that encourage other people to also invest their love and attention. Together, we can cultivate wellbeing in metamodernity.

# Endnotes

## Introduction

1 This comes from Carol Diener's foreword to Diener and Biswas-Diener (2011).
2 Vermeulen and Van Den Akker (2010).

## 1. Disposition

1 Ford et al. (2014), Mahmoodi et al. (2020) and Mauss et al. (2011).
2 Cummins, R. (2014).
3 Fabian et al. (2024)
4 Heinrich (2020).
5 For a popular exploration, see Robin Wall Kimmerer's *Braiding Sweetgrass*, which explores these themes in the traditional cultures of Indigenous American Indians.
6 Tolle, E. (2001).
7 Brooks (2022).
8 Whillans (2020).
9 Taleb's longest discussion of 'f**k you money' is in *The Black Swan: The Impact of the Highly Improbable*, but he talks about it often in social media, blogs, speeches and other fora.
10 Bellet et al. (2024).
11 Wilson et al. (2014).
12 Whitehead, N. (2014).

13 https://x.com/DollyParton/status/3198693707277796736
14 For an accessible overview of this literature, see Clark (2023).
15 Burke et al. (2010).
16 Holbrook et al. (2011).
17 Pyszczynski et al. (2012), p. 389.

## 2. Character

1 See especially Popper's *The Logic of Scientific Discovery* (1953) and *Conjectures and Refutations* (1963).
2 See especially Kuhn's *The Structure of Scientific Revolutions* (1962).
3 For a much more intellectual and exhaustive analysis of other ways of knowing, I highly recommend Ian McGilchrist's two-volume magnum opus *The Matter with Things: Our Brains, Our Delusions, and the Unmaking of the World,* especially book one, *The Ways to Truth.* Following on from the work of philosophers like Nietzsche, Heidegger and Wittgenstein and artists like Milton and Blake, McGilchrist argues that knowledge comes not just from reason but also from intuition, imagination and the body.
4 It is worth noting that many of the ideas discussed in *Thinking, Fast and Slow* have failed to replicate as part of the replication crisis engulfing psychological science since about 2015 onwards. For a discussion on this, see https://replicationindex.com/2020/12/30/a-meta-scientific-perspective-on-thinking-fast-and-slow/#comments. What this means is that when laboratories have copied the designs of studies cited in *Thinking, Fast and Slow* their results have differed from those in the original studies. This suggests that the phenomena these studies claim to identify are not real. Many of these studies are not Kahneman's own, and his central idea – prospect theory – has replicated (Ruggeri et al. 2020). The cognitive and behavioural biases literature is also enormous, and it is impossible that all of it is erroneous. Nevertheless, we need to be very careful about taking the claims of popular science books seriously. This is before we get into discussions of fraud, which has engulfed some of the most successful academic writers of popular psychology books, notably Dan Ariely and Francesca Gino. This is a

big part of why I say that this book is a work of wisdom not popular science – the science can't (yet) be trusted.
5   Hoorens, V. (2011). There is some evidence that illusory superiority is mostly a feature of Western psychology and that in East Asian cultures the opposite is quite common, namely underestimating one's own abilities (Heine and Hamamura 2007). This, of course, might in both cases be partially explained by social desirability bias, which is the tendency to report to researchers what you think they want to hear.
6   Svenson (1981).
7   Zuckerman and Jost (2001).
8   Alicke and Govorun (2005).
9   Cross (1977).
10  Strauss et al. (2016).
11  These lines do not appear in Aurelius' *Meditations*. The closet passage is the following, from chapter 8, s. 33: 'Receive [wealth or prosperity] without arrogance; and be ready to let it go.'
12  Aknin et al. (2019).
13  Dolan et al. (2021).

## 3. Emotion

1   https://www.ted.com/talks/matthieu_ricard_the_habits_of_happiness?
2   For a short and accessible discussion of Ladinsky's translations, which came to him in a dream when he didn't speak any Persian, see this article by Omid Safi of the Islamic Studies Center at Duke University: https://www.aljazeera.com/opinions/2020/6/14/fake-hafez-how-a-supreme-persian-poet-of-love-was-erased
3   Incidentally, no such thing exists, at least according to Narens and Skyrms (2020). Their book canvasses psychology, neurobiology and modern measurement theory to find some real candidate for 'pleasure' as utilitarianism conceptualises it. They find no suitable phenomenon.
4   https://plato.stanford.edu/ENTRIES/epicurus/
5   Chatterjee et al. (2019).
6   Easterlin (1974).

7 Knell and Stix (2020).
8 See, for example, Stevenson and Wolfers (2013) and Killingsworth et al. (2023).
9 Kahneman et al. (2004).
10 Dolan's popular book *Happiness by Design* (2014) covers a lot of this research accessibly.
11 Sheldon and Lucas (2014).
12 Hetschko, Knabe, and Schöb (2019).
13 Armenta et al. (2014).
14 Schwarz et al. (2006).
15 Fabian et al. (2024).
16 See Shin and Lyubomirsky (2014).
17 Emmons (2008).
18 Connolly (2014).
19 This is the broad thrust of Ian McGilchrist's *The Master and His Emissary* (2009), which I think is one of the most important books ever written but is too dense for me to discuss here.
20 Nietzsche, *The Gay Science* (1882), book 5, s. 346.
21 Kabat-Zinn (2006).
22 Baraz and Alexander (2013).
23 Cardacitto et al. (2008).
24 Goldstein (2003).
25 Kabat-Zinn (2006).
26 Breines and Chen (2012).
27 Shapira and Mongrain (2010).
28 Schuling et al. (2020).
29 Or at least some forms of Buddhism. Some of my Buddhist friends seem to practise Buddhism in a way that is disassociated from the metaphysical commitments of Tibetan Buddhism and much more oriented towards various techniques and values like meditation and altruism. It seems to work delightfully for them.
30 Ricard (2003).
31 Ricard (2003), p. 130.
32 Tolle, E. (2001).
33 For an investigation into the origins of this quote, see https://

quoteinvestigator.com/2023/09/06/imagination-preview/#:~:text=Albert%20Einstein%20said%2C%20%E2%80%9CImagination%20is,works%20both%20positively%20and%20negatively

## 4. Self-Actualisation

1. Higgins (1987).
2. Crabb, A. (2015).
3. Crocker and Park (2012).
4. Ryan and Deci (2017).
5. Showers and Zeigler-Hill (2012).

## 5. The Inner Empire

1. Foa et al. (2022).
2. See Sheldon et al. (2004) and Kasser and Ryan (1996).
3. Kasser and Ahuvia 2002, Vansteenkiste et al. 2006.
4. Murdock (1998).
5. Russell (1973/2004).
6. Ryan and Deci (2004).
7. The differences between system 1 and 2 thinking is the subject of Kahneman (2011).
8. Kuhl and Koole (2004), Oyserman et al. (2012).
9. Crowley et al. (1997), Crowley and Siegler (1999).
10. Newport (2016).
11. Nietzsche, *The Gay Science* (1882), s. 290.
12. Russell (1930/2014).
13. Csikszentmihalyi (1992), p. 32.
14. Csikszentmihalyi (1992), p. 214.

## 6. Better Together

1. Dunn (2023).
2. Nick Cave, *The Red Hand Files*, issue #6, October 2018. https://www.theredhandfiles.com/communication-dream-feeling/
3. https://www.oecd.org/en/data/indicators/health-spending.html

4 See Helliwell et al. (2020) for a summary of this research.
5 Gneezy and Rustichini (2000).
6 Rogers (1980).
7 Thornton (2020).
8 See Stevenson (2019).
9 Grahn (1984).
10 Thornton (2020).
11 *Thus Spoke Zarathustra*, Part I, s. 11, 'The New Idol'.
12 Putnam and Romney Garrett (2020).
13 See Fabian and Breunig (2018) for a book-length treatment of the bright side of neoliberalism.
14 Davies (2016).

## 7. Nihilism

1 Fromm (1941/2011).
2 Martela and Steger (2016).
3 Nietzsche, *Twilight of the Idols*, s. 8.
4 McGregor (2004), p. 183.
5 De Beauvoir (1947/1986), p. 53
6 De Beauvoir (1947/1986), p. 126.
7 De Beauvoir (1947/1986), p. 25.
8 For a longer and more academic but still accessible discussion of these ideas, see Oakley (2008).
9 If you want some recommendations, I would start with Bertrand Russell's *Why I am Not a Christian*. It strikes a balance between rhetorical appeal and strong reasoning. On the other side you have Ed Fesser's *Five Proofs for the Existence of God*. From there I would go to YouTube for the various debates between Arif Ahmed, a philosopher at Cambridge University, and theologians, both Christian and Muslim. While you're on YouTube, you can check out the debate between William Lane Craig, a Christian apologist and professor of philosophy at Houston Christian University, and Shelly Kagan, professor of philosophy at Yale. I find this debate interesting both for Kagan's presentation of the 'morality is rational' view and Lane Craig's

very quick and admirable move to motivating faith from nihilism and meaning rather than metaphysical propositions. For more accessible arguments, Christopher Hitchen's *God is Not Great* is a classic. I'm afraid I can't speak for the religious side.

10 I am referring here especially to the Thomistic tradition that follows the work of St Thomas Aquinas, but there are analogues in all major monotheistic religions. Fesser's *Five Proofs of God* is a very accessible introduction and well worth reading. Suffice to say that I find Thomistic arguments unconvincing, especially those concerning God's goodness. They seem to always rely on a linguistic sleight of hand between 'perfection' and 'goodness'. God is perfect, so everything God does is good. The comedian Tony Martin inadvertently offered a witty repost to such arguments on Australia's *The Late Show*: 'My mother's obsession with the good scissors always scared me a bit. It implied that somewhere in the house there lurked the evil scissors.'

11 See Kierkegaard (1843/2005).

12 These different versions reflect quite different Gods, one tyrannical and the other loving. One could write a book on the significance of the difference, but it is outside the scope of this one.

13 Bellet et al. (2024).

14 Lansing (1987).

15 Dawkins (1993).

16 Haidt (2012), p. 38.

## 8. The Free Spirit

1 From *The Essential Rumi*, translated by Coleman Barks and John Moyne (1995).

2 De Beauvoir (1947/1986), p. 159.

3 De Beauvoir (1947/1986), p. 158.

4 Nietzsche (1882), book 5, s. 347.

5 Nietzsche, *The Genealogy of Morals*, essay 2, s. 1.

6 Hitchens (2005).

7 Valentim (2024).

8 Wesley (1774).

9   This is often mistranslated as 'To think is easy, to act is hard, but the hardest thing of all is to act in accordance with your thinking.' I agree with that sentiment more, but it's not at all commensurate with the original German: '*Handeln ist leicht, Denken schwer; nach dem Gedanken handeln unbequem.*'
10  Hitchens (2011).
11  Russell (1927), see especially the section 'The Moral Problem'.
12  Spoken in a debate with David Berlinkski at the Fixed Point Foundation, available here: https://www.c-span.org/video/?295467-1/atheism-poison-everything
13  Card and Krueger (1993).
14  Manning (2021).
15  See https://medium.com/newco/what-do-economists-know-199bf5793ae6 and https://www.econtalk.org/roberts-and-hanson-on-truth-and-economics/
16  https://twitter.com/jenniferdoleac/status/1350255741274349570?lang=zh-Hant
17  Brecht (2008), p. 27.
18  https://epodstemology.buzzsprout.com/1763534/9666644-everything-you-ve-ever-wanted-to-know-about-migration-policy
19  Fabian, Breunig and De Neve (2023).
20  Sides, Tessler and Vavreck (2019), p. 8.
21  Chetty et al. (2016).
22  Pew Research (2016).
23  Pew Research (2013).

## 9. Metamodernity

1  For an analysis of tight/loose culture from the perspective of psychology, see Gelfand (2018). For an analysis of thick/thin cultures in the context of political economy, see Kaplan (2018).
2  This is a very liberal but also popular and evocative translation of Gramsci by Žižek (2010). The original text is closer to: 'The crisis consists precisely in the fact that the old is dying and the new cannot be born; in this interregnum a great variety of morbid symptoms appear.'

3 *Rick and Morty*, series 3, episode 2.
4 De Beauvoir (1947/1986), p. 157.
5 For a treatment of this idea from a political-economy perspective, see Trebeck and Williams (2019).
6 'The Heroine's Journey' is also a body of work (books, workbooks and courses) by the Jungian therapist Maureen Murdock (1990/1998), and a theme of many texts and groups inspired by her insights. One could crudely say that she uses the term to refer to the common structure of most female-led myths, including the ones I call the virgin's promise, but this would do a disservice to the subtleties of her analysis. I don't want to dwell here on what's distinct and valuable in her work, only to acknowledge that I did not invent 'the Heroine's Journey' and that my use of the term is distinct from hers. I use the term mostly because it is rhetorically convenient to describe a recent genre of the hero's journey in which the hero has very many qualities that are usually to be found in the virgin's promise archetype. They are *feminine* heroes, hence heroine. Anyone who finds the content of this chapter stimulating should certainly read Woodman's work – it is excellent and of benefit to men almost as much as women. I found it personally enriching and ideas from it appear elsewhere in this book, notably the discussion of 'the descent' in section 5.5.
7 Li et al. (2023).

## Conclusion

1 Tiberius (2018).

# Bibliography

Aknin, L., Whillans, A., Norton, M. & Dunn, E. (2019). *Happiness and Prosocial Behaviour: An evaluation of the evidence.* World Happiness Report 2019. https://worldhappiness.report/ed/2019/happiness-and-prosocial-behavior-an-evaluation-of-the-evidence/

Alicke, M. & Govorun, O. (2005). 'The better-than-average effect'. In M. Alicke, D. Dunning & J. Krueger (eds), *The Self in Social Judgment* (pp. 85–106). Psychological Press.

Armenta, C., Jacobs Bao, K., Lyubomirsky, S. & Sheldon, K. M. (2014). 'Is lasting change possible? Lessons from the hedonic adaptation prevention model'. In K. Sheldon & R. Lucas (eds), *Stability of Happiness: Theories and evidence on whether happiness can change* (pp. 57–74). Academic Press.

Baraz, J. & Alexander, S. (2013). *Awakening Joy: 10 steps to happiness.* Parallax Press.

Bellet, C. S., De Neve, J. E. & Ward, G. (2024). 'Does employee happiness have an impact on productivity?' *Management Science*, 70(3), 1656–1679.

Bolet, D. (2021). 'Drinking alone: Local socio-cultural degradation and radical right support – the case of British pub closures'. *Comparative Political Studies*, 54(9), 1653–1692.

Brecht, B. (2008). *Life of Galileo.* Penguin Classics.

Breines, J. & Chen, S. (2012). 'Self-compassion increases

self-improvement motivation'. *Personality and Social Psychology Bulletin*, 38(9), 1133–1143.

Brooks, A. C. (2022). *From Strength to Strength: Finding success, happiness, and deep purpose in the second half of life*. Green Tree.

Burke, B., Martens, A. & Faucher, E. (2010). 'Two decades of terror management theory: A meta-analysis of mortality salience research'. *Personality and Social Psychology Review*, 14(2), 155–195.

Camus, A. (1942/1986). *The Myth of Sisyphus*. Citadel.

Card, D. & Krueger, A. B. (1993). 'Minimum wages and employment: A case study of the fast-food industry in New Jersey and Pennsylvania'. *American Economic Review*, 84(4), 772–793.

Cardaciotto, L., Herbert, J., Forman, E., Moitra, E. & Farrow, V. (2008). 'The assessment of present-moment awareness and acceptance: The Philadelphia mindfulness scale'. *Assessment*, 15(2), 204–223.

Carney, T. (2019). *Alienated America: Why some places thrive while others collapse*. HarperCollins.

Cave, N. (2018). *The Red Hand Files*, issue #6. https://www.theredhandfiles.com/communication-dream-feeling/

Chatterjee, K., Chng, S., Clark, B., Davis, A., De Vos, J., Ettema, D., … & Reardon, L. (2019). 'Commuting and wellbeing: A critical overview of the literature with implications for policy and future research'. *Transport Reviews*, 40(1), 5–34.

Chetty, R., Grusky, D., Hell, M., Hendren, N., Manduca, R. & Narang, J. (2016). 'The fading American dream: Trends in absolute mobility since 1940'. NBER Working Paper 22910. http://www.equality-of-opportunity.org/papers/abs_mobility_paper.pdf

Clark, A. (2023). *The Experience Machine: How our minds predict and shape reality*. Allen Lane.

Connolly, W. R. (2014). *Stoicism*. The Ecole Initiative. http://ecole.evansville.edu/articles/stoicism.html

Cottam, H. (2018). *Radical Help: How we can remake the

*relationships between us and revolutionise the welfare state.* Virago Press.

Crabb, A. (2015). *The Wife Drought: Why women need wives and men need lives.* Random House Australia.

Crocker, J. & Park, L. (2012). 'Contingencies of self-worth'. In M. Leary & J. Tangney (eds), *Handbook of Self and Identity* (2nd ed., pp. 309–326). Guilford Press.

Cross, P. (1977). 'Not can, but will college teaching be improved?' *New Directions for Higher Education*, 1977(17), 1–15.

Crowley, K., Schrager, J. & Siegler, R. (1997). 'Strategy discovery as a competitive negotiation between metacognitive and associative knowledge'. *Developmental Review*, 17(4), 462–489.

Crowley, K. & Siegler, R. (1999). 'Explanation and generalisation in young children's strategy learning'. *Child Development*, 70(2), 304–316.

Csikszentmihalyi, M. (1992). *Flow.* Harper & Row.

Cummins, R. (2014). 'Can happiness change? Theories and evidence'. In K. Sheldon & R. Lucas (eds), *Stability of Happiness: Theories and evidence on whether happiness can change* (pp. 75–100). Academic Press.

Dahl, R. (2013). *The Twits.* Puffin.

Davies, W. (2016). *The Limits of Neoliberalism: Authority, sovereignty, and the logic of competition.* Sage Books.

Dawkins, R. (1993). 'Viruses of the mind'. *Free Inquiry*, 13(3), 34–41.

de Beauvoir, S. (1947/1986). *The Ethics of Ambiguity.* Citadel.

—(1970/1996). *The Coming of Age.* W. W. Norton & Company.

di Lampedusa, G. T. (1958). *The Leopard.* Feltrinelli.

Diener, E. & Biswas-Diener, R. (2011). *Happiness: Unlocking the mysteries of psychological wealth.* Wiley.

Dillard, A. (1989). 'Write till you drop'. *New York Times.*

Dolan, P. (2014). *Happiness by Design.* Penguin.

Dolan, P., Krekel, C., Ganga, S., Lee, H., Marshall, C. & Smith, A. (2021). 'Happy to help: The welfare effects of a nationwide micro-volunteering programme'. *IZA Discussion Papers.* https://docs.iza.org/dp14431.pdf

Dostoevsky, F. (1879/2009). *The Brothers Karamazov.* Project Gutenberg. https://www.gutenberg.org/files/28054/old/28054-pdf.pdf

Dunn, J. (2023). 'When someone you love is upset, ask this one question'. *New York Times.* https://www.nytimes.com/2023/04/07/well/emotions-support-relationships.html

Easterlin, R. (1974). 'Does economic growth improve the human lot? Some empirical evidence'. In D. David & M. Reder (eds), *Nations and Households in Economic Growth: Essays in honour of Moses Abramovitz* (pp. 89–125). Academic Press.

Emmons, R. (2008). *Thanks! How practicing gratitude can make you happier.* Mariner.

Epicurus. (2006). *Principle Doctrines* (E. Anderson, trans.). https://blogs.ubc.ca/phil102/files/2013/08/Epicurus-PrincipalDoctrines-epicurusinfo.pdf

Fabian, M. & Breunig, R. (2018). *Hybrid Public Policy Innovations: Contemporary policy beyond ideology.* Routledge.

Fabian, M., Breunig, R. & De Neve, J. (2023). 'Worldview defense and self-determination theory explain the return of racial voting: Evidence from the 2016 US election'. *European Journal of Social Psychology*, 53(1), 147–166.

Fabian, M., Kaiser, C., Funk, S., Panasiuk, S. & Brett, C. (2024). 'Evidence against the simple statistical validity of life satisfaction scales from long form cognitive interviews'. Working paper prepared for the IARIW conference. https://iariw.org/wp-content/uploads/2024/08/FINAL-Fabian-et-al.-Cognitive-Interviewing-IARIW.pdf

Fesser, E. (2017). *Five Proofs of the Existence of God.* Ignatius Press.

Feynman, R. (2005). *Perfectly Reasonable Deviations from the Beaten Track: The letters of Richard P. Feynman.* Basic Books.

Foa, R., Fabian, M. & Gilbert, S. (2022). 'COVID-19 and subjective well-being: Separating the effects of lockdowns from the pandemic'. *PLoS ONE*, 17(2), e0163570.

Ford, B. Q., Shallcross, A. J., Mauss, I. B., Floerke, V. A. & Gruber, J. (2014). 'Desperately seeking happiness: Valuing happiness is associated with symptoms and diagnosis of depression'. *Journal of Social and Clinical Psychology*, 93, 891–906.

Foster-Wallace, D. (2009). *This is Water: Some thoughts, delivered on a significant occasion, about living a compassionate life.* Little, Brown and Company.

Fromm, E. (1941/2011). *Escape from Freedom.* Ishi Press.

Gelfand, M. (2018). *Rule Makers, Rule Breakers: How culture wires our minds, shapes our nations, and drives our differences.* Robinson Press.

Gneezy, U. & Rustichini, A. (2000). 'A fine is a price'. *Journal of Legal Studies*, 29(1), 1–17.

Goldstein, J. (2003). *Insight Meditation: A psychology of freedom.* Shambhala.

Grahn, J. (1984). *Another Mother Tongue: Gay words, gay worlds.* Beacon Press.

Gramsci, A. (1929/2011). *Prison Notebooks: Volumes 1–3.* Columbia University Press.

Greene, J. (2014). *Moral Tribes: Emotion, reason and the gap between us and them.* Atlantic Books.

Gustav-Wrathall, J. (2006). 'A gay Mormon's testimony'. *Sunstone*, 141, 52–57. https://sunstone.org/wp-content/uploads/sbi/articles/141-52-57.pdf

Haidt, J. (2012). *The Righteous Mind: Why good people are divided by politics and religion.* Penguin.

Haidt, J. & Lukianoff, G. (2019). *The Coddling of the American Mind: How good intentions and bad ideas are setting up a generation for failure.* Penguin.

Heine, S. J. & Hamamura, T. (2007). 'In search of East Asian self-enhancement'. *Personality and Social Psychology Review*, 11(1), 4–27.

Heinrich, J. (2020). *The WEIRDEST People in the World: How the West became psychologically peculiar and particularly prosperous.* Farrar, Straus, and Giroux.

Helliwell, J., Huang, H., Wang, S. & Norton, M. (2020). *Social Environments for World Happiness*. World Happiness Report: https://worldhappiness.report/ed/2020/social-environments-for-world-happiness/

Henley, E. (1920). *Poems*. Macmillan and Co.

Hetschko, C., Knabe, A. & Schöb, R. (2019). 'Looking back in anger: Retirement and unemployment scarring'. *Demography*, 56(3), 1105–1129. https://doi.org/10.1007/s13524-019-00772-7

Higgins, T. (1987). 'Self-discrepancy theory: A theory relating self and affect'. *Psychological Review*, 94(3), 319–340. https://doi.org/10.1037/0033-295X.94.3.319

Hitchens, C. (2005). *Letters to a Young Contrarian*. Basic Books.

—(2007). *God is Not Great: How religion poisons everything*. Twelve.

—(2011). *Hitch-22: A memoir*. Atlantic Books.

—(2013). *Mortality*. Atlantic Books.

Hochschild, A. (2016). *Strangers in Their Own Land: Anger and mourning on the American right*. The New Press.

Holbrook, C., Hahn-Holbrook, J. & Sousa, P. (2011). 'Unconscious vigilance: Worldview defense without adaptations for terror, coalition, or uncertainty management'. *Journal of Personality and Social Psychology*, 101(3), 451–466. https://doi.org/10.1037/a0023982

Hoorens, V. (1993). 'Self-enhancement and superiority biases in social comparison'. *European Journal of Social Psychology*, 23(1), 113–139. https://doi.org/10.1002/ejsp.2420230109

Jung, C. G. (1995). *Memories, Dreams, Reflections: An autobiography* (R. F. C. Hull, trans.). Fontana Press. (Original work published 1957)

—(2008). *Letters* (G. S. K. M. H. O. T. H. McGuire, trans.). Princeton University Press. (Original work published 1975)

Kabat-Zinn, J. (2006). 'Mindfulness-based interventions in context: Past, present, and future'. *Clinical Psychology: Science and Practice*, 10(2), 144–156. https://doi.org/10.1093/clipsy/bpj075

Kahneman, D. (2011). *Thinking, Fast and slow*. Penguin.
Kahneman, D., Krueger, A. B., Schkade, D. A., Schwarz, N. & Stone, A. (2004). 'A survey method for characterizing daily life experiences: The Day Reconstruction Method'. *Science*, 306(5702), 1776–1780. https://doi.org/10.1126/science.1103572
Kaplan, S. D. (2018). *Human rights in Thick and Thin Societies*. Cambridge University Press.
Kasser, T. & Ryan, R. (1996). 'Further examining the American dream: Differential correlates of intrinsic and extrinsic goals'. *Personality and Social Psychology Bulletin*, 22(3), 280–287. https://doi.org/10.1177/0146167296223006
Kierkegaard, S. (2005). *Fear and Trembling* (A. Hannay, trans.). Penguin. (Original work published 1843)
—(2008). *The Sickness unto Death* (A. Hannay, trans.). Penguin. (Original work published 1849)
Killingsworth, M. A., Kahneman, D. & Mellers, B. (2023). 'Income and emotional well-being: A conflict resolved'. *Proceedings of the National Academy of Sciences*, 120(10), e2208661120. https://doi.org/10.1073/pnas.2208661120
Kimmerer, R. W. (2020). *Braiding Sweetgrass: Indigenous wisdom, scientific knowledge, and the teachings of plants*. Penguin.
Knell, M. & Stix, H. (2020). 'Perceptions of inequality'. *European Journal of Political Economy*, 65, Article e101927. https://doi.org/10.1016/j.ejpoleco.2020.101927
Kuhl, J. & Koole, S. (2004). 'Workings of the will: A functional approach'. In J. Greenberg, S. Koole & T. Pyszczynski (eds), *Handbook of Experimental Existential Psychology* (pp. 431–448). Guilford Press.
Kuhn, T. S. (2012). *The Structure of Scientific Revolutions* (4th ed.). University of Chicago Press. (Original work published 1962)
Ladkinsky, D. (1999). *The Gift: Poems by Hafiz, the great Sufi master*. Penguin.
—(2011). *A Year with Hafiz: Daily contemplations*. Penguin

Lansing, S. J. (1987). 'Balinese "water temples" and the management of irrigation'. *American Anthropologist*, 89(2), 326–341.

Li, P., Yang, J., Islam, M. & Ren, S. (2023). 'Making AI less thirsty: Uncovering and addressing the secret water footprint of AI models'. https://arxiv.org/pdf/2304.03271

Lincoln, A. (1953). *The Collected Works of Abraham Lincoln*. University of Michigan Library.

Machado, A. (1912). *Proverbios y cantares*. https://biblioteca.org.ar/libros/158144.pdf

Mackie, J. L. (1990). *Ethics: Inventing right and wrong*. Penguin. (Original work published 1977)

Mahmoodi, K. B., Bower, J. L., Glover, F. M. G. Q., et al. (2020). 'Wanting to be happy but not knowing how: Poor attentional control and emotion-regulation abilities mediate the association between valuing happiness and depression'. *Journal of Happiness Studies*, 21, 2583–2601.

Manning, A. (2021). 'The elusive employment effect of the minimum wage'. *Journal of Economic Perspectives*, 35(1), 3–26.

Martela, F. & Steger, M. (2016). 'The three meanings of meaning in life: Distinguishing coherence, purpose, and significance'. *Journal of Positive Psychology*, 11(5), 531–545.

Maslow, A. (1993). *The Farther Reaches of Human Nature*. Penguin.

Mauss, I. B., Tamir, M., Anderson, C. L. & Savino, N. S. (2011). 'Can seeking happiness make people unhappy? Paradoxical effects of valuing happiness'. *Emotion*, 11(4), 807–815.

McGilchrist, I. (2009). *The Master and His Emissary: The divided brain and the making of the Western world*. Yale University Press.

—(2012). *The Divided Brain and the Search for Meaning*. Yale University Press.

—(2023). *The Matter with Things: Our brains, our delusions, and the unmaking of the world*. Perspectiva Press.

—(2004). 'Zeal, identity, and meaning: Going to extremes to be one self'. In J. Greenberg, S. Koole & T. Pyszczynski (eds), *Handbook of Existential Psychology* (pp. 182–199). Guilford.

McKenna, T. (1990). 'Opening the doors of creativity'. https://www.organism.earth/library/document/opening-the-doors-of-creativity

Murdock, M. (1990). *The Heroine's Journey: Woman's quest for wholeness*. Shambala.

—(1998). *The Heroine's Journey Workbook: A map for every woman's quest*. Shambala.

Narens, L. & Skyrms, B. (2020). *The Pursuit of Happiness: Philosophical and psychological foundations of utility*. Cambridge University Press.

Newport, C. (2016). *Deep Work: Rules for focused success in a distracted world*. Piatkus.

Nietzsche, F. (1882). *The Gay Science* (W. Kaufmann, trans.).

—(1883). *Thus Spoke Zarathustra* (W. Kaufmann, trans.).

—(1886). *Beyond Good and Evil* (W. Kaufmann, trans.).

—(1887). *On the Genealogy of Morals* (W. Kaufmann, trans.).

—(1888). *The Antichrist* (R. J. Hollingdale, trans.).

—(1888). *The Twilight of the Idols* (R. J. Hollingdale, trans.).

Oakley, B. (2008). *Evil Genes: Why Rome fell, Hitler rose, Enron failed, and my sister stole my mother's boyfriend*. Prometheus.

Oyserman, D., Elmore, K. & Smith, G. (2012). 'Self, self-concept, and identity'. In M. Leary & J. Tangney (eds), *Handbook of self and identity* (2nd ed., pp. 21–49). Guilford.

Pessoa, F. (1982). *The Book of Disquiet* (M. J. Costa, trans.). Penguin.

Pew Research. (2013). 'Breadwinner moms'. https://www.pewresearch.org/social-trends/2013/05/29/breadwinner-moms/

—(2016). 'Gender gap in religious service attendance has narrowed in U.S'. https://www.pewresearch.org/short-reads/2016/05/13/gender-gap-in-religious-service-attendance-has-narrowed-in-u-s/

Pollan, M. (2018). *How to Change Your Mind: The new science of psychedelics*. Penguin.

Popper, K. (1945/2011). *The Open Society and its Enemies.* Routledge Classics.

—(1953/2002). *The Logic of Scientific Discovery.* Routledge Classics.

—(1963/2002). *Conjectures and Refutations.* Routledge Classics.

Putnam, R. (2000). *Bowling Alone: The collapse and revival of American community.* Simon and Schuster.

Putnam, R. & Romney Garrett, S. (2020). *The Upswing: How we came together a century ago and how we can do it again.* Swift Press.

Pyszczynski, T., Greenberg, J. & Arndt, J. (2012). 'Freedom versus fear revisited: An integrative analysis of the dynamics of the defense and growth of self'. In M. R. Leary & J. P. Tangney (eds), *The Handbook of Self and Identity.* Guilford.

Ricard, M. (2003). *Happiness: A guide to developing life's most important skill.* Atlantic Books.

Rich, A. (1983). *Sources.* Heyeck Press.

Rilke, R. M. (1929/2014). *Letters to a Young Poet.* Penguin.

Robbins, T. (1984). *Jitterbug Perfume.* Bantam.

Rogers, C. (1961). *On Becoming a Person: A psychotherapist's view of psychotherapy.* Constable.

—(1980). *A Way of Being.* Houghton Mifflin.

Ruggeri, K., Ali, S., Berge, M. L., Bertoldo, G., Bjorndal, L. & Cortijos-Bernabeu, M. (2020). 'Not lost in translation: Successfully replicating prospect theory in 19 countries'. *Preprint.* https://osf.io/2nyd6

Russell, B. (1927). 'Why I am not Christian'. Lecture delivered in Battersea Town Hall.

—(1930/2014). *The Conquest of Happiness.* Routledge Classics.

—(1973/2004). *In Praise of Idleness.* Routledge Classics.

Ryan, R. & Deci, E. (2004). 'Autonomy is no illusion: Self-determination theory and the empirical study of authenticity, awareness, and will'. In J. Greenberg, S. Koole & T. Pyszczynski (eds), *Handbook of Experimental Existential Psychology* (pp. 431–448). Guilford.

—(2017). *Self-determination Theory: Basic psychological needs in motivation, development, and wellness*. Guilford.

Sartre, J. P. (1944/1958). *No Exit*. Concord Theatricals.

Schuling, R., Huijbers, M., van Ravesteijn, H., Donders, R., Cillessen, L., Kuyken, W. & Speckens, A. (2020). 'Recovery from recurrent depression: Randomized controlled trial of the efficacy of mindfulness-based compassionate living compared with treatment-as-usual on depressive symptoms and its consolidation at longer term follow-up'. *Journal of Affective Disorders*, 273(1), 265–273.

Schwarz, C., Bode, R., Repucci, N., Becker, J., Sprangers, M. & Fayers, P. (2006). 'The clinical significance of adaptation to changing health: A meta-analysis of response shift'. *Quality of Life Research*, 15(9), 1533–1550.

Shapira, L. B. & Mongrain, M. (2010). 'The benefits of self-compassion and optimism exercises for individuals vulnerable to depression'. *The Journal of Positive Psychology*, 5(5), 377–389.

Sheldon, K. M. & Lucas, R. E. (2014). *Stability of Happiness: Theories and evidence on whether happiness can change*. Academic Press.

Sheldon, K. M., Ryan, R., Deci, E. & Kasser, T. (2004). 'The independent effects of goal contents and motives on well-being: It's both what you pursue and why you pursue it'. *Personality and Social Psychology Bulletin*, 30(4), 475–486.

Shin, L. & Lyubomirsky, S. (2014). 'Positive activity interventions for mental health conditions: Basic research and clinical applications'. In J. Johnson & A. Wood (eds), *The Handbook of Positive Clinical Psychology* (pp. 349–363). Wiley.

Showers, C. & Zeigler-Hill, V. (2012). 'Organisation of self-knowledge: Features, functions, and flexibility'. In M. Leary & J. Tangney (eds), *Handbook of Self and Identity* (2nd ed., pp. 105–123). Guilford.

Sides, J., Tesler, M. & Vavreck, L. (2019). *Identity Crisis: The*

*2016 presidential campaign and the battle for the meaning of America*. Princeton University Press.

Simmel, G. (1903/1950). *The Metropolis and Mental Life*. Free Press.

Smith, A. (1759). *The Theory of Moral Sentiments*. Project Gutenberg. https://www.gutenberg.org/ebooks/67363

Stevenson, B. & Wolfers, J. (2013). 'Subjective well-being and income: Is there any evidence of satiation?' *American Economic Review*, 103(3), 598–604.

Stevenson, C. (2019). 'Social prescribing: A practice in need of a theory'. *British Journal of General Practice*.

Strauss, C., Taylor, B., Gu, J., Kuyken, W., Baer, R., Jones, F. & Cavanagh, K. (2016). 'What is compassion and how can we measure it? A review of definitions and measures'. *Clinical Psychology Review*, 47(1), 15–27.

Svenson, O. (1981). 'Are we all less risky and more skilful than our fellow drivers?' *Acta Psychologica*, 47(2), 143–148.

Taleb, N. (2010). *The Black Swan: The impact of the highly improbable*. Penguin.

Thornton, C. (2020). *The Hologram: Feminist, peer-to-peer health for a post-pandemic future*. Pluto Press.

Thurston, Z. N. (1937/2020). *Their Eyes Were Watching God*. Virago.

Tiberius, V. (2018). *Wellbeing as Value Fulfilment: How we can help each other to live well*. Oxford University Press.

Tolle, E. (2001). *The Power of Now: A guide to spiritual enlightenment*. Yellow Kite.

Trebeck, K. & Williams, J. (2019). *The Economics of Arrival: Ideas for a grown-up economy*. Policy Press.

Valentim, A. (2024). 'Repeated exposure and protest outcomes: How Fridays for Future protests influenced voters'. *OSF Preprint*. https://osf.io/preprints/socarxiv/m6dpg

Vermeulen, T. & Van Den Akker, R. (2010). 'Notes on metamodernism'. *Journal of Aesthetics and Culture*, 2(1), 5677.

Weil, S. (1949/2001). *The Need for Roots*. Routledge Classics.

—(1947/2002). *Gravity and Grace*. Routledge Classics.
—(2015). *First and Last Notebooks: Supernatural knowledge*. Wipf & Stock.
Wesley, J. (1774). *Thoughts Upon Slavery*. Joseph Crukshank.
Whillans, A. (2020). *Time Smart: How to reclaim your time and live a happier life*. Harvard Business Review Press.
White, T. H. (1958/1987). *The Once and Future King*. Ace Books.
Whitehead, N. (2014). 'People would rather be electrically shocked than left alone with their thoughts'. *Science*, 3 July 2024. https://www.science.org/content/article/people-would-rather-be-electrically-shocked-left-alone-their-thoughts
Wilson, D. (2002). *Darwin's Cathedral: Evolution, religion, and the nature of society*. University of Chicago Press.
Wilson, T. D., Reinhard, D. A., Westgate, E. C., Gilbert, D. T., Ellerbeck, N. & Hahn, C. (2014). 'Just think: The challenges of the disengaged mind'. *Science*, 345(6192), 75–77.
Žižek, S. (2010). 'A permanent economic emergency'. *New Left Review*, (64).

# Acknowledgements

I live amidst an extremely thick intellectual community, and so there are an enormous number of people to thank for ideas and inspiration in this book. Unfortunately, because a lot of my wisdom was gained by osmosis, I often don't know who is directly responsible. Let's have a go, and my apologies to anybody I forgot.

The person I have to thank the most is the inimitable R Meager. They are a titan of twenty-first-century intellectual, cultural and emotional thought (and feeling) leadership and I'm so privileged to have them as a friend. Get on their Substack: 'The Universal and Vacuous Events'. It is a moving, stimulating and insightful mash-up of social science, pure maths, literary analysis, earnest shitposting (it's a thing), autoethnography and just straight up truth bombs. And it's free. A (meta)modern miracle.

I want to thank the other people who proofed part or all of this book: Sofia Panasiuk, Cherise Regier, Michael Wijnen, Flint O'Neill, Caspar Kaiser, Indi Dissanayake, Matthew Iasiello, Mitsue Akiba, Patrick Harding, Nolan Bryce, Jamie Freestone, Daniel Glover, Stephanie Badman and Patricia Marino.

Many of these people have known me since I was a very young adult and have seen the ideas here grow from shower thoughts and diary scribblings into things someone thought worthy of publishing. I'm very glad that I managed to get this to print while we still vaguely remember those days and what we were like. So often these sorts of books are driven by the urgency and vitality of youth but can't be written because their authors have to establish themselves professionally first. That takes freakin' ages as an academic (compare it to something like music, where people are recruited, bankrolled and supported primarily in their raw youthful era). By the time they're secure enough to turn to popular writings, they've forgotten what it is they wanted to say and academic conventions have eradicated the electricity in their writing. I hope I didn't forget any of the things I knew when I was younger.

I want to thank some people who I have lost touch with but who were with me when many of these ideas germinated. Zara Maxwell Smith, Dan Glover, Pete G. Res, Nicolas Lema Hebash, Sebastian Willis, Madeleine Willis and Nora Fredstie (also Madeline Goldie to whom the book is dedicated).

I must thank my therapist, Sara Hagerman, who helped me work through a lot of the ideas that came to me through my emotions rather than my reasons, especially Chapter 6.

The Australian-American Fulbright Commission must be acknowledged for giving me a scholarship to do a short postdoc at the Brookings Institution. Were it not for them I would probably be a bureaucrat now and this book might never have made it to print. Life is very random – don't ever forget how large a role luck played in your achievements.

I must of course thank Jamie Hodder-Williams and Laura Fletcher, my publishers at Bedford Square, who took a big punt on *Beyond Happy* as one of their first non-fiction books; Jonathan Conway, my agent, who polished the book pitch to a shine I did not think possible; James Nightingale, my copyeditor, who is an artist with the pruning shears; and Sam Gilbert for putting me in touch with Jonathan. Also, everyone who endorsed the book (I had to write this acknowledgements sections before these were finalised!)

Finally, I want to thank Nietzsche, who had to be alone with all this. Rest in peace.

## About the Author

Dr Mark Fabian is Associate Professor of Public Policy at the University of Warwick, and an Affiliate Fellow at the Bennett Institute for Public Policy at the University of Cambridge. He hosts the podcast ePODstemology, which interviews junior academics about their paradigm shifting research. *Beyond Happy* is his debut book for a general readership; his academic book, *A Theory of Subjective Wellbeing*, was published in 2022 by Oxford University Press.

Bedford Square Publishers is an independent publisher of fiction and non-fiction, founded in 2022 in the historic streets of Bedford Square London and the sea mist shrouded green of Bedford Square Brighton.

Our goal is to discover irresistible stories and voices that illuminate our world.

We are passionate about connecting our authors to readers across the globe and our independence allows us to do this in original and nimble ways.

The team at Bedford Square Publishers has years of experience and we aim to use that knowledge and creative insight, alongside evolving technology, to reach the right readers for our books. From the ones who read a lot, to the ones who don't consider themselves readers, we aim to find those who will love our books and talk about them as much as we do.

We are hunting for vital new voices from all backgrounds – with books that take the reader to new places and transform perceptions of the world we live in.

Follow us on social media for the latest Bedford Square Publishers news.

@bedsqpublishers
facebook.com/bedfordsq.publishers/
@bedfordsq.publishers

https://bedfordsquarepublishers.co.uk/